Hai Van

François Houtart
and
Geneviève Lemercinier

Hai Van

Life in a Vietnamese Commune

François Houtart
and
Geneviève Lemercinier

Zed Books Ltd.

Hai Van was first published by Zed Books Ltd.,
57 Caledonian Road, London N1 9BU, in 1984.

Copyedited and proofread by Mark Gourlay
Typeset by Jo Marsh
Cover design by Jacque Solomons
Cover photo courtesy of John Spragens, Jr.

Printed by The Pitman Press, Bath

British Library Cataloguing in Publication Data

Houtart, Francois
Hai Van: life in a Vietnamese commune.
1. Collective farms — Vietnam
2. Vietnam — Rural conditions
I. Title II. Lemercinier, Genevieve
959.704'4 HD1492.V5

ISBN 0-86232-234-0
ISBN 0-86232-235-9 Pbk

US Distributor
Biblio Distribution Center, 81 Adams Drive, Totowa,
New Jersey, 07512.

Contents

Preface	i
1. Towards a Sociology of Socialist Transition	1
The Role of Sociology in a Socialist Society	1
The Concept of Transition in Sociological Terms	3
Agrarian Reform (1945–47)	9
Radical Agrarian Reform (1953–57)	11
Balance Sheet of the Reform	18
2. Economic Structure	21
The Village Before the Revolution	21
The Agrarian Reform	23
The Co-operative	23
Active Population and Production	30
Domestic Economy	39
Towards Large-Scale Production	43
Sociological Reflections on the Transition	45
3. Leaders, Personnel and Participation	52
The Election of the Personnel of the Co-operative	52
The Organization of Work	59
4. Collective Organization of Leadership	71
The Organigram of the Commune	71
The Bureaucracy as a Social Process	73
The Social Aspects of Leadership	76
5. Education and Health Services	80
The Educational Services	80
The Health Services	90
6. The Family and its Function	94
Social Practices, Cultural Models and Demographic Structures	96

The Position of Women and their Role in the Family 103
The Organization of Domestic Work 107
Decision-Making in the Family 115
The Transformation of Social Relationships 122

7. Cultural Transformation 131
The Home: Present and Future Forms 133
The Use of Free Time 151

8. Transformation of Religion 162
The Evolution of the Catholic Group during the Period of Transition 163
The Cultural Models of the Catholic Population 181
Conclusions 188

9. The Sociology of Social Transition 193
Relations Between the Infrastructure and the Superstructure 193
The New Dimension of Social Space 196
The Collective Aims 197
Objective Conditions Versus Consensus 198
The Formation of the Consensus 200
A Pedagogy of the Planned Transition 202

Index 205

Tables

1.1, 1.1a	Redistribution of Lands After Agrarian Reforms	19
1.2	Growth of Agricultural Production	20
2.1	Evolution of Resident and of Active Population in the Commune	31
2.2	Evolution of Active Population According to Sexes	31
2.3	Evolution of Active Population According to Sectors of Activity	32
2.4	Comparison Between Distribution of Active Population Between 1973 and 1978	33
2.5	Distribution of People Employed in Local Industry According to their Activities	33
2.6	Indicators Showing Evolution of Agricultural Production	34
2.7	Indicators Revealing the Development of the Technical Base	35
2.8	Raising of Pigs and Production of Meat	36
2.9	Evolution of Sales of Produce of Local Industry and Handicrafts	37
2.10	Distribution of Total Production of Food	38
2.11	Distribution of Net Revenue of the Co-operative	39
2.12	Average Annual Revenue of a Worker in the Co-operative	39
2.13	Time Given Weekly to Private Economy According to Categories of Population Studied	41
2.14	Annual Revenue Derived from Private Economy	41
2.15	Use of Domestic Revenues	42
2.16	Comparison Between Hours Spent in Domestic Work and Revenue Derived therefrom	43
3.1	Criteria for Choice of President of the Co-operative and Head of Production Group	53
3.2	Criteria for Choice of President of Co-operative and of Head of Production Group According to Categories of Population Studied	54
3.3	Most Important Criteria for the Election of President of Co-operative and Head of Production Group According to Categories of Persons Questioned	54
3.4	Correspondence Between Criteria Used in Electoral Choices and Level of Awareness of Influencing Elections	56
3.5	Correspondence Between Criteria Underlying Choices and the Level of Awareness of Influencing Elections of Heads of Production Groups	57
3.6	Evaluation of Management of the Co-operative	58
3.7	Evaluation of Head of Production Group	59
3.8	Agents to Whom Decisions on the Designation of Members of the Work Team and Opinions on these Decisions are Attributed	60

3.9 Agents to Whom Decisions Regarding Choice of Products are Attributed, and their Evaluation 61
3.10 Agents to Whom Decisions Concerning Fixing Norms of Work are Attributed, and their Evaluation 62
3.11 Agents to Whom the Elaboration of the System of Points, and their Evaluation are Attributed 64
3.12 Agents to Whom the Distribution of Points and the Evaluation of the System are Attributed 65
3.13 Participation at Co-operative Meetings, and their Evaluation 66
3.14 Opinions on the Outcome of Debates at Co-operative Meetings 67
3.15 Perception of Conflicts Within the Co-operative 68
4.1 Distribution of the 41 Cadres Questioned According to Type of Institution and Function Exercised 76
4.2 Demographic and Socio-Cultural Characteristics of the Cadres Interviewed 78
5.1 Level of Education of the Population of Hai Van 1945/6 81
5.2 Level of Education of the Population of Hai Van, 1960 82
5.3 Level of Education According to the Sexes, 1946 and 1960 83
5.4 Level of Education of the Population of Hai Van, 1978/79 85
5.5 Distribution of Schools, Staff and Students According to Study Cycles 85
5.6 Programme of Studies of 1st and 2nd Cycles of General Education in Course Periods, by Year of Study 86
5.7 Distribution of Library Users According to Age, Sex and Occupation 89
5.8 Frequency and Type of Books Borrowed by Library Users 89
6.1 Educational Level of Women and of their Husbands: Compared 97
6.2 Distribution of Women According to Age, Occupation, and that of their Husbands 98
6.3 Distribution of Women According to Age at Marriage and Duration of the Marriage 99
6.4 Duration of Marriage 100
6.5 Distribution of Women According to their Age and Number of Children 101
6.6 Number of Children per Married Woman and the Duration of Marriage 101
6.7 Size and Structure of Families of Women Questioned 102
6.8 Number of Hours in a Working Day for Which the Women Could Not Accurately Account 104
6.9 Use of Time by Women Aged Less than 30 105
6.10 Average Distribution of Time for Women Aged 30-40 106
6.11 Average Distribution of Time for Women Aged 40 and over 107
6.12 Principal Agents in Management of the Family Budget, According to the Woman's Age 108

6.13	Agents Intervening in Domestic Agricultural Production and Small Scale Cattle Rearing According to the Woman's Age	109
6.14	Agents Intervening in Domestic Agricultural Production, According to Occupation of Married Partners	110
6.15	Domestic Agricultural Work Done by Husbands, According to Job Category	111
6.16	Quantum of Husbands' Participation in Domestic Agricultural Production, According to Education and Job Category	112
6.17	Agents Responsible for Household Tasks, According to Task and Size of Family	113
6.18	Work Sharing in Relation to Members of the Family	115
6.19	Agents Responsible for Basic Decision-Making	117
6.20	Repositories of Decision-Making in Cultural and Socio-Political Activities	119
6.21	Social Relationships, According to Age, Sex, Occupation and Political Activity	123
6.22	Institutions or Social Agents to Whom Recourse is made by Villagers in Difficulties: Outline of Population Studied	125
6.23	Difficulties Confronting at Least 15% of Families, According to Age of Wives	128
6.24	Institutions or Persons to Whom Recourse is made in Case of Difficulties	129
6.25	Type of Relationships Established with Certain Officials	129
7.1	Opinions For and Against Maintaining the Single Family Home with Garden and Pond	134
7.2	Motives of Persons Favouring Retention of Present Form of Home	136
7.3	Opinions in Favour of House with Several Rooms, and in Favour of Two Storey Building	137
7.4	Motivations Justifying Opinions For and Against an Extension of Present Home	138
7.5	Motivations Justifying Opinions For and Against General Extension of Homes	139
7.6	Social References of Persons Questioned	142
7.7	Motivations Underlying Opinions For and Against Construction of Single Family Two Storey Houses	141
7.8	Motivations Underlying Opinions For and Against Construction of Two Storey Houses According to Characteristics of Sample	142
7.9	Types of Motivation Advanced	144
7.10	Opinions Concerning Urbanization of the Villages	145
7.11	Motivations Underlying Opinions For and Against Urbanization of the Rural Habitat	146

7.12	Motivations Underlying Opinions For and Against Urbanization, According to Characteristics of Sample	147
7.13	Types of Socio-Economic and Cultural Preoccupations in Function of the Home	148
7.14	Positions and Predominant Justifications with Regard to Changes in Housing	149
7.15	Capacity to Choose Among Free Time Activities	153
7.16	Opinions on Different Uses of Free Time, According to Sex and Age	155
7.17	Choice of Free Time Activities, According to Characteristics of Sample	157
7.18	Selections of Free Time Activities by Categories of Population	158
7.19	Characteristics of Preferred Activities, According to Categories of the Sample	160
8.1	Persons Sharing in the Three Cultural Models Concerning the Relations Between Christianity and Communism	182
8.2	Persons Without Systematized Cultural Model Concerning Relations Between Christianity and Communism	183
8.3	Attendance at Sunday Mass and Reception of Communion	184
8.5	Opinions on Certain Types of Prayer	186
8.6	Opinions on Mixed Marriages	187

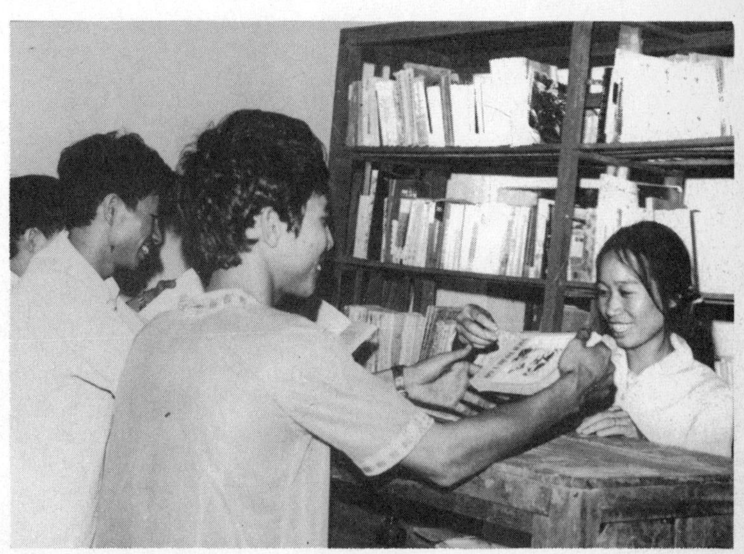

Preface

During July and August 1979, research students of the Institute of Sociology, attached to the Committee of Social Sciences of Vietnam, undertook a research project on a commune situated in the Red River Delta, in the district of Hai Hau, in the province of Ha Nam Binh. The task had a threefold purpose: to give the young research students an opportunity to confront reality, i.e. concrete social reality; to verify some hypotheses in the field of rural sociology, and finally, to prepare, through a pilot research project, a broader programme with a view to gaining a better knowledge of the mechanisms involved in social transformation, at a time when new initiatives were under way, especially with regard to production on a large scale.

The collaboration of responsible individuals in the area, as well as of the district and of the commune, and the welcome given to the research students by the inhabitants of Hai Van, have enabled us to bring this work to fruition and it is our wish to thank them most heartily. It is to their school that the research students were attached and they learnt much. The following pages contain the results of their work and analysis. In the summer of 1980 the results of the inquiry were discussed by the plenum of research students of the Institute, and verified and completed on the spot with the members of the commune.

The commune chosen for the inquiry comprises a single co-operative which covers practically the entire territory. Thanks to these verifications done at the district level, it was possible to establish that the social and cultural aspects of Hai Van are not exceptional situations; and this furnishes us with a sufficiently solid basis for investigation.

F. Houtart and G. Lemercinier

1. Towards a Sociology of Socialist Transition

Before proceeding with this analysis of the commune we studied, it is essential to define the frame of reference within which we worked. In order to approach the reality of a commune – which corresponds to a single collective unit of production – we have adopted a specifically sociological perspective.

Being entirely a pilot project, i.e. an attempt to pin-point methods and specify theoretical perspectives, the study of Hai Van is of interest for its own sake. One must not consider this study as typical of all communes in Vietnam or even of those in the Red River Delta. Further, some of the inquiries made in the commune could not measure up accurately to the stringent norms of truly representative sampling. But the principal contribution is twofold: on the one hand this research project reveals the existence of real tendencies even if one cannot say in what measure, exactly, they are to be found in the whole of Vietnam; on the other hand, it enables us to bring into relief hypotheses which will help further sociological research in Vietnam.

The Role of Sociology in a Socialist Society

Sociology, in so far as it is a discipline, sets itself, as its fundamental purpose, the discovery of a *social logic* through socially treated facts taken as indicators. In other words, one seeks to transcend reality immediately visible in order to get at the reasons behind it. The sociological approach is distinguished from philosophy, the purpose of which is more comprehensive since the latter envisages the totality of the real, not simply its social aspect, and, further, since philosophy is concerned with ultimate ends. According to the well-known sociological principle, the social must be explained by the social. Consequently, the problem of origins is defined sociologically as a search for the genesis of collective constructions, while that of ends is bound with the reproduction of social groups and of social systems of collective constructions. One could also say that sociology has for its end the discovery of the concrete dialectic of societies.

Sociology cannot, however, be allowed to degenerate into empiricism, i.e. the search for explanations in what is immediately visible, for this would limit it to a field essentially descriptive even if this is effected by statistically elaborate devices. Theory and empirical research are, in fact, linked together dialectically. On the one hand, facts do not speak for themselves, they must be questioned, and for this one must use a system of questioning, which is sociological theory. On the other hand, this theory is not a pure invention of the mind: it can exist and develop only in the measure in which one comes to grips with reality through a primarily inductive approach. In this sense the method which Marx used in *Capital* coincides with such an outlook, since he attempted, above all else, to discover the trans-empirical laws of the capitalist system (the constitution of value, surplus value, surplus labour, etc.) by starting with a concrete case, that of capitalist development in England. Although he described in detail the British economic reality, his real pursuit was the construction of a theory to interpret and explain the facts. From this point of view Marxist sociology seeks to explain and not only to describe. Further, it takes as the central hypothesis of its approach that of historical materialism which establishes at the very beginning of the chain of social causes the primacy of the production of the means of existence (economic function) – means indispensable to life and to the survival of any human collectivity. The role of the sociologist is to unswervingly pursue this hypothesis through the study of history in order to discover the numberless variations by which such a process is realized; to establish the logic which controls it, and finally to elaborate intermediary theories indispensable for the formulation of subsequent hypotheses and their verification.

There could evidently exist, in a sociology internal to socialist societies, the temptation to adopt a sociological perspective that is exclusively functionalist, or at least predominantly so. The underlying presupposition of functionalism is to look upon the existing stage of the social system as an autonomous entity and therefore to make a fetish of it and ask how to make it function, how to avoid dysfunctions, how to prevent deviations, and how to adapt the behaviour of social agents to the structures. In a transitional situation such a perspective is contradictory, for transition signifies as much a pursuit of change as a consolidation of solid acquisitions, and demands as much of interrogation about the social processes 'in via' as questioning on the nature of social relations. It is not a question of rectilinear movement, a fact which the sociological approach must contend with. Although functionalist approaches are useful as intermediary theories, as the work of Soviet and Polish sociologists has shown, the perspectives as such, if they are not revitalized, run the risk of reifying reality. It cannot take account of the dialectical dimension which is indispensable to a sociology of transitions. In this sense functionalism is the diametrical opposite of Marxism's specific contribution to sociology. It is necessary to rediscover the twists and turns, and, eventually, even the contradictions (contradictory effects of the same cause) which exist in a transitional situation, and that too in a dynamic fashion. This must be done in function of the double relation between the social affinities of production and the state of the forces of production on the one hand, and the infrastructure and the superstructure on the other. This is what we will attempt to do in the pages that follow.

In the measure in which society of any kind is more than a mere aggregate of individuals, it becomes a fit object for study from a specific scientific point of view and therefore such a scientific approach has a place in a socialist society. Social relations are never perceived integrally and in all their complexity by the social agents themselves. Fruthermore, planning, which is the proper characteristic of socialist societies, is always confronted by two realities: the first is the fact that social processes are not always amenable to voluntary decisions, and therefore, they are not always the end-product of planned decisions. There do exist 'social invariables' ('objective laws') which it is important to know if one is not to unleash effects not intended, though foreseeable in some measure. Sociological knowledge can contribute to a better understanding of those laws. Consequently, apart from its place as a scientific discipline in the totality of knowledge, sociology is also functional in a socialist society. The second aspect is the fact that not all the spheres of social life are necessarily covered by planning, and this applies to their effects as well.

In summary, we may say that sociology enables us to confront reality as it is constructed by deliberate planning. It is necessary to keep in mind that the probability of effects, induced voluntarily or otherwise, covers in the social domain a wide span which will always be an object of investigation and sociological reflection. On the other hand, planning remains always an action of a dialectical nature, which countermands itself when it reifies itself.

The Concept of Transition in Sociological Terms

The concept of transition, if it is not accurately defined, runs the risk of becoming a veritable omnium gatherum which will include practically every reality; for what society is there which is not in transition? Marx studied in very detailed fashion the transition of societies from feudalism to the state of capitalist production. He wrote: 'The capitalist economy has sprung from the entrails of the feudal economy. The dissolution of the former has released the constitutive elements of the latter'.[1] Our task is to study another reality – that of the transition from the capitalist mode of production to socialism, by using the same methodological procedure. And to this must be added that Vietnamese society has been peripheral in its relation to the centrality of capitalism, and that capitalism in consequence, has been channelled to it in numerous and complex forms relevant to both pre-capitalist and capitalist societies. Further, we must utilize these concepts with reference to a society which has entered into the process of transitional change only very recently and which was subjected to the ravages of successive wars for almost the entire duration of this period.

Let us recall, first of all, that a social process is not a total rupture with the past, as if at a given moment everything went back to square one. Obviously the transition to a socialist mode of production was not effected in the same manner as the transition from feudalism to capitalism – by the progressive transformation of economic, social and cultural, and finally, political forms, (the change in social relations sometimes getting ahead of the forces of production and vice versa) and eventually arriving at the transformation of political structures. In the case of Vietnam it was a question of political change, a seizure of the state apparatus, its transformation and its utilization as a tool for the transformation of the social relations of production. The study of this transition is therefore a study of beginnings, i.e. the study of the construction of a new social whole as well as a study of the social structures of production and of the political and ideological superstructures. One must not in any way minimize this aspect of the question.

The transition from feudalism to capitalism was a progressive and endogenous transformation, pertaining to the dynamic peculiar to that society and it signifies the birth of the latter from the former by decomposition and natural dissolution; the social forms of production were modified with corresponding changes in the forces of production. It is quite different, however, in the transition to a socialist mode of production. This type of social formation is foreign to the emergence of the constitutive elements of the new mode of production deriving from the progressive decomposition of the state of affairs prior to it. It is, rather, an introduction, deliberately provoked, of a process of dissolution and emergence of what M. Godelier speaks of, a deliberately willed transformation, where the political agents attempted to replace the former state of affairs with a new form of the social bonds of production, which, at the time the changes were introduced, did not correspond to the level of development of the prevalent forces of production. This unleashed a new dialectical process where it was the change in the social relationships of production which was the driving force.

It is a question here of a new social form of production which, as M. Godelier expressed it, is established on the old material base (formal subsumption); one begins to walk, as it were, with the legs of another. This stage must be necessarily and progressively transcended (to pass on to that of real subsumption). The role of the superstructure is very considerable, even more so than in other transitions. In the transition to socialism, politics is dominant, for the process is deliberately willed. This means that the underlying cultural model plays a dynamic role. The risk of 'voluntarism', which is only a new form of idealism, is evidently not absent, no less than the risk of centring one's attention too exclusively on the infrastructure.

However, whatever the well-defined relations of production are – e.g. capitalist, colonialist, feudal or tributary – the new revolutionary regime created nothing: they made use of an existing social fabric to build the future. There survive, therefore, through all the processes of change, older forms – there is never a total rupture – and at the same time a dissolution of some forms. It is the task of the sociologist to determine which forms have dissolved most rapidly and which have survived, and then to search for the laws. The emergence of new forms is not automatic; they are subject to the same laws as the older forms, but in an opposite sense; they are the convex side of the lens. The double process – dissolution and emergence – is the proper object of sociological research of transition.

Certain Marxist authors utilize the concept of 'the dominant mode of production' to avoid the problem of survivals 'which history has not been able to efface'.[2] These forms which survive are, in fact, integral parts of the new structures. Is it necessary to speak of a combination of several modes of production of which one is the most dominant? This is not to be believed. It seems clearer to speak of the dominant mode of production in the sense of a specific structure of socialist relations of production, which integrate forms which are not necessarily proper to it, without losing their specificity. Thus, the capitalist mode of production in Latin America is grafted on to feudal forms of slavery. In India it fits in perfectly with the caste system, precisely in the transitional stages, or, to put it differently, at certain moments of the development of the forces of production in the framework of a peripheral capitalism.

In this case of transition to a society the end of which is socialist, there is a rupture, namely that of a certain totality or of a social formation, in the sense given by Marx in the *Grundrisse* to this concept, i.e. the entirety of the interactions between the infrastructure and the superstructure. The rupture is to be found in the very heart of the structure, i.e. in the grouping of the elements, not necessarily in each of the component parts. A new social constellation is created, completely abolishing the fundamental relations of the feudal type (agrarian reform) and of the capitalist type (private ownership of the means of production: fixed capital and finance capital). But these social relations are not to be established at a single stroke. The development of the forces of production plays a key role in the rhythm of this evolution, for it presides over the possibilities of a transition to new relationships, though it does not depend solely on political volition.

Political and juridical structures change rapidly but not totally, in so far as prior forms of social relationships abide (agricultural production in small plots, mixed enterprises, petty free enterprises, etc.), whether one believes or not that the final socialist relationships ought to abolish them, or on the contrary, to subsume them. As for the entirety of the symbolism which covers the ideological dimension, the matter is still more complex, for cultural schemes possess their own rhythm of transformation, which is far from being parallel – one tends to forget this sometimes – to changes in the infrastructure and which cannot in any case be considered as modelling itself automatically on the infrastructure. In fact, there exists a dialectical relationship between them.

In brief, a period of transition is one that follows a period of rupture, or, to use Marx's expression, a period of 'social consolidation of the mode of production'.[3] We are not going to deal with this highly complex problem here, for our purpose is more modest: that of introducing a pilot research project conducted on a commune of the Red River Delta. However, it is not possible to broach this subject empirically without some kind of theoretical framework. Seen from the point of view of a theory of transition, a double problem is clearly posed: on the one hand, that of the non-correspondence between the forces of production and the social relations of production, and, on the other hand, the tension between the infrastructure and the superstructure. Thus posed, the question is very abstract and needs to be made more precise.

Social Relations of Production and the Forces of Production

The seizure of political power in Vietnam took place in the very thick of a struggle which was not only national but also social, i.e., in the guise of a very specific project for the transformation of society. Further, when this stage was accomplished, there had to follow a formal imposition of a mode of production which, though progressive, was new to the framework of the society in its entirety. But, as Bettelheim has remarked apropos of other socialist societies, the real change in nature continues to be made at the level of the collective (the co-operatives for example) as the nature of the forces of production will scarcely permit any other mode. Therefore, there is to be found a non-correspondence (rather than a contradiction defined as such: contradictory effects of the same cause), which can be corrected only by a development of the forces of production, both in their technical and cultural aspects. In its turn such a development calls for a new transformation in the organization of the relations of production. The transition in the commune of Hai Van of the five small co-operatives, from the size of a former village (*lang*) to what is equivalent to a commune, presents us with a stage of this kind. This effect will reappear when we pass on to what is called in Vietnam today, production on the grand scale, i.e. to the framework of the whole district. The dialectic between these two aspects of social reality dominates the whole of political reality and it is very important to respect its rhythm if one is not to fall into errors the repercussion of which could be very grave at the practical level.

In effect – and Marx showed this when he studied primitive societies[4] – the relations of production which are built up in the process of production can only be modified in parallel with the development of the forces of production. It would be illusory to try to establish an organization which does not correspond to such a development. One can think of it theoretically; one can even impose it from above without reckoning with the realities of the case, and it cannot be said that all socialist regimes have always resisted the temptation to do so. But the 'objective laws' of the development of societies – in other words, inexorable social logic – will oblige those responsible to lag behind. This is the central problem of transition and the importance of its sociological study is clear.

We must bear in mind that, in speaking of the forces of production, one is not considering merely the material aspect of reality. Doubtless, one has to do so with questions of the means of production, and therefore of the technical state of production (irrigation, mechanization of agriculture, fertilizers, etc.), but the concept of the forces of production necessarily includes the inventiveness of the collective human mind, and therefore of the state of knowledge, of its diffusion among the people; the acceptability of the techniques at the mental level; the capacity for economic, social and political organization; the mastery of the instruments used for work. And this must cover not only production properly so-called, but the political field as well. It should be evident that reality is complex and this is one of the reasons why an empirical study at the microcosmic level of a commune, or even of rural groups of production, is not a luxury for the development of a sociology of transition to socialism.

This having been premised, we are not postulating that society in Vietnam has already established the social relations of socialist production. It has certainly abolished capitalist relationships such as those which began to appear with the introduction of French colonization. It has also suppressed every form of exploitation caused by the private ownership of the means of production, and likewise relations of servitude between the peasants and 'notables' or private proprietors. We do not wish to enter into a general debate for the simple reason that it would require still other factors of knowledge. Our purpose is more limited – limited for the most part to clarifying the interaction between the three elements of the new relations of production – namely the state, the co-operatives, and the individual producers. And our point of departure will be a rural commune in the Red River Delta. We are, therefore, conscious of the limits of our contribution.

Infrastructure and Superstructure

Another dialectical relationship, inseparably bound up with the one discussed above, is that between the infrastructure and the superstructure. Much attention will be paid to this aspect in this study, for it is here, it seems to us, that there will be found a particularly rich vein that has scarcely been mined. It is well known that distortions at the level of the superstructure can seriously handicap both the evolution of social relations and the development of the forces of production. Marx, in *The Eighteenth Brumaire of Louis Bonaparte*, analysed the non-correspondence between the objective interests of the peasant class and its political behaviour of supporting the monarchy in France, owing to a clear lack of social and political consciousness. The patriarchal family structure, typical, among other things, of the tributary mode of production, could also be an obstacle to transition either to a socialist or to a capitalist mode of production although the objective needs of economic production demand transformations. One could supply other, similar examples, and some of them could be borrowed from the domain proper to the sociology of religion.

In a peasant population such as the commune of Hai Van, which we are going to study, the representations both of relationships to nature as well as social relationships form a very important subject of study. Here we are touching on a reality which forms a complex structural whole. How can one change over, for example, to economic planning with mass production if the cultural model of the family is constituted on the patriarchal pattern; or if the vision one has of one's habitation is identified with the representation of an individual house, surrounded by a small garden, a pool and parents living in houses nearby? How can one introduce women to economic and social responsibilities if the image of their role is limited to domestic activities and to lower forms of production? How can one make the progressive change-over to collective mastery at the concrete level of production and of political organization if those responsible model their behaviour according to Confucian principles or if the centralism of the state has the monopoly of making decisions?

Such are some of the difficulties that can come between a project and its realization. Sometimes one tends to believe that the changes at the level of symbols follow automatically those of the infrastructure. Relations no doubt change, but a caveat is in order here: change is not linear, it is dialectical. In other words, the two elements can be set up in opposition, one against the other, and can thus contribute to creating tension which, after it is resolved, will be a source of transformation, even if in this last instance, the ultimate conclusion will lead us to establish the determining character of the relation at the materialist base. Therefore one ought not to confound fundamental logic with the innumerable divarications of the process, otherwise the approach becomes dogmatic and the research is sociological only in name.

But one ought not to give the impression that the process is solely mechanical and that there is no dynamic function of the superstructure with regard to the infrastructure. This is the case in socialist transition in which the new state, gripped by what is defined as representative of the objective interests of the subordinate classes, namely the workers and peasants, dominates the process of transformation of the infrastructure, according to lines defined by a cultural political model which consists precisely in the socialist project. And from this one will not mistake the phenomenon of the change of the representation of social relations, comprised here in certain rural populations, while the material bases of change have not yet been established at this juncture; the tension of which we spoke, between the infrastructure and the superstructure, is manifested in another sense. It is precisely the coexistence of these two types of tensions which goes to make up the complexity as well as the interest of the study of socialist transition. For, let us not forget that sociology, even more perhaps than philosophy, cannot be content merely to observe society, but that it also must, according to a celebrated expression, 'contribute to change it'.

Such is our concept, made specific, and in some sense, operative, of transition. What we have to do in the following pages is to uncover the mechanisms of transformation, the bonds or even the contradictions which result from the tensions, without excluding anything of it, while allowing ourselves to be guided in our questioning by the theoretical framework outlined above. Let us note finally that we are considering Vietnamese society such as it is, in its present state of organization without pretending, even when one speaks of a socialist society, that the ultimate objectives have already been reached, even in the transformation of the relations of production, nor do we claim to consider the theoretical discussion underlying this question, although we believe that this type of research has its contribution to make at this level. Having thus set out the limits of our field of study, it now remains for us to approach the results of our research.

Agrarian Reform (1945–57)

Vietnam is overwhelmingly a peasant country. In order, therefore, to win independence from the French, it was necessary to rely on the peasants, to politicize and arm them. But such a task called for a higher degree of awareness than a mere call to retrieve the ancient national heritage would be able to muster. Educated persons took upon themselves the task of mobilizing the peasants. But, blissfully ignorant of the progress of the modern world, they summoned the peasants to battle for King and Confucius against an enemy equipped with weapons and the full armoury of modern ideas. The westernized elite knew only the life and culture of the city; to them capitalism in its French version appeared as the ideal for society. Of the peasants, who constituted 90% of their people, they had only the vaguest notions.

That they saw the links between the question of independence and the question of the peasantry is to the lasting credit of the Vietnamese communists. From its foundation in 1930 the Vietnamese Communist Party aimed at worker-peasant unity under the leadership of the working class.[5] Part of its consciously adopted programme was that in the first phase of the Vietnamese revolution should strive towards the accomplishment of two fundamental tasks: the national task, which was anti-imperialist, and the democratic task, which was anti-feudal.

Both tasks had to be fulfilled simultaneously, the one reinforcing the other. Without the victory over imperialism, the anti-feudal struggle would not be successful. Without the anti-feudal struggle, it would not be possible to mobilize the masses against colonialism. Among the anti-feudal tasks was that of agrarian reform. The Vietnamese Communist Party at the time ordered total confiscation of the lands of the landowners – whether they were foreigners, Vietnamese or ecclesiastical personages – and that they should be handed over to the poor and middle peasants.

In practice, Vietnamese communists encountered several difficulties. The national task, which called for an alliance of classes, was in contradiction to the democratic task which called for a class struggle. The Party had to decide, given the circumstances, which task was more important. In 1941 during the Second World War the Party judged that the contradiction between the Vietnamese people and French or Japanese imperialism was more crucial than ever before. With the objective of uniting all social groups in the National Front of the Viet Minh, therefore, the earlier order, namely, total confiscation of the lands of the landowners was temporarily suspended. The new order was couched in the following terms: confiscate the lands of the imperialists and the traitors and give those to the poor peasants; redistribute common lands; reduce rents and interest.

According to the analysis of the Vietnamese Communist Party, classes in a colonized country other than the working and the peasant classes may also be revolutionary, or at least anti-imperialist; and these would include the national bourgeoisie of the cities, the intelligentsia, rich and middle peasants and some landowners. To make as few enemies as possible was the golden rule of the Vietnamese revolutionaries, and from this rule the Party drew the conclusion that if the anti-imperialist and the anti-feudal tasks were to be seen as one on the level of ultimate strategy, they had to be separated on the level of immediate practical policy. To bring about the alliance between workers and peasants, it was necessary to meet the demands of the peasants. To promote the interests of the National Front, comprising diverse elements, united only in their anti-imperialism, it was necessary for the agrarian reform to proceed by way of successive stages. This would also help to exploit to the full the contradictions between the imperialists and the landowners and among the landowners themselves.

Partial Agrarian Reforms (1945-53)

After the capture of power by the Vietnamese Communist Party in 1945 and almost throughout the entire period of the first resistance (1946-54) the agrarian policy was a moderate one. In 1953, after self-criticism of this policy, the Party proceeded to a more radical stand. This meant the abolition of the rights to property of the landowners and the liquidation of their political power. Before 1953 the agrarian policy had as its objectives merely the reduction of rents and interest.

When it seized power in 1945, the Vietnamese Communist Party realized that the immediate danger was the presence of Chiang Kai Shek's Chinese troops in the North, the British in the South, and the prospect of the return of the French. The Party comprised less than 5,000 militants scattered all over the country. The poor peasants – their class consciousness less acute than their national consciousness – were still subject to the influence of the village notables. Central power was not yet solidly established; still less was regional and local power. Popular committees at village level were still composed of a majority of the former notables. The cadres were young intellectuals, desirous of winning national independence and ushering in a new era, but for the most part were children of landowners and rich or middle peasants.

The Vietnamese Communist Party, therefore, did not go beyond a moderate agrarian policy. This meant the confiscation of the lands of imperialists and traitors, and the temporary lease of this land to poor peasants; equitable repartitioning of common lands; a reduction of 25% in rents from the levels existing before 1945; a reduction of interest, now fixed at 13% p.a. for money loans and 20% p.a. for loans in kind. Between 1945 and 1953 only 17% of peasant households in North Vietnam benefited from land reform and received 15% of cultivable lands. All efforts were geared to the struggle for independence. The anti-feudal task suffered in comparison. Fearful of weakening national unity in any way, the Vietnamese Communist Party contented itself with appeals to the good sense of the landowners. With few exceptions, however, the landowners did not submit to even the moderate prescriptions of reform.

In 1949 the government published a new decree further reducing rents and interest. Like the measures of 1945, this new decree too met with only partial success. The political cadres still tended to underestimate the importance of the anti-feudal task. On the other hand, the landowners continued to exercise great authority in the countryside, and often maintained control over the committees of local administration. They used various means to obviate the implementation of the laws and those peasants who claimed their rights were arraigned for sabotaging the Party policy of a National Front. In these attempts they found allies in local party cadres, drawn from the families of landowners or rich peasants.

The war mobilized millions of peasants. Numberless poor peasants slowly but surely learned to read, to write, to organize, to discuss political and other questions. Young intellectuals – even those who came from rich families – were propelled by the force of prolonged war to take their stand ever more closely with the masses and were steadily won over to the idea that, side by side with the national revolution, a social revolution was also necessary.

Radical Agrarian Reform (1953–57)

Motivations and Objectives

From 1953 the Vietnamese Communist Party launched its massive campaign for the mobilization of the peasant masses. The demands were a decisive reduction of farm rents and the abolition of the rights of landowners to private property.

The Party was impelled to this policy of radical reform by reasons both internal and external. On the one hand, the Party had become stronger, while on the other, the war, which, with the United States' assistance to the French colonialists from 1950, had lasted for six years, threatened to escalate. Between 1945 and 1951 the efforts of the government of Bao Dai to bring together all those – traditionalists, landowners, anti-communist nationalists – who feared the internal revolution had spent themselves. To the extent that it was found to be impossible to continue the war without the enthusiastic support of the poor peasants, merely moderate agrarian reform was seen to be futile. Ninety per cent of the soldiers and the people's army came from the ranks of the poor peasants. Indeed, the factor that contributed most to the final and most sensational victories of the war, culminating in Dien Bien Phu, was the mass mobilization of the peasantry for the implementation of agrarian reform.

In January 1953, at the first National Conference of the Vietnamese Communist Party, its Secretary-general, Truong Chinh, made the following self-criticism:

Hai Van:

> The policy of forging national unity was necessary and just. Yet we underestimated the role of the peasantry, the importance of the struggle against feudalism. We did not realize that the success of the struggle against feudalism was the indispensable condition of the struggle against imperialism and the means of hastening its success . . .
>
> The weakness of our agrarian policy has had its influence over the whole range of our tasks . . .
>
> . . . there has been some slowness in the widening and the consolidation of the National Front based on the unity of workers and peasants; in several places the Front has been abused to the advantage of the landowners;
>
> . . . power at the base, especially at the level of the commune, has been in numerous places exercised by landowners and notables; the worker peasants have not been the centres of power in the countryside.

On 4 December 1953, when the war of resistance was at its peak, the National Assembly passed the law of agrarian reform with the declared objective of 'abolishing the system of the buying up of land by the colonialists, abrogating the rights of the colonialists to property, abrogating the system of feudal property rights . . . in order to achieve the task of national liberation.'

In his speech before the Assembly, Ho Chi Minh indicated the intended effects of the reform:

1) On the military level, the peasants will now take a more active part in the resistance;
2) On the political level, political and economic power in the countryside will now be in the hands of the worker peasants;
3) On the economic level, the peasants will be freed forever from the dead-weight of feudal exploitation; the forces of production in the countryside will be liberated; the peasants will increase production; the whole economy will be stimulated; the standard of life in general will improve; the way to industrial and commercial development will open.

The Agrarian Law

Composition of the rural sector: The law categorizes the rural sector as follows:

– landowners, defined as those who possess land in large extents, who are not themselves cultivators and live on rent and interest;
– rich peasants, defined as those who possess land sufficient in extent to enable them to employ hired labour in addition to their own labour;
– middle peasants, defined as those who live solely from the produce of their land without exploiting hired labour;
– poor peasants, defined as those who have little land and live without exploiting the labour of others;
– landless labourers who live solely by hiring out their labour power.

The reason for such a categorization is that agrarian reform should have a precise strategic objective. The strategy was to isolate the landowners and organize 'an anti-feudal front' with a regrouping of worker peasants and the rural bourgeoisie (including the rich peasants). The class alignment visualized by the Vietnamese Communist Party is thus meant

> to rest squarely on the poor and the landless peasants, to link closely with the middle peasants, to seek alliance with the rich peasants, in such a way as to make the class of landowners stand on its head and gradually, though diversely, liquidate the system of feudal exploitation.

The poor peasants and the peasants with no land constituted 60% of the population. Severely oppressed and exploited by the colonialists and the landowners, they were active elements in the resistance movement and had special stakes in the struggle against the landowners. For these reasons it was necessary to develop their role of leadership and to meet their demands while simultaneously educating them politically.

The poor and the landless peasants had to unite with the middle peasants who constituted 30% of the population; they were also oppressed and exploited. Their unstable economic situation was a vulnerable one, continually menaced by the covetous designs of the landowners. Nonetheless, given their economic situation, the middle peasants could join ranks equally well with the bourgeoisie as with the proletariat. The strategy, therefore, of linking with the middle peasants would be possible 'only to the extent that it rested squarely on the poor peasants and on the peasants with no land'. As the position taken by the middle peasants, either for or against the revolution, would be absolutely crucial, the Vietnamese Communist Party envisaged, that in the agrarian reform from the economic point of view, it was necessary to give land to the middle peasants of the lower ranks, while from the political point of view, it was necessary to give them a share in the administration and in the organization of the communal masses.

With the rich peasants, according to the Vietnamese Communist Party, it was necessary to work towards an alliance in order 'to draw them into the resistance movement, to keep them from the landowners and to give some sense of security to the middle peasants'. For these reasons the lands and the properties of the rich peasants were not expropriated; they were even allowed to employ hired labour for their production.

The class of landowners, estimated at 5% of the population,[6] as the target of attack, had to be completely abolished and its economic base utterly destroyed. However, with a view to the all-nation character of the resistance movement, which sought to attract a part even of the landowner class on the principle of 'making the highest possible number of friends and the lowest number of enemies', it was necessary to distinguish between various groups in the feudal landowning class according to their attitude to the resistance. Thus were distinguished:

– the landowning traitors, the landowning reactionaries and the tyrannical notables; these were guilty of crimes against the country and the peasants; their lands had to be confiscated;

– the other landowners who lived mainly on rents: their lands to be requisitioned without compensation;[7]
– the landowners who took part in the resistance, those who had children in the resistance and those who were known to be democrats: their lands were to be requisitioned with the payment of compensation. The amount due in compensation was the value of the average annual production of the land plus the local market value of cattle and equipment. At the same time, landowners were invited to offer their lands as free gifts to the State. Payment was made in 10-year treasury bonds, with interest at 1.15% p.a.

The beneficiaries of the reform: Art. 25 of the law enumerated the beneficiaries according to the following order of priority:

– landless labourers, poor peasants and middle peasants possessing insufficient lands;
– other rural workers (artisans, vendors etc.) whose productivity was insufficient for a livelihood;
– those engaged in actual combat or their heirs, the administrative cadres, workers in state enterprises – provided their families lived in the village;
– the unemployed and refugees in the countryside;
– religious communities which were allowed to keep a part of their lands for the needs of worship.

The law further envisaged the possibility of special awards to special landowners, to soldiers of the French regime with a rural background, and to foreign claimants, but this clause remained of symbolic value only.

Principles of land-distribution: The principles of land distribution were the following: the urgency of the needs of each family; the rights of the peasant possessor; the quality and location of the lands; the number of dependants (not the number of workers) in each family. The beneficiaries received full title and were not liable to make any payment either to the State or to the former owners.

Organization of the reform: The implementation of the reform was entrusted to the people themselves: reform committees were set up composed of poor and landless peasants at central, regional and provincial level under the direction of cadres sent by the government, independently of local party cells. These agrarian reform committees encouraged the people to set up peasant assemblies and special tribunals to make decisions in cases of criminal acts of landowners and of a divergence of claims. Because of the shortage of cadres and the heterogeneous nature of the base organizations, the agrarian reform took place in successive stages: first in those regions where the required conditions were present – the conditions being political stability and effective demand for reform on the part of a sufficient number of peasants equipped to take over the management of the reform – and then in other regions. The first stage began in 1953 in the liberated territories.

The Implementation of Agrarian Reform

From March 1953, and before agrarian reform began to be effectively implemented, the Vietnamese Communist Party organized a campaign of ideological education for the political cadres and the soldiers of the people's army in order to prepare them for the role that they would have to play in the transformation of the countryside. At the same time, the Party mobilized the masses to force the landowners effectively to reduce all land rents. To obtain this last objective, thousands of specially trained cadres were sent out into the countryside by the Party to create awareness among the peasants.

Each militant cadre lived with one of the poorest of the poor peasants. Every morning he would work on the fields with his host, live, like him, on rice and simple curry, and return at night to sleep on a torn mat spread on the floor. For several days the range of conversation between guest and host was very limited. But gradually the ice began to melt and one day the peasant would begin to tell the story of his life, and all his sufferings. The cadre then felt that the first part of his task had been accomplished: to make the peasant aware of his life of misery and humiliation. Having won his confidence, the cadre had next to lead the peasant to see that the source of his misery was not some decree made up in the sky but rather lay in the landowner's exploitation of his condition – the landowner whom he had so long taken to be the lord and master of his commune and his clan.

That ignorance disappeared was less important than the reawakening of the consciousness of class. It was the strategy of the 'three togethers' that paid dividends: work together, live together, eat together. The militant cadre may have been of city origin – now he had become a peasant in peasant surroundings. To reach the point, however, where the difference between the peasant and himself disappeared was easier said than done. How often did the militant cadre – a young student from the city – notice that the peasant offered him a full bowl of rice, only to realize that in fact he was being treated as if he were a mandarin. It was a difficult task to bridge the gap between the cadre sent by the Party and the peasant in the field.

Obviously, one could not wait for the creation of such awareness in every Vietnamese peasant. In practice, in each commune, the militants succeeded in forming a few poor peasants into what would become the nucleus of the Party and the peasant union in the commune.

The campaign for the reduction of farm rents meant a reorganization of the village administrative set-up and of the local branch of the Party. The rich peasant and the landowners were thrown out; their places were taken by the poor peasants and the landless labourers gained importance in the affairs of the Party: in 22 villages their representation in the Party increased from 3.7% to 53%, though the middle peasants, with 44% representation in local Party cells, also continued to play an important role. The campaign of mobilization of the masses for the reduction of farm rents was a useful rehearsal for radical agrarian reform which began only in December 1953.

Before the redistribution of lands and goods could begin, it was necessary to categorize each person in accordance with the categorization envisaged in the law of agrarian reform. This was done by the Council of peasant delegates but had then to be ratified by the provincial administrative committee. People's popular tribunals began to be set up in several places. Before a peasant audience numbering hundreds, sometimes thousands, the most rapacious landowners and notables had to face public accusations for their past misdeeds. The accusers were their former tenants or labourers. Landowners found guilty of grave crimes, could be executed on the spot. The aim of these sessions was to produce an emotional shock and the awakening of a collective consciousness of their liberation among the peasants. They who had always lived in fear of the landowner in a master-servant relationship and who always believed that their very life and labour depended on the landowner now had a sense of liberation and power. For the first time in their lives they found the notables humiliated and cowering for mercy. The people's tribunals had also the effect of building deep solidarity among the peasants and gave the agrarian reform its special stamp and character.

The agrarian reform was not merely an economic act – it was an act of the class struggle. This struggle had to lead to a complete abolition of the existing structures of village life and to the complete destruction of the ancient psychological links between exploiters and exploited. But once the poor peasant found that the fetters that bound him to the past were finally broken, he went very far. The collective emotional upheaval experienced by the poor peasants made it difficult for them to distinguish between the landowner who was an enemy and the landowner who was a nationalist, between the rich peasants and the middle peasants.

Mistakes in Implementation

The agrarian reform went through several successive phases – from the trial phase of 1953, which involved 10,792 peasants, to the fifth and last phase of June 1956, which involved 6,140,127 peasants. Implementation of the reform, however, was not without mistakes. These were taken so seriously that, three months after its achievement, in September 1956, the Vietnamese Communist Party met in general session to evaluate the results of the reform. The leaders did not seek to hide their mistakes. Self-criticism of the Party was again the theme of General Vo Nguyen Giap's speech (a member of the Politbureau) on 29 October 1959. According to the Party, the errors committed called attention to the practical implementation of the official policy and to the purification of the rural cells of the Party.

From the left-wing of the Party mistakes arose from the fact that the reform cadres had insufficiently 'adapted the principles of Marxism–Leninism to the particular conditions of the country'. They had not paid sufficient attention to the close connection between the anti-imperialist struggle, which called for inter-class alliance, and the anti-feudal struggle, which called for inter-class struggle. Inter-class alliance went somewhat by default.

Practically, these mistakes of the left were those that had their source in the desire to satisfy the immediate demands of the poor and the landless peasants at the expense of the interests of the other strata of the peasantry. The mistake was to have forgotten the need to ally with the middle peasants, and thus to have harmed their legitimate interests. A fair number of these latter found themselves categorized with the rich peasants and the landowners.

The policy of alliance with the rich peasants was often ignored. Reform cadres and poor peasants unhesitatingly tended to class the rich peasants with the landowners. Even as regards the landowners, they were mistakenly lumped together into one undifferentiated mass. Their number was exaggerated, with the result that those in charge of the reform tended to see a landowner behind every bush. There was a tendency to undervalue the old party structures in the villages. Middle and rich peasants and landowners were indiscriminately attacked, even if they supported the resistance and had had their children in the movement. Given the hierarchical and separate organization of the agents of the reform, which made it difficult for efficient and quick control to be exercised over the use of powers which, at times, were excessive, mistakes often could not be detected in time.

These mistakes are a pointer to the practical difficulty of judiciously and tactically combining the anti-imperialist with the anti-feudal struggle. It was seen to be as difficult to avoid leftist deviations as to avoid rightist ones. Between 1945 and 1953, the undervaluing of the anti-feudal struggle was a case of deviation to the right. Between 1953 and 1957, during the years of radical agrarian reform, failure to keep the class struggle within the limits of the anti-imperialist struggle was a case of deviation to the left. To the extent that the poor and the landless peasants formed the *avant-garde* of the class struggle, the question became much more complex. The concepts of class line, alliance of classes, different social categories (four categories of peasants, three of landowners) were defined as part of party strategy for various stages of the revolution and of public demand. Thus the landowners were held to be social parasites at a time when the rich peasants still had a role to play in the stage of transition to socialism. Impatient for retribution after years of exploitation, and clinging tenaciously to their simple theory of a two-class (rich-vs-poor) society, the poor peasants found these concepts, however much they were part of a long-term strategy, difficult to comprehend. The distinction between landowners and rich peasants was one they found particularly difficult to grasp. The exploitation they had suffered at the hands of the rich peasants was more within their immediate experience than exploitation by the landowners. Moreover, there are grounds for believing that the simple two-class theory of society was encouraged by some reform cadres, and even by some members of the Politbureau. These were those whose task was to get agrarian reform going. They took a dogmatic approach to the class struggle and were anxious to proceed with their task without giving sufficient attention to the specific politico-economic context of the country.

Balance Sheet of the Reform

After its self-criticism the Vietnamese Communist Party undertook a campaign of rectification. Its objectives were freedom, reclassification of persons into categories, moral rehabilitation and indemnification of those unjustly condemned, and criticism and education of erring cadres. At the Central Committee those directly responsible for the agrarian reform were relieved of their duties. Truong Chinh, director of the reform, was removed from his post of General Secretary of the Vietnamese Communist Party, and this was taken by Ho Chi Minh himself, in September 1956. The Minister of Agriculture was also replaced. These decisions did not remove all tension; there was trouble, for instance, in November 1956 in the Catholic region of Nghe An.

It is impossible to give exact figures of the number of deaths caused by the agrarian reform. Bernard Fall, a conservative American university specialist on Vietnam, estimated that 50,000 people were executed during the reform, and that at least twice that number were imprisoned.[8] In an interview with Ernst Utrecht in Indonesia Ho Chi Minh admitted to 10,000 deaths.[9] The journal of the Vietnamese Communist Party, *Nhan Dan*, admitted that 30% of landowners condemned were innocent.

The storm raised by the violence of the reform could not be stilled in one day. To consolidate the unity of the local party cells was a crucial and delicate task. It was a question of uniting the middle peasants – old Party hands and members of the resistance – with the poor peasants and landless labourers – new Party members and activists of the reform. On 22 November 1956, *Nhan Dan* published an article entitled, 'Our task when we return to the villages', which contained what may be called a code of good conduct for those who had been imprisoned and were now released. In numerous instances, these latter refused to have anything to do with the cadres who had sent them to jail. In other instances they induced the cadres to attend the sessions of self-criticism. President Ho Chi Minh – his reputation unassailed in the midst of all that had taken place – exhorted his countrymen to reconciliation. On 16 February *Nhan Dan* reported that at Hung Yen the reinstated members of the party had a plan to arrest those who had denounced them. When their plans were foiled, they went on strike and refused to work with the Party. On 19 February *Nhan Dan* wrote that 'the mistakes of agrarian reform and its omissions had seriously affected the grass-roots unity of the Party in the countryside' and exhorted the peasants 'to forget their personal grievances and continue to work for unity'.

The rectification campaign which began in the summer of 1956 was completed by the end of 1957. Thus ended agrarian reform and with it the national, democratic and popular revolution in North Vietnam. It embraced all the rural areas, comprising 1.5 million hectares of cultivated land and 10 million persons. More than 810,000 hectares, 1,846,000 head of cattle, 148,565 houses were distributed to 2,104,000 peasant households, comprising eight million persons or 73% of the rural population.

For a fair evaluation of the agrarian reform in North Vietnam, it is necessary to bear in mind both the mistakes committed and the results achieved.

The following positive results may be listed:

– from a political standpoint, the reform had placed definite limits on the landowners as a class and had transformed the poor peasants into middle peasants (see Table 1); the people's power, founded on worker-peasant unity, was thus consolidated;
– from a military standpoint, agrarian reform lay behind the victory of Dien Bien Phu and marked the final collapse of French colonial power;
– from an economic standpoint, the reform had liberated the rural forces of production, increased agricultural production (see Table 2) and paved the way for industrial development.

Table 1.1
Redistribution of Lands After Agrarian Reforms

	Average Holdings per Capita (in sq. metres)	
	1945[1]	*After the Reform*[2]
Landowner	10093	738
Rich Peasant	6393	1547
Middle Peasant	1372	1610
Poor Peasant	431	1437
Agricultural Worker	124	1413

[1] Situation in 3,653 communes in 1945 (against a total of 5,673), *Kinh tê Viêt Nam 1945–1960*, Hanoi, p.49.
[2] *Ibid*., p.86.

Table 1.1a
Redistribution of Lands After Agrarian Reforms

	Distribution of		*Families*	*Average*
	Lands (1000 ha.)	*Cattle (1000 head)*	*Benefited (in 1000s)*	*per Family (in sq.m.)*
Agricultural Workers	170.4	38.8	416.0	4,095
Poor Peasants	440.4	31.0	1,059.8	4,155
Middle Peasants	179.0	2.5	539.6	3,317
Paupers	8.5	1.4	35.0	2,282
Other Workers	11.7	0.3	52.9	2,216
Total	*810.0*	*74.0*	*2,104.1*	*3,848*

Source: *Cuc thông kê trung uong, 5 nam xây dung kinh tê và van hoa*, Hanoi, 1960, p.83.

Table 1.2
Growth of Agricultural Production

	1939	1955	1956	1957
Cultivated Area (1000 ha.)	2125	2627	2874	2637
Irrigated Area (1000 ha.)	365	923	1571	1528
Paddy Yield (cwts per ha.)	13	16	18	18
Food Yield per capita (in Kg.)	228	287	335	286
Paddy Yield per capita (in Kg.)	221	260	294	272

Sources: *Etudes vietnamiennes*, No 44, p.90.

Notes

1. K. Marx, *Le Capital*, Vol.III, Ed. Sociales, Paris, 1950, pp.154-5.
2. Charles Bettelheim, *La Transition vers l'économie socialiste*, Maspero, 1977, p.13. The author has studied in particular Soviet agriculture, on which he bases his theoretical reflection.
3. K. Marx, *Le Capital*, Vol. VIII, Ed. Sociales, Paris, 1950, p.257.
4. K. Marx, Lettre à Vera Zassoulitch, Vol. XXVII des Oeuvres de 18 Marx et Engels, en Russe, Moscow, p.681.
5. 'The peasantry cannot be relied upon to direct the revolution. The main reason is that their mode of production is that of the individual craftsman and to that extent is not an advanced mode of production. Moreover, the peasantry is not a radically revolutionary class.' (Truong Chinh, *Ecrits*, 1953, p.373).
6. The figures here were overestimated and this led to certain abuses in the implementation of agrarian reform. The reform cadres made every effort to find landowners, in order to arrive at the declared total of 5%. In reality landowners in 1949 did not exceed 2%.
7. Land confiscation without compensation and land requisition without compensation had the same effect on the economic plane, but not on the political. Land confiscation made the landowner an object of scorn and was meant to be politically a punitive measure.
8. Bernard Fall, *Les Deux Vietnam*, Ed. Payot, Paris, p.184.
9. Ernst Utrecht, 'Interview with Ho Chi Minh', in *Journal of Contemporary Asia* 3 : 2, 1973, p.220.

2. Economic Structure

The commune of Hai Van is situated in the district of Hai Hau, some 120 km. to the east of Hanoi and below the principal tributary of the Red River. It is a region which has made gradual inroads into the sea through alluvion. The majority of human settlements have been spontaneous in this region, beginning in the 13th Century, except under the Nguyen, with Nguyen Cong Tru, who organized migrations of the populace. Even though it is situated on the edge of the sea there are few fishermen there, for all immigrants have come from the interior. The commune of Hai Van, which is near the sea, is composed exclusively of agriculturists and consisted, in 1979, of 5,200 inhabitants, of whom 85% are Catholics. They are made up of five former villages which today form the hamlets of the commune.

The Village Before the Revolution

Being a part of the structure of a tributary mode of production (Asiatic), the Vietnamese village, the *láng*[1] , has guarded through the years its very high degree of internal autonomy in relation to the central political power, bound to it only indirectly by the payment of tribute, it is a little world of its own with the regrouping of only a few families. It would be wrong to believe, however, that we have here a village with an egalitarian form of society. There have been proprietors, 'notables', litterati, temples, churches, etc. which have been the chief sharers of the land. In fact, the sharing of the village land held in common, was the basis of the organization of production and of social life. It is this which preserved the Vietnamese villages from disintegration, through the development of a pre-capitalist society, and fostered the conservation of the patriarchal system of families and the system of blood-relationship as the backbone of their internal structure. Gradually, however, the litterati, and the notables' began to arrogate to themselves feudal rights, and later, the colonial regime made good use of such persons as middlemen for the exercise of their power. These structures passed over into the villages which now constitute the commune of Hai Van.

Prior to 1945 the land, in theory, was held in common and the head of the village was charged with the task of making annual allocations of the land to families according to their capacities for cultivating it. In practice, however, only the land which had not already been acquired by private landlords, according to very singular criteria, was in fact distributed. One of the present hamlets is a former village of beggars or of tares (*tareau*), a name derived from the fact that the inhabitants of the village were so poor that they had to live by begging and had only the tares for nourishment, not being able to afford rice. The land surface is 750 *meaux* in extent, of which 500 *meaux* are rice fields. All this land was held in common and every male worker between 18 and 60 years of age was bound, at least in theory, to see to the cultivation of two *chas* (370 sq. metres). The young sometimes had to wait for several years before sharing in the work, and large numbers had to migrate to find work elsewhere: to the coal mines of the Hong Hai region in the North, the French rubber plantations in the South, the port of Hai Phong. In fact, in this village, seven landed proprietors had seized, in the course of years, 70% of the land held in common. A variety of subterfuges had been made use of to bring this about. The head of the village conceded two *meaux* to each head of the clan. Moreover, the sons of the 'notables' received a portion of the land as a title of honour, but they were dispensed from working the land, though they enjoyed the fruits of its exploitation. The chief of police and each of the police officers enjoyed similar privileges. In addition, 80 *meaux* were kept in reserve for the unforeseeable needs of the 'notables'. In short, from the head of the village to the 'notables', from the litterati to police officers or to some other functionaries, the peasant saw the common land, which had to be distributed, shrinking away. Obliged to work for a miserable wage, they were scarcely able to survive.

The magnates increased their wealth by dispossessing the petty landlords and even the middlemen, by the subterfuge of usurious loans; and this often brought about the surrender of the land to clear the debt. And this was not all: the Catholics of the village had to cultivate the land of the parish and each of them had to furnish a tithe on the land they cultivated. The non-Catholics had to do likewise for their temples. And, last of all, they had to cultivate the 'rice fields of death', the revenue of which served to pay for the religious services in commemoration of the dead.

The implements of agricultural production were primitive – a very small hoe or plough. Irrigation and manuring were practically unknown. Yields were very low despite the richness of the soil – around a tonne of rice per hectare. A large number of inhabitants fell victim to the famine which afflicted Vietnam in 1945. In the commune, of some 2,500 persons, around 1,000 disappeared. The material situation was precarious (only three brick houses as against more than 300 today, two bicycles for 70% of the people as against 970 today) and the level of education was scarcely better – there were only six children in the village attending primary school.

The inhabitants of the former village of beggars (now one hamlet of Hai Van) are today filled with indignation at the conditions they experienced before the revolution. It is not difficult for them to make a comparison with the past for they lived through the transition. Neither the village nor the hamlet represents extreme cases; it was the common lot of the peasants of Vietnam. When the inhabitants of Production Group No.1, which corresponds today to this hamlet, compare their present situation with that of the past, there is scarcely need to question them to get them to speak.

The Agrarian Reform

The prolongation of the war reined in the movement of reform organized in 1945 and it was restarted only in 1954. As we will have occasion to specify in the pages that follow, the history of the commune was very chequered at this time. The exodus of Catholics was a hard blow for Hai Van, almost half of its families leaving. But the reforms went ahead regardless: each peasant received an area of 300 sq. metres to cultivate – land expropriated from the landlords. The landlords were tried; in the village of beggars they were all 'notables', and, being Catholics, they exercised responsibilities in the parish. Two of them were executed for collaboration with the French; five others were pardoned and today they have accepted the new conditions of production and even demanded that they be allowed to enjoy the same rights as other citizens. This was acquiesced to, according to each case, after three, five or seven years and their children were allowed to enlist in the army. At present they are fully enfranchised members of the co-operative.

But at Hai Van agrarian reform has not been a simple process. The political-religious backwash had its repercussions which extended over a period of several years. A section of the Catholics were reluctant to take part in the new processes of production and the clergy scarcely encouraged them. The personnel of the party of the village were not always men of experience, either in agricultural technique or in social organization. Some of them were penalized for their short-comings but they have all been reinstated today. All these difficulties exerted their repercussions on production to such an extent that yields became very low and it was necessary, in consequence, to have recourse to exemption from the payment of taxes. Patient efforts were needed to restore the situation to normalcy.

The Co-operative

Evolution of the Co-operative

The co-operative movement began in the village in 1959. It was centred exclusively on the hamlets which remained not only basic units of the social and cultural life of the village but also of agricultural production. The first stage was terminated in 1960. The peasants pooled together all their implements of work and organized themselves into teams of mutual self-help. The bases of the organizations were constituted by the new units of small co-operatives of the neighbourhood. The second stage dates from the period 1963-64. It was a question this time of the collectivization of the means of production, viz. the land, and of the transformation of production itself in the direction of a diversification of agricultural production (rice is not cultivated exclusively). Nine basic units were fused into five co-operatives which now acquired the dimensions of hamlets (four villages or *lángs*).

It was necessary to wait for about a decade to elapse in order to pass on to the next stage. In 1970–77 a co-operative was set up within a communal framework. But this transformation was not only the result of the fusion between the five existing co-operatives, the reform bore on the two following elements: on the one hand, new material and technical bases by irrigation works and the gradual electrification of the pumping system; and on the other, a new division of labour. Ten working groups were organized, and, at the infrastructural level, footpaths and roads were made, cultivated surfaces were levelled, and a reorganization of living space took place in some hamlets. New collective equipment was fabricated, at the level of the commune and at the hamlet level; space for drying, stables for buffaloes, libraries, schools, crèches, dispensaries, etc. were organized.

Production increased from about one tonne per hectare before the agrarian reform to about five tonnes when the only co-operative of the commune was established. Yet things have not been easy: there has been political resistance to the establishment of new structures on the part of the Catholic population, and managerial disorders have not always favoured evolution in a positive direction. Also, during this period, peasants regularly took up cultivation of their little individual plots, and this lasted, though with diminishing frequency, up to 1977. Added to this was the war, with the departure of many men to the front, and five bomb attacks which killed two children, but did not cause much damage to the material side of the organization.

The reorganization of production was effected according to the following stages: first of all an attempt was made to place land, and the rice field in particular, on a rational basis. Then a detailed study was made of the surface area of the land and of the quality of the soil. In the second phase, a transformation was effected on the structure of the varieties of rice according to each harvest. It was then that, in the third stage, the hydraulic system was studied and gradually established. From there another step was taken to increase the sources of fertilizers, especially green manure – chemical fertilizers were a luxury. Finally, a redivision of the rice fields for the work-groups had to be undertaken. Some of them were close to their homes and others far away; some were situated in very fertile areas and others not. Each group was entrusted with two or three sections consisting of about 10–15 hectares of rice fields. In 1977 a new regrouping took place and there was a change-over from 10 work-groups to six – five corresponding to the hamlets and one special group, that of the aged, who decided to continue to work even after the age of retirement on a pension, by occupying themselves with the production of fruits and lentils.

It must be added that the population of the village grew; youth could no longer find enough employment in the co-operative or in the economic activities of the district, and so emigration had to come into the picture.

Departures were organized in the direction of the High Plateaus, and also towards the New Economic Zones of the South. In 1979, 26 families set out towards the South; they comprised 40 workers and 160 persons all told; the commune organized the departure, selecting only families that volunteered, the co-operative providing them with the necessary means of living till the time of self-sufficiency.

The Co-operative as an Economic Subject

The concept of an economic subject, such as that elaborated by Charles Bettelheim in the work cited above, is very useful for an analysis of what the co-operative represents with regard to the work-group. This is indeed an important question, for we will see below that the work-group, corresponding to the hamlet, is, from the sociological point of view, a concrete social unit which, for the persons who live and work at this level, delimits their horizon. Even the co-operative, at the level of the commune, in itself, constitutes a little world of its own, which escapes their grasp, at least partially. For the organization to acquire collective control, one must reckon with the factors the importance of which ought not to be minimized, especially when the way is being prepared for production on a vast scale.

One can speak of an *economic subject* when there is an entity that is such that it is possible to exercise effective control over the forces of production and to make non-subordinate choices. These are either centres of appropriation of nature or centres of distribution for the products. According to Bettelheim, these are centres of such a nature that, 'there would be no other similar agent capable of making a socially influenced decision more efficiently than this economic subject'.[2] It cannot be doubted that, in the present state of the forces of production, the co-operative can be defined in this manner, while the work-group cannot. It has been so to such an extent that small co-operatives (that of the hamlet) have been able to satisfy the needs of the organization of production. Today it has become a collective for work or a technical unit.

For each economic subject there ought to be a corresponding juridical subject, i.e. a possibility of taking a decision which has both administrative and juridical value. This obtains in the organs of the co-operative. But let us study the questions of the organization of production in greater detail, in so far as we have been able to observe them in the co-operative of Hai Van.

The Level of the Work-Group

It is among the members of Group no.1 that our study has been deepest. And so, we will look at this group in some detail, based on an interview with the head of the group. A son of poor peasants, the head of the group comes from a family of four children. His father had to leave the village in order to go and work in the mines of Hong Gai; his mother came from a very poor peasant family of the beggars' *láng*. She had four children of whom the eldest son terminated his studies with the second cycle and the daughter married a career soldier. He has been head of the group for eight years and has been re-elected each time, even though he wished to be relieved of his responsibilities in favour of another. He is a member of the Party and a practising Catholic.

The work group is a union of 228 households, the surface area of which social unit covers 228 hectares, 37 of which are set aside for the cultivation of rice, secondary cereals and other forms of agriculture and to dwellings. A little less than 5% of the land is set aside for private gardens. From 1967 production has been on the increase uninterruptedly apart from 1977 when a slight diminution was experienced on account of unfavourable climatic conditions. But now it has returned to a satisfactory level, and for four years in succession it has been awarded the district certificate of 'socialist group'. Within the territory of the group there are two granaries for cereals, a place for drying the grain, a crèche, a school for mothers, a dispensary, a church and a co-operative store. The rearing of cattle is not done on a collective basis, except for 18 draught buffaloes. There are also four brick-kilns employing 140 workers and a tile-kiln employing 11 workers. Plans are afoot to set up a unit for carpet weaving. But it is the cultivation of rice in which most of the workers are gainfully employed; 180 of them work in the rice fields. Further, 40 workers are employed on the land belonging to the group.

To modernize the hamlet it is necessary to diversify employment. Several concrete bridges have been built and roads metalled. There is no mechanization other than some electric pumps. On the other hand, irrigation canals run throughout the territory and facilitate transport by sampan and one can say that the mastery of the water problem is an accomplished fact. But all this has necessitated new criteria for the geographical redistribution of the economic functions, and especially for the distribution of dwellings. Further, a rearrangement of the rural habitations was undertaken and only ten families have not yet entered into this scheme. Three of them will be settled before the end of the year 1979. This spatial reorganization of the habitations has been made along the length of the canals and the new roads, thus making possible a more rational utilization of the land at a time when families are beginning to build houses. All this is not easy to realize; patience and persuasion are necessary from time to time, according to the head of the group.

The function of the head of the group is to be especially concerned with the organization of production. This is measured in function of norms which have been elaborated on the basis of recommendations made by the work group, by the committee of management of the co-operative, and is subject to constant revision and adaptation. They have therefore the assent of the heads of the work groups as well as of the peasants. There is a system of points by which the remuneration for work and for the distribution of the produce is calculated. The scheme of reallocation is discussed between the members of each team for distribution in the form of paddy or of money, and the results produced by each member of the team are published. This is how things work in theory, but at times there are discussions and disagreements and it pertains to the head of the group to offer solutions to them.

The organization of work under the co-operative system has definitely improved the living conditions of the peasants. Not only has the yield from the land increased, but so have the comforts available in the homes. Practically all the houses are now built of brick. Today there is an average of 1.4 bicycles per family and almost every house possesses a chiming clock – the status symbol, *par excellence*, of success. The incomes of the families vary, but the average is around 1,500 dongs per annum, going up to a maximum of 3,500 dongs. Domestic economy accounts for a large part of the revenue. Only 20 households do not derive any revenue from it, and most of those who live in them are the aged who enjoy various advantages according to their condition, going even so far as to receive a free ration of paddy. The head of the group says that he produces in his garden, by way of rearing animals on a small scale, 20 pigs, poultry, and 500 fish and also keeps pigeons and four dogs.

As for the future, the head of the group talks of mechanization and electrification as the stages being looked forward to. Everyone is hopeful, he says, but at the same time he has his fears, for employment will diminish and then some will have to leave for the New Economic Zones, although the people are very attached to their native places. Obviously, there will always be people here. The transition to production on a vast scale is always a prospect to stir up a certain fear in the hearts of the peasants. However, management is well organized and difficulties are ironed out as they have always been when there has been a transition to a new stage of work by the team from the time when eight specialist teams were organized. It is quite clear from the foregoing that if the work group is not an economic subject in the sense defined above, one could call it, in a paraphrase of Bettelheim, a *social subject*, i.e. that the satisfaction of the social needs and cultural and interpersonal relations go beyond the level of the family and find their firm basis there for their concrete realization. This means that no one can live at this level without being obliged, except in an accessory capacity, to have recourse to a higher rung in the administrative ladder; for those who live at this dimension, this constitutes the level of social consciousness, as symbolic of the totality of their daily life. It is their world in every sense of the word.

As we will have occasion to say later, in studying in more detail the phenomenon of the levels of awareness at which the peasantry participate, at least in the commune under study, and perhaps because the groups correspond to the former villages, this unity remains still a very strong source of identity and it constitutes, further, a bond of psychological security. At this level, consciousness of participating in the making of economic decisions is very real. It is definitely much more so than at the co-operative level. It is, in the present state of the development of the forces of production, the real and objective bond of the 'collective ruler', at least for the majority of peasants. Needless to say, some have gone beyond this level of immediate identification, and in the measure in which they have been integrated into sharing in the responsibilities which surpass the limits of the work-group or in function of the development of the general services rendered by the commune. It appears already that for some whose work-place is elsewhere, for school children, for ex-servicemen, etc., their horizon clearly extends beyond the hamlet. The vice-president of a district committee, while protesting that the former village continues to remain a particularly strong point of anchorage adds that a sense of communal belonging is also becoming just as real: 'It is sufficient to notice the reactions of the peasantry when the commune is criticized', he declares.

The mere prevention of the concentration of social activity at the level of the former village does not yet yield a well founded sense of consistency. Let us not forget the existence of the former *láng*, i.e. let us not forget the cohesive power of the native habitat where the greater part of the clan is concentrated and which formerly constituted the basis of the land communally held. Today it corresponds, in the commune of Hai Van, to the work brigade with its appropriate economic equipment.[3] One can find there the former parish and its church, as well as the basis of religious organization. It is also the centre for the functioning of the conciliation group and of the security force. In short, in spite of the existence of a new dimension – the commune – the former *láng* exists as a focus of *social identification*.

It is quite evident that the development of the forces of production demands from the peasants a social awareness that goes beyond the boundaries of the hamlet, but at the same time, not to reckon with this reality is to risk running into a whole host of difficulties. How is one to combine the economic subject with the social subject? This is certainly a key question for the success of a change-over to a superior stage of production.

A second reflection suggested itself to us after interviewing the head of the group, and it concerns the quality of leadership. It appears, in fact, that the exigencies with regard to the chief of the work-group extend far beyond the mere execution of piecemeal tasks within the co-operative. His role is a complex one, combining, at the same time, economic, social and cultural aspects. Possibly it is here, for the time being, in every case, that resides the key role of the whole social rural structure of today; that is our guess. Those who exercise responsibility in the co-operative, have, in fact, functions that are indubitably economic, and they are already further away in relation to the daily life of the peasant. The administrative functions of the commune devolve on those who hold responsibility there. Only the head of the group gathers together in his person the multiple responsibilities, and plays, in consequence, an overall role, even if this is done only at the local level.

Another type of work-group which we have already mentioned above, is Group no.6 or that of the aged. A woman is the head of this group; she is the former vice-president of the executive committee and former political commissar of the unit of the militia of the commune. She, therefore, has a militant past. Born of a family of poor peasants, she has had no schooling and learnt the alphabet only after the revolution; she has also followed a Party course. Of her three children, one is in the army, and her husband is also a soldier. Full of animation despite her 67 years she explained the working of the group. Founded in 1963, the group of the aged began to produce results in production from 1968. At this time there were 12 people over the age of 60, in charge of two hectares of mulberry trees. In the first year they produced 1,950 kg. of silk cocoons. Gradually the surface area was increased and the produce sold to the state. In 1968 the type of production was changed and the team was put in charge of what is called secondary production – i.e. fruits, lentils, cereals other than rice and the rearing of pigs. A hectare was given to them and in the first year after the change 12 men and five women earned 45,000 dongs. Later, ten other men and nine women joined the group. Today their annual earnings very between 80,000 and 90,000 dongs. In terms of cash, says the one responsible for the group, with pride, this is the work-group which contributes the most to the commune. This is quite correct, for, in fact, an important part of the produce can be sold in the open market. Thus raising pigs contributes about 15,000 dongs, and sericulture another 15,000.

At the time of the survey, the group comprised 30 men and nine women. The head of the group is elected by all the members of the co-operative. Work begins at 6 a.m. and ends at 5 p.m. (from 6 a.m. to 11 a.m. and from 2 p.m. to 5 p.m.). The secretary of the group who explained the statistics of the weekly production in tabulated form, in the group's hall of reunion, is an old man who was illiterate before 1954. Son of a poor peasant, he lost his parents at the age of nine. He emigrated to the South in search of work and was employed in a French rubber plantation there. In 1954, after the Geneva Accords, he took advantage of the occasion to return to his village in the North with his wife; both of them are Catholics. He was taught to read and write and was integrated into the co-operative on his return. When he reached the age of 60 he asked to be transferred to the group of the aged. Indeed, economic activity is not obligatory for the aged. They can also retire and there exists in the commune a rest home for invalids, but many prefer to continue their productive activity.

The Level of the Co-operative

The organization and functioning of a rural co-operative is sufficiently known to dispense with a detailed description of it.[4] In the inquiry made at Hai Van, our aim was not to make an economic study; our attention was centred rather on a specifically sociological aspect. As everywhere else in the district, the co-operative is based on the following scheme. On the one hand, the president and four vice-presidents have specialized responsibilities, for the commissariat, cultivation, cattle-rearing, and commerce. On the other hand, there are work-groups (sometimes called brigades), in our case, six in number, five of which are of dimensions geographically determined by the former villages, more than eight specialized units and work teams. Among the specialized units there is one for sowing, two for labour, one for hydraulics, two for fertilizers, one for transport and one for construction. To this fundamental structure must be added a section depending on the director of the committee, whose task is planning, fixing norms of work, statistics, accounts and technical questions.

While the members of the committee of management of the co-operative are elected directly by the members of the co-operative, those with responsibility, i.e. the president, the vice-presidents, etc., are elected by the committee and therefore elected by second remove.[5] It will be recalled that, at the level of the group, the head of the group is elected directly. This will be of some importance when we study the social awareness at the level of participation of peasants in the co-operative.

As everywhere else, the fixing of norms is done in collaboration with all the co-operatives of the district. Effects are monitored regularly by observing the work of a team in each domain of production according to quantity and time. The results are compared with those of other co-operatives at the district level. The general norm is then again adapted to the particular circumstances of the co-operative, if necessary. This is then discussed in a general assembly of the members of the co-operative. In the district of Hai Van the table of norms comprises 382 different levels: 165 for agriculture; seven for raising livestock; 178 for diverse trades; seven for transport; 25 for afforestation. In each co-operative – and this is the case for Hai Van – a final table is prepared in function of the different harvests, different kinds of terrain and different work teams. They comprise, in all, 80 norms. The individual norms are the basis for the award of points. For instance, a day's work by a carpenter is given ten points. Let us suppose that he can make a chair normally in a day. This will be equivalent to ten points. If he has not finished a chair in a day he will be given eight or nine points, according to the circumstances. It is the same for agricultural work. When the work is collective, the award of points is discussed between the members of the work team and in case there is no agreement, the norm is fixed by a majority vote. On several occasions the members of the co-operative have said that this sometimes provokes conflicts. Each one is paid according to the work done, measured in points.[6] In cases where the norms are not achieved, except for medical reasons and in case of exemptions for good reasons (for example, visiting one's parents on the occasion of a death), the ration of paddy is diminished.

The accountant of the co-operative keeps a record on the fulfilment of norms and the award of points. He maintains a weekly balance sheet and makes a report to the management committee of the co-operative. The revenues of the sale of produce of the different work groups sold either to the state or in the open market[7] is centralized at the level of the co-operative which makes advances to the different teams, and these are distributed according to the norms established. But, beyond collective work there is also the economic activity which the peasants develop in the domestic sector.

Active Population and Production

Between 1973 and 1978, the population of Hai Van increased from 4,620 to 5,503, i.e. an increase of 19.1%, and the growth has been chiefly by natural increase. Faced with the increase of mouths to be fed and, *a fortiori*, of the density of population, the common policy was to favour, ultimately, the emigration of young families into the New Economic Zones of the South (261 persons in 1978). This migratory movement, coupled with an increase in temporary emigration to schools of higher studies, has pushed back the growth in population to 12.9%. The population charts given in Table 2.1 refer to the resident population.

Table 2.1
Evolution of Resident and of Active Population in the Commune

Year	*Resident population*	*Index*	*Active population*	*Index*	*% Active population*
1973	4,589	100	2,641	100	57.6
1974	4,806	104.7	2,856	108.1	59.4
1975	4,912	107.0	2,987	113.1	60.8
1976	5,154	112.3	3,091	117.0	60.0
1977	5,211	113.6	2,834	107.3	54.4
1978	5,179	112.9	2,827	107.0	54.6

The comparison of the evolutions of the resident population and of the active population, indicates, on the one hand, that since 1976 a stabilization of the resident population has been achieved. On the other hand, the active population has decreased since 1977. This decline corresponds to the beginning of the migrations of the young families to the South. But this is not the only reason for the decline in the active population. An analysis of the structure of the table, according to the sexes, will show (Table 2.2) that since 1975 there has been a growth in the active male population, while the number of women workers in the co-operative or in the commune has diminished by 20.3% during the period 1975-78. One may surmise that after the liberation of South Vietnam, some women who had continued to work in the co-operative beyond the age of retirement, did actually retire then from active life.

Table 2.2
Evolution of Active Population According to the Sexes

Year	*Women*	*Index*	*Men*	*Index*
1973	1,407	100	1,234	100
1974	1,695	120.5	1,167	94.6
1975	1,700	120.8	1,287	104.3
1976	1,647	117.1	1,444	117.0
1977	1,434	101.9	1,400	113.5
1978	1,355	96.3	1,473	119.4

Sectors of Activity

Has the diminution of the active female population, partially compensated for by the increase of the active male population, affected the organization of work, and if so, to what extent? Table 2.3 looks at this.

The comparison between the three parts of the table indicates that the

Table 2.3
Evolution of Active Population According to Sectors of Activity

Total Active Population

Year	Agriculture		Livestock Rearing		Handicrafts		Hydraulics		Services		Management	
1973	1,371	100	139	100	951	100	104	100	51	100	25	100
1974	1,463	106.7	134	96	1,040	109.3	136	130.8	58	113.7	25	100
1975	1,589	115.9	113	81	1,048	110.2	154	148.1	60	117.6	23	92
1976	1,345	90.7	114	82	1,366	143.6	275	264.2	60	117.6	31	124
1977	945	68.9	155	111	1,423	149.6	191	187.7	64	125.5	56	224
1978	727	53.0	168	121	1,607	169.0	187	179.8	65	127.4	73	292

Active Female Population

Year	Agriculture		Livestock Rearing		Handicrafts		Hydraulics		Services		Management	
1973	842	100.0	71	100.0	394	100.0	48	100.0	45	100.0	7	100.0
1974	887	105.3	75	94.7	597	157.5	74	154.2	54	120.0	8	114.3
1975	963	114.4	56	79.0	548	139.1	71	147.9	54	120.0	8	114.3
1976	709	84.2	65	86.7	690	175.1	119	247.9	54	120.0	10	142.8
1977	548	65.1	90	120.0	647	164.2	77	160.4	58	128.9	16	228.6
1978	435	51.7	96	135.0	675	171.3	75	156.3	58	128.9	16	228.6

Active Male Population

Year	Agriculture		Livestock Rearing		Handicrafts		Hydraulics		Services		Management	
1973	529	100.0	68	100.0	557	100.0	56	100.0	6	100.0	18	100.0
1974	576	108.9	59	86.8	443	79.5	62	110.7	4	66.6	17	94.4
1975	626	118.3	57	83.8	500	89.8	83	148.2	6	100.0	15	83.3
1976	536	101.3	49	72.0	676	121.4	156	278.6	6	100.0	21	116.7
1977	397	75.0	65	95.6	776	139.3	114	203.6	6	100.0	42	233.3
1978	292	55.2	72	105.9	932	165.3	112	200.0	7	116.0	57	316.7

diminution of the active female population is manifested in the domain of agriculture. Nevertheless, because a diminution of the active male population has been recorded in this very sector, it is clear that it is a question here of a policy of the co-operative seeking to reduce the number of the agricultural workers. This is the reason for the reduction of the female work force. The question which arises is what the effect of this new orientation was on agricultural production. We will seek an answer to this question in what follows. Let us emphasize, finally, that the diminution of the work-force in the agricultural sector is on an equal footing with the strengthening of the work force in small scale local industries, and handicrafts, and in a lesser measure, in the hydraulic sector. In the last few years there has been a restructuring of the work force, which is apparent in Table 2.4.

It will be observed that in 1978 the majority of the active population of the

Table 2.4
Comparison Between Distribution of Active Population Between 1973 and 1978

Sectors of production	*1973*		*1978*		*Index of growth*
Agriculture	1,371	51.9%	727	25.7%	– 53.0%
Livestock rearing	139	5.3%	168	5.9%	+ 20.9%
Handicrafts	951	36.0%	1,607	56.8%	+ 69.0%
Hydraulics	104	3.9%	187	6.6%	+ 79.3%
Collective services	51	1.9%	65	2.3%	+ 27.4%
Management	25	0.9%	73	2.6%	+ 192.0%

Table 2.5
Distribution of People Employed in Local Industry According to their Activities (%)

Activities	*1973*		*1978*		*Index of growth*
Brick-making	480	50.5	815	50.7	+ 69.8
Carpentry and construction	62	6.5	148	9.2	+ 138.0
Mechanics	27	2.8	58	3.6	+ 114.8
Jute, matting	289	30.4	162	10.7	– 44.0
Lacework	0	–	154	10.2	–
Basket-making	5	0.5	6	0.4	–
Needlework and hairdressing	13	1.4	13	0.8	–
Forestry	75	7.9	91	5.7	+ 21.3
Transport	–	–	60	3.7	–

co-operative was no longer employed in agriculture properly so-called. In the space of five years the proportion of manpower between the two principal sectors of the commune had been reversed. Before analysing the effects of this restructuring of the work force on production, we must clarify the importance of the different industrial and artisan activities, according to the work-force employed.

It will be seen from Table 2.5 that the policy of the co-operative in the sector of small industries and handicrafts is orientated in three directions: 1) the strengthening of the work force occupied in brick-making and construction and, in a lesser measure, in mechanics and the fabrication of metal tools; 2) the diminution of effective hands in the jute and carpet industries. It is not a matter, in this case, of abandoning this type of activity, but of transferring it from the domain of collective economy to that of domestic economy and; 3) the creation of new sectors of activity.

During the years 1976–78, the co-operative created and developed a specialist team for the transport of its products by waterways and by road (in 1980 it acquired a lorry). Further, during the same period the co-operative was faced with the problem of finding employment for the younger generation, who were finishing their secondary school studies. The limits of the extent of cultivable land made it impossible to absorb even a hundred youths a year in agriculture, especially young girls. This meant for the co-operative the need to diversify the avenues of employment.

In 1976 youths who had just graduated from secondary school were promoted to cattle-rearing. In 1977 a workshop for embroidery and lace-making was set up where young girls received a professional training for one year before launching out into production for export, chiefly to west European countries. It is evident that so long as industrial development at the regional and district level is weak or non-existent, rural co-operatives will be faced every year with the problem of a workforce in excess of their needs and for whom new forms of employment will have to be found, requiring neither sophisticated equipment nor primary raw materials difficult to obtain. The products, however, will find outlets in local or foreign markets. The managers of the co-operatives believe that this is a problem difficult to solve.

Development of the Forces of Production

A decrease in the work-force in certain sectors of production must lead to a decrease of production, unless there is a development of the forces of production which ensures that production will not suffer from a decrease in the workforce. This is the hypothesis we are seeking to verify, and from this proceeds the first question on the evolution of production during the period under review.

The greatest diminution in the agricultural sector work-force has been recorded as 47% between 1973 and 1978. Since the purpose of this inquiry

Table 2.6
Indicators Showing Evolution of Agricultural Production

Surface area of:	*1973*	*1974*	*1975*	*1976*	*1977*	*1978*
Land cultivated (ha.)	439.53	439.52	439.52	439.52	451.62	460.26
Indices	100	100	100	100	102.8	104.7
Rice fields with three harvests	212.18	212.18	212.18	212.18	227.31	230.11
Indices	100	100	100	100	107.1	108.5
Rice fields with two harvests	183.45	183.45	183.45	183.45	180.42	187.00
Indices	100	100	100	100	98.3	101.9
Land under cereals	5.11	5.11	9.20	9.20	9.20	9.20
Indices	100	100	180	180	180	180
Land under vegetables	1.44	1.44	7.60	7.60	7.60	7.60
Indices	100	100	527.8	527.8	527.8	527.8
Rice yields						
Tonnes/ha.	6.2	8.0	6.2	8.9	8.8	7.1
Average for two years	7.1	7.1	7.5	8.8	7.9	

is not the economic order, only some indicators will be considered here.

These figures, as a whole, reveal that the diminution of the work-force since 1977 has not had a negative influence on the extension of the cultivated land; and it has been the same for rice fields producing three harvests a year. The diminution of the yield per ha. is due to adverse climatic conditions (drought and floods). This increase of the cultivated zone, especially the increase in extent of the intensely exploited rice fields, indicates very forcefully an increase in work. To what extent was this assured by the development of the technical base? Table 2.7 refers.

Table 2.7
Indicators Revealing the Development of the Technical Base

	1973	*1974*	*1975*	*1976*	*1977*	*1978*
Land irrigated (ha.):	258	238	260	265	280	280
Indices	100	92.2	100.8	102.7	108.5	108.5
by canals	130	130	153	153	153	153
by pumping	21	21	20	20	35	35
mechanized irrigation	58.5		66.5	65.3	67.1	67.1
Mechanization:						
Diesel	3	3	3	3	4	4
Pumping	2	2	2	2	4	5
Rice threshing machines	1	1	3	4	4	4
Machines for labour	–	–	–	–	–	1
Harrowing machines	–	–	–	–	–	1
Hand ploughing	89	106	105	105	110	130
Fertilizers:						
In tonnes/ha.	18.5	19	15	22	n.a.	21

If the figures in Table 2.7 indicate the beginnings of the process of mechanization of the means of production – beginnings which coincide with the diminution of the work-force in agriculture – they nevertheless appear insufficient to permit a substantial reduction in the work-force. The council of management of the co-operative estimates that it would be useless to introduce to Hai Van excessively sophisticated machinery, for it is certain that one of the effects would be at least partial unemployment of the effective personnel in agriculture. On its part, the industrial sector is not yet geared to mass production at the district level.

The diminution in the number of agricultural workers in the co-operative is due, in the last analysis, to a rationalization of the production. It is a fact that the introduction of new crops has led, since 1976, to the total abandonment of the rice crop of the fifth lunar month, thus increasing the spring harvest when the yield per ha. is much greater. In fact, the rice fields are used twice a year for the cultivation of rice. During the time when the soil is being turned, the members of the co-operative who so desire, may cultivate, at their own expense, a piece of collectively held land for the production of lentils which can serve as fodder for pigs raised at home and also serve to fertilize the soil.

The collective rearing of livestock at Hai Van is limited to pigs. In spite of the growth of the work-force occupied in raising livestock, the number of pigs has diminished. The diminution has not entailed a parallel diminution of meat sold to the state (in fact 2.4 times more) but there has been a diminution of pork given by the co-operatives to its members.

Table 2.8
Raising of Pigs and Production of Meat

	1973	*1978*	*Index of Increase*
Number of pigs	752	585	77.8
Quantity of meat sold to the state	4,570 kg.	11,351 kg.	239
Quantity of meat furnished to the co-operatives	22,322 kg.	12,050 kg.	54
Average weight of pigs sold	36 kg.	40 kg.	111.1
Number of pigs reared by members of the co-operative	1,215	1,953	160.7
Quantity of meat sold to the state	17,275 kg.	34,022 kg.	196.9
Quantity of meat consumed locally	19,955 kg.	44,655 kg.	224.8

The policy followed was to limit this distribution of meat to certain categories of persons – children in crèches, the inmates of homes for the aged and families with an insufficient revenue. In addition, the co-operative has gone ahead with the development of domestic husbandry and has furnished the members of the co-operative with piglings. Therefore, the task of the selection of the breeds of pigs and their reproduction devolves on the co-operative. Young animals are distributed gratis against an annual contribution of a determined quantity of dung to serve as fertilizer. This policy gives the co-operative the advantage of a fixed quota of manure without having to increase the space reserved for raising livestock, nor of having to invest in the construction of sties; for the members of the co-operative it is an appreciable source of certain revenue, the co-operative being responsible for the contribution to the state, the demand for which is growing and the price of which is agreed upon and fixed at a level midway between the government price and that of the free market (the latter fluctuates according to the vagaries of supply and demand).

With regards petty local industry and handicrafts, the available statistics refer to tables of sales of different products. They give, nevertheless, a general view of the probable evolution of production, the fluctuations in prices being almost insignificant. Table 2.9 refers.

Table 2.9
Evolution of Sales of Produce of Local Industry and Handicrafts

	1973	*1978*	*Index of growth*
Limestone	10,095	75,471	747
Bricks and tiles	135,920	92,489	68.0
Metal tools	4,412	6,344	143.8
Woodwork	6,703	18,307	274.4
Transport	20,930	30,225	144.4
Forest products	8,034	13,044	162.6
Carpets	59,861	41,305	69.0
Needlework	2,200	5,240	238.2
Total	*248,155*	*282,515*	*113.8*

When compared with the figures of 1973, the gross returns from sales have increased by 13.8% over five years and would have been higher still but for the decline recorded in the brick-making sector. One ought not to conclude that there has been a diminution in this domain or that, in so far as the work-force has been strengthened during the last year. Certainly, when the needs are considered the demand for building material is unlimited. However, other factors intervene – a lack of cement, for instance, can hold up construction. Further, in the commune itself, some peasant families postponed their building projects, while waiting to see the interim results of the experience gained by two families who have constructed a house in two stages.

All in all, one may say that the transfer of the most important part of the work-force to small industries can have positive effects on the economic development of the co-operative, in the measure in which the state is a regular buyer of the produce, for it is evident that the local market is rapidly reaching saturation point. Add to this that the transfer of the work-force to small industries is producing another effect – the increase in the number of working days. In 1973, the 2,641 active workers put in 491,938 days of work, i.e. an individual average of 174 days – which means an average increase of 10.1% for each worker. The growth in the duration of co-operative work – a phenomenon which is simultaneous with the change of policy in the distribution of the work-force – is caused precisely by this factor. In effect, this induces the agricultural workers to work for a greater number of days in the co-operative, and offers to the workers engaged in small industry a more regular work schedule.

Distribution of the Social Product

Let us consider in this last part some indicators of the redistribution of the social product.

This distribution reveals that almost 70% of the production returns directly to the co-operative producers. The contributions to the state represent 20% of the whole. However, three-quarters of the contributions are sold at an 'agreed' price which is midway between the state price and the open market price. The

Table 2.10
Distribution of Total Production of Food (tonnes)

	1973	%	*1978*	%	*% Increase*
State					
Taxes	69.4		70.0		0.86
Selling price to the state	2.4		2.6		8.3
Agreed selling price	27.2		208.9		668
Hydraulic reimbursement	1.5		1.5		–
Total	*100.5*	*9.15*	*283.0*	*20.4*	*181.6*
Co-operative					
Sowing	38.7		39.0		0.77
Collective cattle rearing	40.1		71.2		77.6
Cattle rearing by the family	35.2		27.0		–23.3
Reserve, welfare, management	10.5		12.0		14.3
Total	*124.5*	*11.3*	*149.2*	*10.8*	*19.8*
Members of the Co-operative					
Compensation	3.0		6.4		13.3
Gifts to low income families	82.1		65.6		–20.1
Exchange for fertilizer	70.6		56.1		–20.5
Work points	717.4		826.8		9.4
Total	*873.1*	*79.5*	*954.9*	*68.8*	*9.3*
Grand total	*1,098.1*	*100.0*	*1,387.1*	*100.0*	*26.3*

proceeds of these sales are also an indirect return for the members of the co-operative. Hence, the contribution in kind from the co-operative to the collectivity (state) does not exceed 5% of the food produced agriculturally. The deductions made by the co-operative amount to 11%. Three-quarters of these deductions are reinvested in production either as a reserve for sowing or as animal fodder. Finally, it should be noted that the co-operative, as such, has no commercial dealings with the free market. This does not hinder the individual members of the co-operative from selling to the free market a part of their produce in kind.

It should be noted that three-quarters of the net revenues of the co-operative is distributed to the members, that 8% constitute taxes paid to the state to be converted into cash, and that 17.6% is retained at the co-operative; 82% of the surplus financial deductions made by the

Table 2.11
Distribution of Net Revenue of the Co-operative (dongs)

	1973	*%*	*1978*	*%*	*% Growth*
State					
Agricultural taxes	27,843		39,814		43
Industrial taxes	2,757		4,000		45.1
Total	*30,600*	*8.1*	*43,814*	*8.0*	*43.2*
Co-operative					
Accumulation	41,650		79,361		90.5
Welfare	13,020		12,874		–1.2
Reserve	–		4,400		–
Total	*54,670*	*14.4*	*96,635*	*17.6*	*76.8*
Members of the Co-operative					
Compensation	483		10,650		21.4
Work-points	293,310		398,488		35.8
Total	*293,793*	*77.5*	*409,138*	*74.4*	*39.26*
Grand total	*379,063*	*100.0*	*549.587*	*100.0*	*45*

Table 2.12
Average Annual Revenue of a Worker in the Co-operative

	1973	*1978*	*% Growth*
From the Co-operative			
In kind (rice)	500 kg.	574 kg.	14.8
In cash	110 dongs	174 dongs	58.2
From the domestic economy	310 dongs	495 dongs	59.7

co-operative is added to the capital; 13%, i.e. 2.3% of the total net revenue, is meant for welfare, i.e. for school equipment, for health, and for cultural activities. These figures are relatively low and ought, without doubt, to increase in the coming years, if one takes into account the state of the buildings and equipment.

Domestic Economy

The organization of the collective economy of Hai Van is being effected on a surface area that is a little less than 5% of the arable land of the commune. It was in 1963 that a new survey was made; 5% of the land has been allocated to families at the rate of 36 sq. metres per person, and generally the land lies around the house of the family. Almost the whole of the surface area is equally fertile. The problem, in such a case, is created by change in the composition of the families. The same problem crops up when there is question of the distribution of non-transferable land when agrarian reform takes place in non-socialist societies. Prior generations wither and die away. The young are employed in military service or they marry. The number of children varies after a generation. As these changes are progressive it is difficult to establish strict norms that work automatically. It is the duty of the commune, therefore, to attempt to settle matters amicably, but without adding to the surface area of privately held land. At Hai Van, there does not seem to have been any abuse in this field. When a family can dispose of more than 36 sq. metres per person, the commune allocates the surplus to someone else. But the situation of the garden and the pond close by the house does not always make the task easy.[8]

The average proportion of cash revenue of families yielded by domestic economy is evaluated in Hai Van at 45%, which is greater than the average estimate of the district, which is 38%. When the peasants are questioned they say that the work done on their private plot of ground is definitely more intensive than that done on collectively held land, and that by as much as twice or thrice. It is true that the type of production is different: e.g. mulberry trees, lentils, fruit, animal raising, etc. And it is the same with regard to the use of fertilizer. The average per *sâ* (360 sq. metres) for green fertilizer (*azolle*) is about four quintals for land belonging to the co-operative, and from five quintals to a tonne for private gardens. It is nine to ten quintals per *sâ*, and ten to 14 respectively for artificial fertilizer.

In our inquiry, we have included some questions concerning domestic economy – what it represents for the peasant in terms of investment of time, of revenue and of consumption possibilities. The results are shown in Tables 2.13–2.15.

These three tables furnish interesting indicators, which we have interpreted only provisionally because the extent of the sampling does not permit us to do more, but they seem to indicate some existing tendencies. First of all, there is an important differential level of productivity and this can be deduced from a comparison between the average number of hours spent in the home garden and the revenue which is derived from it. The results are shown in Table 2.16.

The tendencies which Table 2.16 reveals are very striking. It is clear that social and cultural factors are very important. Persons of middle-class peasant origin seem to have a better knowledge of production than others; they are much better informed than those who come from poor peasant families. There are also significant differences between the young and the aged, between those who have had only a primary school education and those who have passed out of secondary school. Political participation also seems to affect productivity. Whether one is a Catholic or not is hardly significant.

Production from private gardens depends on a variety of factors, and one should not try to press on to conclusions which go beyond the premises contained in the statistics. Some villagers may prefer this or that kind of

Table 2.13
Time Given Weekly to Private Economy According to Categories of Population Studied

	0-10hours	*10-20hours*	*20-30hours*	*More than 30 hours*	*Average in hours*
Sex: Males	28.1	40.6	18.8	3.1	14.5
Females	46.2	46.2	7.7	–	11.2
Age: 35 and less	50.0	27.8	22.2	–	12.2
35–49	22.2	55.6	11.1	–	13.75
50 and over	22.2	44.4	11.1	11.1	15.6
Political Participation:					
Party and organizations	40.0	46.7	13.4	–	10.3
Non-members	30.0	40.0	15.7	3.3	14.1
Religion:					
Catholic	33.3	39.4	12.2	–	12.6
non-Catholic	33.3	50.0	8.3	8.3	13.8
Education:					
Primary	35.3	58.0	–	5.9	13.5
Secondary	38.1	33.3	28.6	–	14
Origin:					
Poor peasant	38.7	38.7	16.1	3.2	13.2
Middle-class peasant	33.3	66.6	–	–	11.6

Table 2.14
Annual Revenue Derived from Private Economy (dongs)

	Less than 100	*101-200*	*201-300*	*301-400*	*More than 400*	*Average**
Sex: Males	6.3	34.4	25.0	18.8	3.1	228
Females	7.7	38.5	15.4	15.4	–	205
Age: 35 and less	5.6	33.3	33.3	22.2	–	229
35–49	11.1	38.9	16.7	16.7	5.6	219
50 and over	–	33.3	11.1	11.1	–	210
Political Participation:						
Party and organizations	–	46.7	13.4	26.8	–	227
Non-members	10.0	30.0	26.7	13.3	3.3	215
Religion:						
Catholic	9.1	36.4	12.2	12.2	3.0	235
non-Catholic	–	33.3	33.3	16.7	–	225
Education:						
Primary	11.8	29.4	23.5	–	–	177
Secondary	–	47.5	23.8	23.8	4.8	226

Origin:						
Poor peasant	9.7	48.4	9.7	12.1	–	196
Middle peasant	–	8.3	58.3	33.3	–	263

* Calculated solely on the number of persons who made a declaration of their revenues.

Table 2.15
Use of Domestic Revenues (% calculated on the total of persons belonging to each category)

	Habitation	*Food*	*Other consumer goods*	*Savings*	*Investme in private economy*
Sex: Males	96.9	90.6	75.0	21.9	34.4
Females	100.0	100.0	84.6	23.1	38.5
Age: 35 and less	100.0	100.0	72.2	11.1	61.1
35–49	100.0	68.9	77.8	22.2	5.6
50 and over	88.9	88.9	88.9	44.4	11.1
Political Participation:					
Party and organizations	100.0	100.0	66.7	13.3	66.7
Non-members	96.7	90.0	73.3	26.7	20.0
Religion:					
Catholic	97.0	90.9	69.7	21.2	39.4
Non-Catholic	100.0	100.0	100.0	25.0	25.0
Education:					
Primary	100.0	100.0	88.2	41.2	23.5
Secondary	100.0	95.2	76.2	9.5	38.1
Origin:					
Poor peasant	96.8	90.3	72.2	45.2	19.4
Middle peasant	41.7	41.7	33.3	33.3	33.3

production for reasons other than plain, economic benefits. Apart from the figures cited there seem to be certain indications that factors of economic rationality are influenced either by past experience, or by education, or by age, or by political participation, often combined with the educational factor. This expresses a certain logic, perhaps to be expected, but interesting, all the same, when it is revealed by the facts. Let us add that if all classes of villagers utilize this revenue for the betterment of their homes and for nourishment, in a practically similar way, (except for the middle-class peasants about whom we have very unconvincing statistics), the differences of behaviour in the sphere of savings, or of investment in private gardens are appreciably greater. The younger generations and the members of political and other mass

Table 2.16
Comparison Between Hours Spent in Domestic Work and Revenue Derived therefrom

Category	*Average number of hours per week*	*Average annual revenue*	*Index**
35 years and less	12.12	229	18.9
50 years and over	15.36	210	13.7
Political participation (Party and organizations)	10.18	227	22.3
Non-members	14.06	215	15.3
Primary education	13.30	177	13.3
Secondary education	14.00	226	16.1
Poor peasant origin	13.12	196	12.9
Middle peasant origin	11.36	263	23.2
Catholic	13.30	235	17.6
Non-Catholic	13.48	225	16.7

* Average annual revenue divided by the number of hours per week.

organizations seem to invest more in their private gardens. Contrariwise, the level of savings scarcely reveals any particular tendency in respect of variable reserves. This element depends, very probably, on other factors such as the size of the family, the fact of having built a permanent home, etc.

Towards Large-Scale Production

It is important to understand that large-scale production signifies at once, a stage in the growth of the forces of production and an evolution in the social relations effected by production. It is, therefore, a political decision of very great importance. Preparation for this stage has been going on now for several years, and it was in 1974 that a conference was held at Thai Binh on this question, and a broad plan of action was decided upon. We will recall here some aspects, relevant to our inquiry, to help us to understand what such a step will mean in reality.

In an exposition at this conference, Le Duan, the Secretary of the Party, explained the reasons behind the wished-for evolution, in these words:

> At present, though the co-operatives are socialist economic units, they still have a markedly corporate character. Each of them is an almost independent organization, bound by gossamer threads to other co-operatives and to the national economy. Worse still, it is the same for each production brigade, at the very heart of one and the same co-operative. Even though collectivized, our agriculture still bears the

characteristics of piecemeal production.[9]

Later on, Duan remarked that: 'Every day, every hour, capitalism is being engendered even by small-scale production'.[10]

Pham Van Dong recalled that for all progress in agriculture, be it socialist or capitalist, there is a 'point of contact'. It is the growth of the forces of production in agriculture.[11] Such a growth signifies, according to Le Duan, transformations in all spheres. The management of hydraulics, the improvement of the soil, the reorganization of the workforce, a new orientation of production based on a delimitation of the economic zones and a renewal of manufacturing plant.[12] But it is necessary, at the same time, to organize new relations of production and management.

The new dimension of this agricultural reorganization is the district, comprising, on an average, about 12,000 hectares and 40,000 workers. This ought to permit not only the rationalization of the workforce in the various branches of the economy, but also a better organization of education, health care, cultural activities and defence. There will be a new framework for the management of the economy, whereas, up to now, the district formed the organ of co-ordination of the co-operatives while at the same time being a link uniting it with the state for the greater part of its functions.

Such a new phase of economic development must be minutely studied and prepared over a long period of time. Le Duan said, in the course of his exposition at Thai Binh, 'We must possess the scientific knowledge of our age: the social sciences, the economic sciences, the technical sciences . . . to apply them, to make them pass into life'.[13] In fact, the present state of the forces of production corresponds to small-scale production and the transition to a new state presupposes their growth, i.e. a basis, more and more social, of the means of production. This supposes a change-over to superior forms of social ownership; but by whom and by what means?

These questions are not easily answered and experience alone, combined with scientific knowledge, will show us the paths to tread. The same must be said of the plan for cultural superstructures which can become a serious obstacle if one does not respect a certain number of transitions. Ideological transformations and the formation of a new symbolic universe demand a policy the consequences of which one must fully recognize, for all this will not automatically follow changes in the infrastructure. The role of the sociologist consists, especially, of drawing attention to such questions, whilst maintaining awareness of the relative autonomy of symbolic change and of its influence on the entirety of the projects both social and technical.

With regards the transition to production on a vast scale in the territory that concerns us plans are already being realized. In principle, 1985 is the year which will see the definite transition in the district of Hai Van: it will be divided into five economic regions of which one will be reserved for fishing and for salterns. Each of these regions will be about 40,000 hectares in extent and will be administered by a member of the district committee, assisted by a technician. It is necessary to recall that the economic evolution of the country was progressive. In 1975 there were 52 co-operatives in the district, and in 1976, 38. Already then preparations were afoot for a progressive transition to management on a large scale. But such a transformation signifies much preparation. At present the spotlight is being focused on the formation of the cadres of management. Several presidents of corporations have been sent to the institutes of higher studies in the province and to the university and there are also correspondence courses.

On the technical level, the irrigation network is already being managed in a way that corresponds to the new dimension, and the same may be said of livestock rearing. The problem of fertilizers and of seed for sowing is also being organized at this level. At the same time a number of people are being encouraged to settle down in the new rural colonies of the High Plateaus of the South, in order to stabilize the demographic level at 220,000 inhabitants.

In the commune of Hai Van, we are still at the beginnings, and one cannot yet say what effects will follow from the new economic and social dimension. We have already sampled the opinion of the peasants, but the phenomenon has not yet really stirred the consciousness of the village. It remains for us now to make some reflections, rather theoretical in nature, on what has been learnt from our analysis of the infrastructure of the Hai Van commune.

Sociological Reflections on the Transition

At the level of the economic infrastructure of the commune studied we can advance certain hypotheses in the form of conclusions. There exists a double economic reality, in respect of the possession of the means of production (not evidently with regard to its ownership which, of course, remains collective), viz. organization of work and the distribution of the social product. These two sectors intercross, for, at the level of distribution, for instance, a part of the collective product can be diverted to the open market. However, and this is central to the issue, it is the collective level which is dominant, and therefore, one may conclude, this method of producing is articulating the other elements in the productive process.

It is thus that an economic form of a dual mode of production continues to exist, in the present state of transition. This section of the economy is important if one views it from the point of view of the villager (not only the peasant but also the worker), for it constitutes 40–45% of the cash revenue of the family. Its importance is diminished if one views things from the angle of the central sectors of the agrarian economy, since the dual economy signifies only the bridging of the gap in production. However, this too is controlled by the state, since the cultivated surface area of this dual type of production cannot go beyond a certain limit, and because, since 1979, an important part of the produce has been sold through state channels. But in a period of transition, dual economy has a social as well as an economic function. It is, in fact, one of the means which contribute, partially, at least, to the speeding-up of the nuclearization of the family. This last mentioned factor has at its disposal a material base, constituted already by the individual's salary, but reinforced by a revenue which makes up the difference and which is derived from the nuclear family unit itself. In fact, the organization of work on the domestic front ought necessarily to be effected within the group and this will only reinforce the functions of the family.

The nuclear family is, as we will have occasion to verify in the pages that follow, one of the social keys in the process of transition. For many good reasons the remains of the extended family must be done away with. But a process of dissolution can be brought about also through sudden ruptures, but these will have very grave consequences on the social and psychological equilibrium of groups and persons as has been verified by urban capitalist development in Asia. The duality apparent in the economic system has therefore more functions than appears on the surface and it is very important to be aware of this when one is seeking to realize the successive stages of the rural transformation.

When we speak of the dissolution of the extended family, let us not be mistaken into thinking of pre-colonial Vietnam, and of a colonial family system of the type of the clan. The situation is much more complex, and the social history of the transformation of the various forms of the family still remains to be written. In a sense, the nuclear family existed in the Red River Delta owing to the particular kind of dual production in agriculture. However, the character of the relations of production, especially its tributary character, has always maintained the unity of the local village base as a fundamental element of its structure, from which results a persistence of the extended family as a social unit, geographically situated and culturally dominant, even if it does not necessarily constitute a unit of production.

It seems to be quite evident that what some have called feudalism (the feudal system) consisted of relations of dependence between the landlords and the peasants or between the mandarins and the peasants, which did not totally result in individualization of the relationship as was the case with the European feudal system. In fact, in the latter case, the peasant was bound individually (together with his immediate family members) to his lord, for whom he had also to perform various services of a personal nature. In other regions of Asia, in Sri Lanka, for instance, the relationship of dependence was established by means of specialized castes for the performance of services. The process obtaining in Vietnam, with the progressive establishment of socialist co-operatives, has definitely transformed the form of production, and at the family level, it has strengthened its nuclear character by combining the salary of the individual with the revenue derived from domestic production, and by organizing on another base co-operation in collective work. One may say that the extended family still plays a role in the reproduction of the workforce, by means of grandmothers occupying themselves with children in their infancy while the mothers go to work.

The new collective relationship is bound together in the heart of the co-operative. At Hai Van the situation is normal, and one may say that, essentially, the co-operative is functioning with very real success on the plane of productivity, as well as on that of the organization of work. When one places oneself at a higher level of the economic system and studies, for instance, the relations existing between the co-operative and the state, via the district and the province as intermediary rungs in the ladder, one will realize that the organization possesses some points of similarity with that of the tributary (or Asiatic) mode of production. In fact, the contributions to the state reproduce, within the economy, some of the forms of this type of society. In both cases there is a contribution of a certain amount of the surplus produced, made by the unit at the bottom, to the unit at the top. At first sight this may seen strange: if one admits that the fundamental social relationship of the tributary mode of production is that which it establishes between the relatively autonomous entity at the bottom, and the state, by means of a tribute, one will find something similar obtaining in the present situation. But it must be added immediately that despite similarity of form the content is totally different. In fact, there is no structural identity between the two cases, for the tributary mode of production is characterized by an antagonistic relationship between the two terms, which is not the case today, even if the two poles are distinct. On the one hand, the nature of the state is totally different, and on the other, the units at the bottom of the framework have been constituted and continue to reproduce themselves in function of a planned model, the origin of which is to be found in the very heart of the political authority which exercises hegemony (in the sense given to that word by Gramsci) over the state, i.e. the Party of the Workers. This leads us to pose more concretely still the problem of the relationship between the co-operative and the state. It is an exchange which is established between the two; but on what do the terms of this exchange bear? Let us begin with the state. Its contribution in relations to the basic units of the co-operative is threefold.

The State and the Process of Production

Electrification, major hydraulic works, etc. – these constitute the material basis of the infrastructure the nature of which is decided by the state. The state intervenes in the process of planning, for it is the district which suggests to the commune the norms and the criteria of the orientation of production. This is not the only mechanism as all this is submitted for discussion and approval by the commune and the co-operative and finally at the district level. The state furnishes the fertilizer at relatively low prices, the only problem in the commune of Hai Van being the progressively diminishing quotas in the last few years as a result of general scarcity. Thus, the quota of nitrogenous fertilizer decreased from 95 tonnes in 1978 to 80 tonnes in 1979, and from 6 tonnes of limestone to 3 tonnes in the same period. On the other hand, phosphates increased from 24 tonnes to 29 tonnes. The state also leased out mechanical engines (e.g. tractors) and ensured their upkeep and maintenance but in the area the number of mechanical devices so hired out was very small. It is always the state which lays down the broad principles of the organization of work, even if their implementation is left to the initiative of the communes.

Consequently, the state fixes the prices. We have here a very complex and fundamental mechanism: as the state is the buyer there can be no possible discussion of the quotas to be contributed, but, on the other hand, what is called the agreed selling price can be one of the subjects of negotiations between the state and the co-operative. Finally, it is the state which assures the finances, through the bank, by granting loans to meet sudden contingencies, and by permitting the co-operative (as well as its members) to deposit its money on interest (at 5%).

The State and Social Reproduction and Protection of the Group
Three sectors enter into this category. First of all there is education, for the teachers are paid by the province as is their training. For their education at university level, the central government pays the bills. There is then the question of health, with the training of doctors within the framework of the province, and the furnishing of some drugs (when they are not in short supply). The third sector is defence, and the supply of arms to the local militia, the equipment and maintenance of the provincial army and also of the national army.

The State and Redistribution of the Social Product
This consists chiefly of offering to the urban populations (state enterprises, services, state bureaucracy) food at low prices (the salaries are also very low). It is only by a study of the macrostructure that one can find out whether the prices fixed by the state for the purchase of food items for distribution, are, at this point, less than they would be under the agricultural co-operatives which have to bear the brunt of it, or whether the administrative functions and services are excessive when compared with the services actually rendered. The comparison between the levels of rural and urban life of this region do not seem to confirm the first hypothesis in so far as the process of social exploitation is concerned. The peasants of this region live more comfortably than most of the city workers.

The co-operative, in so far as it is the second element of the structure, has to gear its production according to the overall directions given by the state especially as it has to contribute a part of its produce at a fixed price. This contribution corresponds to an appreciable part of its surplus, but to a part only. It is true that this last mentioned part is bought up at the price of poor rewards to the workforce and, in a certain measure, at the price of the overtime work of the women. One must add, however, that it is not the state's only source of revenue, for there is also the levy of an industrial tax, and revenues deriving from state enterprises (farms and factories). Finally, it is necessary to remind the reader that there are no personal taxes. When a study is made of a single commune it is evident that one may not judge the system as a whole; and one must also take into account the state of the forces of production prevailing in the social system taken as a whole.

Briefly, if we attempt to study the state of the social relations of production we will have to come to the conclusion – at least so it appears – that there exists a relative autonomy of the members in the co-operative and of the commune, vis-a-vis the state. And thus these two elements are more than mere cogs in the wheels of a centralized machine.

The Future

This combination of dual forms of production, on the one hand, and tributary forms, on the other, which is to be found at the very heart of a mode of production which is in a state of transition towards socialism, results chiefly from a relatively low level of the forces of production. The lack of technical equipment, of financial resources, of experience in management, are some factors which explain the relatively low level of productivity of the collectivized sector of the agrarian economy, in spite of the progress accomplished. This ought to be compensated for by, among other things, the domestic economy which covers the deficit. Since the war has ended, one may hope for important transformations in these domains, and we have seen that some among them have been fully realized, e.g. the plan for the organization of hydraulics. But political difficulties in the period after 1975, not to speak of natural catastrophes, have, without a shadow of doubt, retarded the realization of those plans, even if they have not been able to bring them to a complete halt. This transition to production on a vast scale, which evidently supposes a substantial growth in the forces of production, but which also comprises important changes in the social relations of production (e.g. the increase in the numbers of the working class in relation to the number of peasants, a reorganization of work and a number of important consequences affecting the plan of social management of living space and, therefore, of interpersonal relations), suggests the following reflections.

The study made of Hai Van permits us to make the hypothetical suggestion that the introduction of new techniques in agricultural production will meet with scarcely any resistance from the peasant population. The experience, gained gradually, of a mastery over the water system, the use of fertilizers, the organization of collective work, the productivity of the family garden – these have prepared the peasant not to resist innovations, but to want them. Let us note, however, that it is a question here of considerations at the level of the use of techniques.

The fear that is being engendered in the minds of the rural population in the face of a transition to a more heavily mechanized form of agriculture, and to its organization on new bases, is founded on two fronts – revenue, on the one hand, and social identity on the other. With regard to revenue it is quite clear that no reform of the system of production and distribution could be permitted to diminish the revenue of rural families or even stabilize them as there would then be the risk of a recrudescence of the traditional means of peasant resistance, e.g. a go slow on collective production, refusal to put into circulation a part of the produce, etc. On the other hand, if the reforms permit an increase in production, they will be accepted without any difficulty, and even a certain number of their socially induced effects such as the transformation of the habitat and women working outside the home, will not meet with large-scale resistance.

The second aspect concerns social identity. It has been established that the hamlet was the locus of this primary identity, which did not exclude in any way its identification with the nation or with the people situated in a different context and which history has forged especially during the last few years. The transformations which the peasants have lived through during the last 30 years have been enormous, and yet, they are not fully emancipated from their niche at the parochial level. Gradually, with the development of education, working away from the areas where they were born, military service, leisure in centres which are fast becoming urbanized, their bond of identification has enlarged. But here too transition is ruled by objective laws. It is important not to destroy their fanciful frames of reference, so long as new material and juridical bases have not been created to help in the transformation. If economic organization is to boldly pass on to a higher level, one must control the stages of the groundplan of the social roles so as to adapt them to the local framework. For instance, we have seen how the role of the head of the group, at least in the case studied, was an important and significant central point of reference for an important part of the population.

Notes

1. Nguyen Tu Chi, *Le tang traditionnel au Bac Bo – Sa structure organizationelle – Ses problèmes*, Hanoi, 1980 (MS).
2. Charles Bettelheim, op. cit., chapter I, (2), p.77.
3. In 1980 two other work-groups were set up by decentralizing the former work-groups.
4. See especially, Etudes Vietnamiennes No.51, *Problémes agricoles (5), La gestion des Coopératives*, Hanoi, 1977.
5. This arrangement has been changed at the end of 1979. The president and vice-presidents were elected by direct suffrage at the level of the work group.
6. The reform of 1979 has altered the system somewhat, for henceforth there is no ceiling for the maximum of work done, and the remuneration in paddy corresponds, without qualification, to the work done. The result has been that during the first few months of the enactment of the change, the work done effectively and collectively has increased from 60% to 80%, in relation to what the co-operative considered an optimum. Thus the commune has exceeded 18 to 24 day-points of work per month and reached 26 to 30 day-points.
7. Since the enactment of these measures the major portion of the production has been sold to the state at a price slightly less than that obtaining in the open market.
8. After the new policy, each family had to give the state, via the co-operative, one kg. of pork per 36 sq. metres per annum at a price equivalent to that

prevailing in the open market. On everything that exceeds 36 sq. metres per person the obligatory contribution is multiplied six-fold. Families have also to give one kilo of fish per year per small pond, and two kg. per large pond. Further, and always to stimulate production, collectively held land can be used by private persons, between two harvests of rice, to cultivate food for cattle (e.g. sweet potatoes) averaging the contribution to the state via the co-operative, of a part of the produce. And this can be eventually exchanged for products furnished by the state at a price less than that obtaining at the open market, e.g. cloth, household utensils, tobacco, etc.

9. Le Duan and Pham Van Dong, *Vers une agriculture de grande production socialiste*, Editions en langues étrangères, Hanoi, 1975, p.42.
10. Ibid., p.55.
11. Ibid., p.71.
12. Ibid., p.43.
13. Ibid., p.29.

3. Leaders, Personnel and Participation

The Election of the Personnel of the Co-operative

The organization of a co-operative implies two levels of responsibility. At the overall level, direction is assured by the Council of Management, elected by the assembly of the members of the co-operative – a council whose members elect, in their turn, the president. At the level of production, each team is placed under the direction of the head of the group of production, elected directly by the workers. As one of the objectives of this inquiry is the measurement of the degree of participation of the rural workers in the management of the co-operative, we will see first how their interest is manifested in the choice and the evaluation of the personnel of the whole organization. Three particular aspects will be dealt with by the inquiry: the criteria underlying the choice of the leaders of the co-operative; the consciousness of influencing the choice by participating in the elections; and the evaluation of the organs of present day management.

The Criteria for the Choice of Elected Personnel

The purpose of this inquiry was to discover in what measure the rural populatio[n] called to choose the managers of local economic life, based their choice on the individual qualities which they deemed the individual leaders ought to be endowed with (and what qualities they thought they had), or whether they based their choices on Party directives. Table 3.1 gives a resume of the position of 45 workers of one of the production groups. We have arranged the replies into certain categories, according to their sociological significance, from the concrete indications furnished by the peasants. Each of the persons questioned belonged to a different family, and this sampling reflects the opinion of the head of the family of five. This explains the disparity between the men and the women (32 men and 13 women). Let it be emphasized that all of them work in the co-operative.

In a general fashion the choice of the personnel elected depends on criteria which reconcile, on the one hand, the expectations with regard to the person who will be the functionary, and on the other, the orientations of the Party. In the case of a choice of president, the personal qualities of the candidate will outweigh the directives of the Party (72.7 – 3 = 24.2 against 21.9); for

Table 3.1
Criteria for Choice of President of the Co-operative and Head of Production Group

Criteria	*President*	%		*Head of Group*	%	
Personal Qualities:						
Technical competence	27	25.5		23	22.5	
Moral integrity	28	26.4		25	24.5	
Social sensitivity	22	20.8	72.7	21	20.6	67.6
Conformity to the directives of the Party	23		21.9	27		26.5
No reply	6		5.7	6		5.9

the head of the brigade, on the contrary, the directives of the Party weigh rather heavily (26.5 against 22.5). It has been made clear, further, that the choice rests generally, on more than one criterion: 2.3 on the average (106 responses 45) for the president of the co-operative and 2.2 for the head of the brigade. In what concerns individual qualities, and always for the entirety of the persons interrogated, it is moral integrity which is most in demand, as much from the president of the co-operative as from the head of the brigade. Then comes technical competence, and lastly, social sensitivity.

The people questioned were heterogeneous as regards sex, age, education, political participation, adherence to a religion, etc., and so it is not without interest to ask in what measure the different categories found themselves variously placed with regard to this social practice which constitutes the choice of the personnel. The replies shown in Table 3.2 reveal much about the expectations with regard to a particularly important position of leadership both at the level of collective and particular instances.

The distributions revealed in Table 3.2 of different hierarchies of values in the criteria for making a choice are detailed further in Tables 3.3 and 3.4.

Table 3.3 confirms the difference between the criteria for making a choice, and therefore, the difference between what one expects of the president of the co-operative and of the head of the production group. With regard to the former, there is a strong insistence on the capacity for management in technical matters. It does not exclude, however, the demand for moral integrity. For the head of group, however, technical competence appears less important than fidelity to the directives of the Party. This difference supposes a wider conception of the role, namely, that it be not limited only to the economic sector. Lastly, it should be noted that when things are considered as a whole, the individual's aptitude for leadership, the 'charisma' in the Weberian sense of the term, is considered less important than the other two elements. In fact, it has never appeared as an essential element, either for the president of the co-operative or for the head of the production group.

Table 3.4 compares the positions taken up by the various categories of persons interviewed. Between the values of +2.5 and –2.5 it was possible to

Table 3.2
Criteria for Choice of President of Co-operative and of Head of Production Group According to Categories of Population Studied

Categories	*Choice of president*				*Choice of head of production group*			
	1	2	3	4*	1	2	3	4*
Sex: Males	56.3	59.4	50.0	50.0	56.3	62.5	48.2	62.5
Females	69.2	69.2	53.8	53.8	38.5	38.5	30.8	53.8
Age: 35 and less	55.6	66.7	55.6	66.7	38.5	50.0	44.4	83.3
35–49	55.6	50.0	33.3	55.6	50.0	50.0	38.9	55.6
50 and over	77.8	66.7	65.7	22.2	77.7	77.7	66.0	22.2
Level of education:								
Primary	64.7	64.7	41.2	47.0	47.1	46.7	41.2	64.7
Secondary	61.9	61.9	57.1	57.1	52.4	57.1	47.6	56.9
Political commitment:								
Party and organizations	80.0	80.0	60.0	60.0	66.7	73.3	60.0	60.0
Non-members	50.0	53.3	43.3	47.0	43.3	46.7	40.0	60.0
Adherence to religion:								
Catholics	48.5	53.3	39.4	55.8	42.4	48.5	40.0	69.7
Non-Catholics	91.7	83.3	75.0	41.7	75.0	75.0	66.0	33.3
Social Origin:								
Poor peasant	55.6	53.3	33.3	55.6	41.9	45.2	32.3	67.7
Middle peasant	75.0	83.3	75.0	33.3	66.2	75.0	66.0	50.0
Average	64.7	66.1	52.3	49.5	54.8	58.6	48.2	56.9

*Key 1 = Technical competence; 2 = moral integrity; 3 = social sensitivity; 4 = party directives.

Table 3.3
Most Important Criteria for the Election of President of Co-operative and Head of Production Group According to Categories of Persons Questioned

	President		*Head of production group*	
Criteria	*Score*	*Categories*	*Score*	*Categories*
Technical competence	8	Women aged 35–49 aged 50 and over Primary and secondary educated Party members Non-Catholics Poor peasants	2	Over 50 years Non-Catholics
Moral integrity	8	Men Women Aged less than 35	6	Men over 50 years Secondary educat

		Primary and secondary educated Members and non-members of the Party and organizations Middle peasant origin		Members of the Party Non-Catholics Middle peasant origin
Social sensitivity	0		0	Men/women
Directives of the Party	4	Aged less than 35 and 35-49 Catholics Poor peasant origin	8	Aged less than 35 and 35-49 Primary educated Non-members of the Party Catholics Poor peasant origin

set up a scale of values: 0, +1, +2, +2.5; 0, –1, –2, –2.5. An examination of the scale makes possible the following conclusions as regards the attitudes of the different groups:

Sexes: While men seem generally less interested than women in elections, the election of the president of the co-operative seems to interest men even less than the election of the head of the production group. The contrary obtains for the women: they evince more interest in the election of the president of the co-operative than in the election of the head of the production group.

Different age groups: The young show relatively little concern for the personal qualities of candidates but are more influenced by Party directives. The older groups, on the other hand, set great store by the professional competence of candidates and manifest indifference as regards Party directives.

Political participation: Party members and members of mass organizations set store both by the personal qualities of the candidates and by Party directives. Non-members show little interest in elections, except for the fact that some of them are somewhat concerned about the head of the production group in whom they look for conformity to Party directives.

Education: The level of education seems to have no effect on the electors.

Social Origin: This seems to be a positive factor. Those of middle peasant origin who have access to the cultivation of plots of arable land, pay great attention to the personal qualities of candidates and especially to their technical competence. On the other hand, the older peasants, especially the landless, base their choice on Party directives. The same difference in attitudes obtains as between Catholics and non-Catholics. The influence of religious affiliation is, however, not direct. It seems rather to come by way of social class divisions. We have to bear in mind that the population under investigation once was a 'beggar village', in which those who were landless were also members of the Catholic religious group.

Table 3.4
Correspondence Between Criteria Used in Electoral Choices and Level of Awareness of Influencing Elections

Categories of persons casting their vote according to personal competence of candidates		*Percentage of those aware of influencing elections of the president of the co-operative*
Men	55.2	59.4
Women	64.1	23.7
Aged 50 and over	70.6	66.7
Primary educated	56.9	41.2
Secondary educated	60.3	57.1
Members of the Party and organizations	73.3	60.0
Non-members	48.9	42.3
Non-Catholics	83.3	75.0
Middle peasant origin	77.7	75.0
		(r = 0.842)

Categories of persons who vote according to the directives of the Party		*Percentage of those who are aware of influencing the election of the president of the co-operative*
Aged 35 and less	66.7	44.4
Aged 35-49	55.8	44.4
Catholics	53.8	39.4
Poor peasant origin	55.6	35.5
		(r = 0.547)

Despite the limitations due to the small number of persons interviewed, this brief analysis does point to a sharp cleavage between two attitudes in the co-operatives; the cleavage expresses itself at the time of elections. On the one side are the older folk, particularly those who, in former times, were small landowners: for them the co-operative is an economic enterprise calling for qualified and competent personnel. On the other side are the younger folk, particularly those who belonged to the poorer classes: for them the economic aspect is secondary, and what is paramount is the political dimension of the enterprise. The members of the Party and of the associations appear as a group which seeks to unite the two dimensions of the organization of the local economy. Let us recall that these are the attitudes found among the workers of a production group.

Political Awareness of the Electorate of the Co-operative

If the two tendencies coexist within the co-operative, and if they appear to have a much greater determining influence than would other characteristics, such as the sex of the members of the co-operative or their level of education, it is of interest to ask how each of them would conceive of the possibility of

Table 3.5
Correspondence Between Criteria Underlying Choices, and the Level of Awareness of Influencing Elections of Heads of Production Groups

Categories of persons casting their vote according to personal competence of candidates		*Percentage of those aware of influencing elections of heads of production groups*
Persons aged 50 and over	73.8	66.7
Members of the Party and associations	66.6	60.0
Non-Catholics	72.0	76.3
Middle peasant origin	69.0	75.0
		(r = 0.408)

Categories of persons who vote according to the directives of the Party		*Percentage of those aware of influencing elections of heads of the co-operative*
Men	62.5	62.5
Women	53.8	92.3
Aged 35 and less	83.3	66.6
Aged 35–49	55.6	77.7
Primary educated	64.7	88.2
Secondary educated	56.9	66.7
Non-members of the Party or organizations	60.0	76.3
Catholics	69.7	69.7
Poor peasant origin	67.7	75.0
		(r = –0.424)

influencing the management of the economy by participating in the choice of cadres. Regarding the elections of presidents, there exists a striking correlation between the percentages of those who base their choice on the competence of the candidate and the level of awareness of influencing the elections, that is to say that those who tend to consider the co-operative as an economic enterprise believe that they must be heard in matters of management, at least in an indirect way. Those who follow the directives of the Party in making their choice, believe, however, (clearly less than the others do) in their power to influence the choice of the cadres of the co-operative. We must remind ourselves that it is a question here of the categories which, either because of their age, or by reason of their social origin, have very little ability to make themselves heard in social matters. The oldest, in particular, saved by the action of the Party from a particularly miserable fate, testify to a great fidelity in following the Party's directives, at the cost, perhaps, of a certain misgiving about their failure to fulfil a personally active role in the collective management of the economy (Table 3.4).

At the level of the head of the production group, the mechanism is quite otherwise. Usually the level of awareness of influencing the elections is very high, but there is no evidence of correlation with the criteria on which the choice of the candidate is based (Table 3.5).

Evaluation of the Head of the Co-operative

If there exists a sizeable majority which expresses its satisfaction with regard to the management of the co-operative and its council, there also exists another section which is critical of the president. However, these two attitudes seem to be independent of each other. It is difficult, all the same, to establish the objective criteria on which this criticism is based. If one compares the percentages of those dissatisfied with the distribution of those who cast their vote for aptitudinal reasons in the candidate, one will find no significant relationship.[1] The same negative result will be obtained if comparisons are made between each of the qualities suggested, i.e. technical competence, moral integrity and social sensitivity. The only observable tendency of some little value is to be found among the categories of persons faithful to the directives of the Party. The greater the fidelity to the Party the weaker grows the criticism of it. This seems to confirm the remark made above with regard to the degree of autonomy of the different categories.

Table 3.6
Evaluation of Management of the Co-operative

	Satisfaction (%)		*Dissatisfaction (%)*	
	Council of management	*President*	*Council of management*	*President*
Men	84.4	25.0	9.3	68.7
Women	84.6	53.8	15.4	46.2
Aged 35 and less	88.8	44.4	11.1	55.5
Aged 35–49	83.4	27.8	11.1	66.7
Aged 50 and over	77.8	22.2	11.1	66.7
Members of Party and organizations	93.3	33.3	6.7	66.7
Non-members	79.9	33.3	13.3	59.9
Primary educated	88.2	35.3	11.8	64.7
Secondary educated	90.5	38.1	4.8	57.2
Catholics	81.8	33.3	12.1	60.6
Non-Catholics	91.6	33.3	8.3	66.6
Poor peasant origin	87.2	35.5	9.7	61.3
Middle class peasant origin	83.3	33.3	8.3	58.3

Evaluation of the Head of the Production Group

If we consider all the persons questioned, 41.4% were totally satisfied with the head of the group, and 23.8% were partially satisfied, with subtle differences between some of the criticisms of lesser importance. Table 3.7 sums up the positions of the different categories of which the sample is composed.

Table 3.7
Evaluation of Head of Production Group

	Total satisfaction	*Partial satisfaction*	*Total**
Men	43.8	21.9	65.7
Women	38.0	30.7	68.7
Aged 35 and less	38.9	38.9	66.7
Aged 35-49	50.0	16.7	66.7
Aged 50 and over	33.3	11.1	44.4
Members of the Party and organizations	46.7	13.3	60.0
Non-members	40.0	30.0	70.0
Catholics	45.5	27.3	72.8
Non-Catholics	33.3	16.7	50.0
Primary educated	29.4	35.3	64.7
Secondary educated	57.1	14.3	71.4
Poor peasant origin	48.4	19.4	67.8
Middle peasant origin	33.3	33.3	66.6
Average	41.4	23.8	65.2

* The balance is constituted here by the percentage of those who gave no reply, the average for the whole of which being 31.2%.

As in the case of the evaluation of the president, there is no observable correlation between the positions expressed and the criteria relative to the personal qualities underlying the voting for the election of the head of the group. On the other hand, there exists a significant correlation (r = 0.745) between the percentages of those who say they follow the Party directives for the election of the head of the production group and the percentages of those who say they are satisfied.

The Organization of Work

In this section of the inquiry, the different phases of the process of work will be studied from a sociological point of view. From now on, we will distinguish three principal moments: the designation of the members of the work team, i.e. the lower unit of the production group, which consists of a dozen workers, the organization of production, and that of the allocation of work. However, we do not mean to describe here the practice of the social agents; our purpose is to extract and bring to light the conceptions which the members of the co-operative have of the organization of work. For this purpose we will concentrate on two particular aspects: that of decision making on the one hand, and on the other, the opinions on the content of the decisions made, and on their implementation. The underlying question that remains to be

Table 3.8
Agents to Whom Decisions on the Designation of Members of the Work-Team, and Opinions on these Decisions are Attributed

	Agents to whom the decisions are attributed			*Opinions on the decisions*	
	Members of the co-operative	*Head of the Group*	*Common agree-ment*	*Agree*	*Dis-agree*
Men	12.5	43.8	34.4	87.5	3.1
Women	15.4	38.5	38.5	69.2	7.7
Aged 35 and less	11.1	50.0	38.5	83.3	11.5
Aged 35–49	16.7	50.0	27.8	83.3	–
Aged 50 and over	11.1	11.1	55.0	77.8	–
Members of the Party and organizations	6.7	33.3	53.3	86.7	6.7
Non-members	16.7	46.6	26.6	80.0	3.0
Catholics	15.1	45.5	30.3	84.8	3.0
Non-Catholics	8.3	33.3	50.0	75.0	8.3
Primary educated	11.8	35.3	47.1	82.4	–
Secondary educated	14.3	57.1	23.8	90.5	4.8
Poor peasant origin	9.7	45.2	38.7	83.9	6.5
Middle peasant origin	16.7	41.7	33.3	83.3	–
Average	12.8	40.8	37.9	82.1	4.2

answered is, in what degree the members of the co-operative are aware of their participation at the level of management – an awareness which ought to powerfully influence the manner in which they evaluate the system.

Designation of the Members of the Work-Team

Of the whole of the population questioned, 13% believed that the designation of the members of the work-team is made by the members of the co-operative themselves; 41% attributed the decision to the head of the production group alone; and another 38% saw it as the fruit of a common decision between the head and the workers. If one considers the different positions of the various categories, once again there appears a clear division between the category of persons more than 50 years old, the Party members, the non-Catholics who acknowledge the direct participation of the members of the co-operative in the decision made, on the one hand, and, on the other, the other categories who attribute it solely to the head of the production group. Feminine opinion is once again much more divided.

The opinions concerning the designation of the members of a team converge in expressing satisfaction as much at the procedure as at the result. One must note here that the decisions directly affect the persons questioned since they make themselves the object of the designation. Moreover, the level of satisfaction does not seem to be influenced by the difference of the perception in the procedure for making the designation. It is necessary to keep in mind that the head of the production group in which the inquiry was conducted was highly thought of by the members on account of his qualities as a leader.

Organization of Production

Regarding production, the questions have a bearing both on the choice of products and on the fixing of norms of production, according to the viewpoint adopted in this study, i.e. from the point of view of decision-making and of the evaluation of the practices. As Table 3.9 shows, 55% of the persons questioned considered that decisions concerning the orientation of production proceed from the council of management of the co-operative while 42% felt that the decisions rested with the assembly of the members of the co-operative. This average reflects the tendency which we have seen to be more or less recurrent among women, persons less than 50 years old, non-members of mass-associations, Catholics, those with only a primary education, and the original members of the co-operative of poor peasant origin. As opposed to them, persons over 50 years old, members of the Party or of mass associations, non-Catholics and those coming from the middle-class peasant families, are found always in the same camp, believing, by and large, that the decisions belong to the assembly of the members of the co-operative.

Table 3.9
Agents to Whom Decisions Regarding Choice of Products are Attributed, and their Evaluation

	Agents to whom decisions are attributed		*The possibility of discussing the orientation of production*		
	Council of management	*Assembly of members of the co-operative*	*Yes*	*'No' on orientation but 'Yes' on execution of the project*	*No opinion*
Men	46.9	50.0	28.1	34.4	37.5
Women	84.6	15.4	15.4	30.8	53.8
Aged 35 and less	55.6	44.4	16.7	38.9	44.4
Aged 35–49	72.2	27.8	16.7	33.3	50.0
Aged 50 and over	33.3	55.6	55.6	22.2	22.2
Members of the Party and organizations	33.3	66.7	53.3	33.3	13.3
Non-members	70.0	26.6	10.0	33.3	56.6
Catholics	66.7	30.3	18.2	27.3	57.6
Non-Catholics	33.3	66.7	41.7	50.0	8.3
Primary educated	70.6	29.4	17.6	35.3	52.9
Secondary educated	52.4	47.6	38.1	28.6	33.3
Poor peasant origin	61.3	38.7	22.6	29.0	33.3
Middle class peasant origin	41.7	50.0	25.0	50.0	25.0
Average	55.5	42.2	27.6	34.3	38.1

Table 3.10
Agents to Whom Decisions Concerning Fixing of Norms of Work are Attributed, and their Evaluation

	Agents to whom the fixing of norms is attributed			*Evaluation of the norms of production*		
	Council of management	*Assembly of co-operative members*		*Too high*	*Too high for women and aged*	*No opinion*
Men	46.9	46.9	6.2	72.2	25.0	2.8
Women	92.3	7.7	–	85.7	7.1	7.1
Aged 35 and less	61.1	38.9	–	76.2	19.0	4.8
Aged 35–49	61.1	33.3	5.6	84.2	10.5	5.3
Aged 50 and over	55.6	33.3	11.1	55.6	33.3	11.1
Members of the Party and organizations	40.0	60.0	–	87.5	12.5	–
Non-members	70.0	23.3	6.7	72.7	24.3	3.0
Catholics	63.6	30.3	6.1	63.6	30.3	6.1
Non-Catholics	50.0	50.0	–	50.0	50.0	–
Primary educated	82.4	17.6	–	82.4	17.6	–
Secondary educated	47.1	47.1	4.8	47.6	47.6	4.8
Poor peasant origin	61.3	32.2	6.5	78.8	21.2	–
Middle class peasant origin	58.3	41.7	–	78.6	22.4	–
Average	60.7	35.6	3.7	71.9	24.6	3.4

These two positions become very clear in the manner in which the persons questioned view the possibility of participation on the discussions regarding the orientation of production. In this regard, the majority say they have no firm opinion on the question; this allows us to suppose that there is a certain indifference towards participation at this level of management. There exists a very high correlation between the percentages of those who attribute the decision to the council of management and those who are not committed one way or another in this discussion. This correlation reveals a certain logic which may be expressed thus: the less one is interested in participating in the discussion (i.e. in the management of the co-operative), the more one tends to attribute the power of decision to the cadres. There also exists a correlation, just as strong, between the percentages of those who maintain that the decision belongs to the assembly of the members of the co-operative and the percentages of those who admit not only the possibility of discussing the orientation of production, but also its execution. One may surmise, therefore, that the idea one has of the role of the cadres of the co-operative rests very heavily on the degree of effectual participation which one has in its management. The question which remains to be thrashed out is whether certain categories of the members of the co-operative share less than the others in the making of decisions at the higher level of the co-operative. We will consider this question at the end of the analysis. It is worth noting that the opinions expressed concerning the content of the discussions, i.e. the difference between the orientation of production or the execution of the project, have no relation to the ideas held about the agents who are believed to be involved in decision-making.

In the same way as we looked at the way decisions regarding orientation of production were attributed, we will now analyse the distribution of opinions relative to the agents to whom the fixing of norms of work is generally attributed, as well as those opinions relative to the positions with regard to the effects of this decision-making.

Here again, opinion is divided between what concerns those responsible for the fixing of norms: 61% attribute it to the council of management, and 37% to the assembly of co-operative members. Whatever may be the content of the opinions, it stands out clearly that those questioned are without influence on the evaluation of the norms of work – deemed too high by 72% of those questioned. Another 25% find them too high only for women and for the aged. In other words, the work is judged too heavy for women and for old people by 96.5%, and for men by 72%. The importance of these figures is indicative of the presence of a real problem with which one must reckon. At Hai Van it is certain that all else being equal, one can scarcely hope for a growth in production.

The Points System

The remuneration for work involves the elaboration of a system which gives due appreciation to the work of the individual, taking into account the particular circumstances peculiar to the co-operative (natural conditions, type of work to be done, etc.), and of the workers (health etc.). The system demands, therefore, local adjustments corresponding to norms of work and to their application just as it calls for the daily evaluation of the daily quota of each worker. We will distinguish, therefore, two aspects – the analysis of opinions concerning decision-making and those relative to implementation.

Faithful to the methods followed in this work, we will seek to disclose whether there exists a correspondence between the ideas of the members of the co-operative concerning the agents involved in decision-making and the evaluation they make of the system. With regard to this latter objective, the opinions expressed will be regrouped into two categories according to the similarity of their significance: on the one hand, admission of the justice of the system, even though with recommended rectifications, and on the other, the demand for a more rational fixing of norms, which takes account of the relative difficulty of the different types of work. For the large majority of persons questioned (68%), the elaboration of the system of points depends on the council of management of the co-operative; less than a quarter considered the assembly of the co-operative to be responsible for it. In this sphere, it was only in the group of the Party members that there was found a majority which attributed the responsibility to the co-operative assembly. As in the case of the fixing of norms of work there was no observable influence

Table 3.11
Agents to Whom the Elaboration of the System of Points, and their Evaluation are Attributed

	Agents to whom is attributed the points system			*Evaluation of the system of points*		
	Council of manage-ment	*Assembly of co-operative members*	*No opinion*	*Just*	*Irra-tional*	*No opinio*
Men	46.9	43.8	9.4	43.8	40.6	15.6
Women	84.6	7.7	7.7	46.0	38.5	15.4
Aged 35 and less	56.6	33.3	11.1	50.0	44.4	5.6
Aged 35–49	61.1	33.3	5.6	61.1	22.2	16.7
Aged 50 and over	55.6	33.3	11.1	–	66.7	33.3
Members of the Party and organizations	33.3	60.0	13.3	46.7	40.0	13.3
Non-members	73.3	20.0	6.7	43.3	40.0	16.7
Catholics	74.2	19.4	6.4	45.5	39.4	15.2
Non-Catholics	93.3	26.7	–	41.7	41.7	16.7
Primary educated	77.8	22.2	–	47.1	35.3	17.6
Secondary educated	76.0	20.0	4.0	42.9	42.9	14.3
Poor peasant origin	76.5	20.6	2.9	51.6	32.3	16.1
Middle class peasant origin	78.6	21.4	–	25.0	58.3	16.7
Average	68.2	23.7	8.1	41.9	41.7	16.4

concerning the identity of those responsible (council of assembly) for the elaboration of the system or the evaluation that was made. Here the interviews are equally divided into two groups according to whether they deem the system equitable in so far as it judged not to take into account sufficiently the different types of work. But one finds that there is, on the average, a cancellation of the three positions when the opinions of the different categories are analysed. In fact, the majority of men, women, persons below 50 years old, members of the Party, those with a primary school education, and those who come from poor families, all expressed opinions favourable rather than unfavourable. Those with secondary school education and Catholics are divided in their opinion. The most critical are, once again, persons above 50 years old and those of middle peasant origin.

The distribution of points for the work done is important not only because it determines the level of the worker's salary but also because it puts a seal (either of approval or disapproval) on the quality of his or her work. It is a question, therefore, of a practice much more significant than the simple distribution of the social product. It seems that there exist two ways of attributing points, either by the head of the team alone, or by the work-team which decides by vote, after discussion. They are, in fact, too different to be a cause of confusion. As for the evaluation, 85% of the sample considered

Table 3.12
Agents to Whom the Distribution of Points and the Evaluation of the System are Attributed

	Agents to whom the distribution of points is attributed			*Evaluation of the distribution of points: they ought to be:*		
	Head of the team	*Team*	*No opinion*	*Made public*	*Effected with the presence of the head*	*No opinion*
Men	56.2	40.6	3.1	40.6	37.5	21.9
Women	69.2	15.4	15.4	30.8	46.2	23.1
Aged 35 and less	55.6	38.9	5.6	55.6	44.4	–
Aged 35-49	72.2	22.2	5.6	22.2	38.9	38.9
Aged 50 and over	44.4	44.4	11.1	33.3	33.3	33.3
Members of the Party and organizations	46.7	46.7	6.6	60.0	40.0	–
Non-members	43.3	40.0	16.7	66.7	26.7	6.7
Catholics	60.6	30.3	9.1	36.4	36.4	27.3
Non-Catholics	58.3	41.7	–	41.7	50.0	8.3
Primary educated	47.1	35.3	17.6	35.3	35.3	29.4
Secondary educated	57.1	42.9	–	47.6	47.6	4.7
Poor peasant origin	58.1	32.3	9.7	56.4	28.2	15.4
Middle peasant origin	58.3	41.7	–	61.1	38.9	6.0
Average	55.9	36.3	7.8	49.8	38.7	16.5

it favourable, even though 44% wanted the distribution of points to be made public, and 39% wanted the head to the team to be present at the distribution. It is evident that if the workers accept that there is a bond between the remuneration for their work and the appreciation which they receive from the head or from the members of the team, they would also wish to be assured of certain guarantees for preserving the equity of those judgements.

Generally speaking, concerning the organization of work, it appears that the workers do not always have a clear idea of the processes of decision-making, particularly with regards the decision-making function of the assembly of the co-operative members. It is certain that a decision taken collectively is always the product of discussions which cannot constitute, for some, a stage in the process. It is observable that the categories of people once very down-trodden have the greatest difficulty in understanding the new process. It may well be that these groups continue to be vehicles of cultural models of power which prevent them from understanding the true import of their participation in the assembly. This is no hindrance, in general, to the evaluation of the organizations of work being positive, especially as the workers themselves are capable of furnishing suggestions to improve its functioning. Certainly the organization of

Table 3.13
Participation at Co-operative Meetings, and their Evaluation

	Participation			*Function of the meetings*	
	Regularly	*Occasion-ally*	*Never*	*Informa-tion and discussion*	*No opinion*
Men	78.1	18.8	3.1	81.2	18.8
Women	46.2	30.8	23.1	38.5	61.5
Aged 35 and less	61.1	33.3	5.6	66.6	33.3
Aged 35-49	77.7	11.1	11.1	66.6	33.3
Aged 50 and over	66.7	22.3	11.0	77.7	22.3
Members of the Party and organizations	62.5	25.0	12.5	81.3	12.5
Non-members	70.0	20.0	10.0	60.0	40.0
Catholics	69.7	21.2	9.1	66.7	33.3
Non-Catholics	66.7	25.0	8.3	75.0	25.0
Primary educated	64.7	17.6	17.6	52.9	47.1
Secondary educated	66.7	20.7	4.8	76.2	23.8
Poor peasant origin	64.5	29;0	6.5	64.5	35.5
Middle peasant origin	75.0	8.3	16.7	75.0	25.0
Average	68.9	22.2	8.8	67.9	32.1

work and its remuneration are matters of the greatest concern to them. But one notes in Hai Van much more than a passive interest which would make them consider the economic organization solely from the point of view of its effects on the workers. Even if they do not have a clear awareness of this, the peasants testify to a will to intervene at the local level of the organization itself.

Participation in Co-operative Meetings

As we advanced the hypothesis that the majority of the members of the co-operative do not, perhaps, have a sufficient awareness of the significance of their presence at the assembly of the co-operative, we wished to sound their opinions concerning those meetings themselves and their outcome. Taken as a whole, 69% affirmed that they assisted regularly at the meetings of the co-operative; 22% admitted partial absenteeism and 9% total abstention. One will note, however, that it is the members of the Party and the organizations, and those less than 35 years old, who are relatively less faithful in attending the meetings of the co-operative (62.5% and 61.1% respectively) while the older people of middle peasant origin are more regular in attending the meetings, excluding the total absence of a small group of them (17%).

So how does one explain the irregularity or total absence, of 32% of the members from the meetings, the role of which is so important for the collective and family economy? Several hypotheses are possible. We tried to find, when we questioned them, first of all in what measure the peasants understand the

Table 3.14
Opinions on the Outcome of Debates at Co-operative Meetings

	Taking into consideration the opinions of those interviewed			*Monopoly of speaking by some persons*		
	Yes	*No*	*No opinion*	*Yes*	*No*	*No opinion*
Men	40.6	34.4	25.0	75.0	9.4	16.6
Women	15.4	30.5	53.8	61.2	15.8	23.1
Aged 35 and less	33.3	33.3	33.3	77.8	11.1	11.1
Aged 35–49	22.2	38.9	38.9	66.7	11.1	22.2
Aged 50 and over	55.6	22.2	22.2	66.7	11.1	22.2
Members of the Party and organizations	53.3	26.7	20.0	75.0	12.5	6.3
Non-members	23.6	36.6	40.0	66.7	10.0	23.3
Catholics	27.3	33.3	39.4	66.7	12.1	21.2
Non-Catholics	50.0	33.3	16.2	83.3	8.3	8.3
Primary educated	17.6	35.3	47.1	64.7	17.6	17.6
Secondary educated	42.0	20.6	20.6	81.0	9.5	9.5
Poor peasant origin	25.8	35.5	38.7	74.2	9.7	16.1
Middle peasant origin	58.3	25.0	16.7	75.0	8.3	16.7
Average	33.3	33.3	33.3	71.1	11.1	17.8

importance of this practice, and the function which they attribute to the meetings of the co-operative. The opinions of 68% of them are convergent in this that they consider the meetings as activities organized to give sure information to the members of the co-operative on the economic projects, and to direct the discussion towards their realization. This stand that they have taken confirms the observation we made above: the majority of the members do not deem it necessary to intervene in the decisions concerning the economic projects themselves; 32%, however, have no opinion to express, i.e. probably, they did not know what the function of the meetings was. Those with 'no opinion' are to be found chiefly among women (61.5%), the non-members of the Party and of mass organizations, and among those who have not completed their course of primary education. This ignorance of the function of the meetings is not a complete explanation of the absenteeism. The rate of correlation between the percentages of those with 'no opinion' and the statistics of absenteeism (partial and total) is in fact only 0.6%. One may therefore ask whether the procedure followed at these meetings is not an obstacle to participation in them. We have, therefore, to try to find how those interviewed considered the debates (i.e. the speaking being monopolized by certain groups and the taking into account of the opinions of each person). Table 3.14 synthesizes the opinions expressed on these questions: a third thought that their opinion was taken into account; a third did not think so and the others did not know. They are always the same groups (the 50 years and over, the

Table 3.15
Perception of Conflicts Within the Co-operative

	Are there conflicts at the level of:									
	the co-operative between the groups of production?			*the production group between the head and members?*				*between members?*		
	Yes	*No*	*No opinion*	*Yes* (1)*	*Yes* (2)	*Yes* (3)	*No*	*Yes* (4)	*Yes* (5)	*No*
Men	18.8	37.5	43.8	6.3	37.5	46.9	50.0	12.5	12.5	75.0
Women	7.7	30.8	61.5	7.7	15.4	38.5	61.2	15.4	7.7	76.9
Aged 35 and less	27.8	38.9	33.3	11.1	38.9	44.4	55.6	5.6	22.2	72.2
Aged 35–49	11.1	33.3	55.6	–	22.2	44.4	55.6	22.2	5.6	72.2
Members of the Party and organizations	33.3	33.3	33.3	13.3	40.0	46.7	46.7	33.3	26.7	40.0
Non-members	6.6	36.7	56.7	3.3	26.7	42.3	56.7	3.3	3.3	93.3
Catholics	18.2	33.3	48.5	3.0	30.3	36.4	60.6	6.1	12.1	81.3
Non-Catholics	8.3	41.7	50.0	16.7	33.3	66.6	33.3	33.3	8.3	58.3
Primary educated	11.8	29.4	58.8	–	23.5	47.1	47.1	5.9	–	94.1
Secondary educated	19.0	42.9	38.1	14.3	33.3	42.9	52.4	19.0	19.0	62.0
Poor peasant origin	20.0	33.3	46.7	6.5	25.8	32.3	64.6	16.1	12.9	71.0
Middle peasant origin	–	50.0	50.0	8.3	41.7	75.0	25.0	8.3	–	91.7
Average	15.6	35.6	48.8	7.7	32.7	45.5	50.0	14.6	9.9	71.0

*(1) bad allocation of work; (2) negligence, go-slow; (3) lack of clarity in award of points; (4) on the subject of work outside the harvest; (5) on the subject of light work.

members of the Party, the non-Catholics, and those of middle peasant origin) who manifest the greatest awareness of being listened to. Conversely, the women, the primary school leavers, and the non-members of the Party say they have no influence.

We have been trying to ascertain whether the importance accorded to domestic economy has an influence on the importance accorded to the co-operative; such influence would be manifested notably by participation at co-operative meetings. In the course of this inquiry, it became clear that the time devoted to domestic work was not an obstacle to participation in the management of the collective economy. This becomes clear if one takes into account the categories of persons whose statistics of attendance at meetings surpass the average; and if, further, one compares them with the revenues derived from the private economy (see Chapter 18 – there is a markedly observable correlation). It is also clear that the revenue from the private garden does not appear to be bound up with the time necessary for its cultivation.

Hence, one may ask whether we are faced at Hai Van with a double conception of the organization of the economy – one, which we would qualify as traditional, which would correspond to a partial mastery of the economy, i.e. to a fundamental attitude of dependence on nature, derived from a feeble development of the forces of production. This attitude is to be found mainly among women, the non-members of the Party and mass-organizations, and former poor peasants. The other is characterized by the development of a rationalization of the economy through awareness of the effects of human intervention not only with regard to the work-force, but in the very organization of economic activity.

R. Bourdieu observed a similar phenomenon among the Algerian peasants. He noted two different attitudes: first, an attitude of 'foresight' corresponding to the traditional forms of agricultural exploitation. The peasant 'foresaw' the necessity of labour, the storing of seed, etc., briefly, a whole host of practices, transmitted non-professionally, and which he reproduced; second, an attitude of forecasting which was geared to a growth in production, and from then the peasant sought to intervene in the natural processes. One can well understand that this latter purpose, the management of production, is important. At Hai Van, it would seem that this process is the special characteristic of those over 50 years old, former middle peasants, and to some degree, the members of the Party and of organizations, and those with a secondary education. Consequently, it would be normal to see the reappearance of those categories of persons who are more attentive to and more interested in participating in the management of the co-operative, and in making their private economic activities more productive. Such a duality in the background of cultural models, and practices which derive from it, is not without its impact on the emergence of a new leadership and on its reproduction (even by the device of the electoral process). Therefore, it is important to study it more systematically than we were able to do in the case of a production group in only one co-operative.

Conflicts in the Co-operative

We will complete this short study of the way in which the members see the functioning of the co-operative by an analysis of their perception of the conflicts. In other words, according to them, will there be conflicts, and if so, about what? The questionnaire distinguishes between two levels of possible conflict: at the level of macrostructure of the co-operative (conflicts between the production groups), and at the level of the production groups (conflicts between the head and the members, and between the members themselves).

Table 3.15 enables us, first of all, to make an observation at the level of the 'places' where these conflicts are perceived. It is observable that nearly 50% of those questioned are incapable of identifying the existence or non-existence of conflicts in the different production groups which constitute the co-operative. On the other hand, we should note that there is no one in the 'No opinion' group at the level of the production group.

In his study of peasant movements in South-east Asia, Scott[2] observed in the majority of rural inhabitants the near-impossibility of perceiving and of representing social structures which transcended the bounds of their village. In a study made in Sri Lanka, the same conclusion was arrived at.[3] Our observations throughout this work incline us to the opinion that a similar phenomenon exists at Hai Van. The co-operative of today is the recent product of the fusion of five very old hamlets which, in a first stage, had organized their own co-operatives. As the new organization of the economy takes into consideration these earlier arrangements, at least at the level of the organization of work and numerous other social activities at the social and geographical level, the hamlet of former times always constitutes the place of social identification of its inhabitants. There is no doubt that this persistence constitutes an important factor of social cohesion. This facilitates, in some way, the integration of the social entity, as such, into a structure of very large dimensions (co-operative, commune). But it is also an omen of a contradiction in the measure in which it restrains, in individuals, the awakening of an interest which transcends the level of the microstructure. The opinions on the subject of conflicts within a production group are available in much greater detail. They indicate relatively few conflicts between the members, and when they exist, they crystallize around a lack of possibilities for work outside strictly agricultural activities. More numerous are the conflicts with the head of the group, particularly on the subject of the award of points, which is objectively a possible source of struggle. But if one recalls the positive evaluation that was made of the head of the group one may suggest that, in the case studied, these conflicts are not of great importance.

Notes

1. The president, who was re-elected for the seventh time in succession, was caught up in the mainstream of the criticisms and then of the discussions of the results of the inquiry at Hai Van. He declared that he was well aware that while some of the criticism could be the result of malice, some was quite justified. He averred that he was in favour of an utterly democratic procedure before decisions were made, but admitted that in implementing the decisions he was authoritarian. The responsible functionaries of the district, knowing quite well the opinions of the members of the co-operative, told the electors to choose another candidate if they so desired, but he was re-elected because, according to the peasants, he was efficient and honest.
2. James Scott, *The Moral Economy of the Peasant – Rebellion and Subsistence in South-East Asia*, Yale University Press, New Haven, 1976.
3. F. Houtart and G. Lemercinier, *The Social Action of the Catholic Church in Sri Lanka*, SEDEC, Colombo, 1979.

4. Collective Organization of Leadership

This chapter gathers together some information and reflections on a subject which we have been unable to study in its entirety. We feel that this compendium of elements could contribute to the formulation of hypotheses for research and that, as such, they have their utility. There is, first of all, the organigram of the commune with an indication as regards the number of persons involved in the tasks of direction. We will then offer some reflections on the bureaucracy as a social process, and finally, some notes concerning the social aspects of leadership.

The Organigram of the Commune

We divide the organigram into two parts: one concerning the structure of the base of the commune, with its three fundamental elements, namely Party, administration, and co-operative; the other constitutes two important institutions in the social life of Hai Van, but does not constitute the fundamental organizations, namely the Patriotic Front and the Catholic parish.

The organigram of the commune of Hai Van corresponds to that of all the communes in the North and of those, which, elsewhere, have reached the stage of the organization of socialist co-operatives. There are, clearly, three sectors of public activity: the Party, the commune and the co-operative. The first is of the ideological and political order, the second of the administrative order, and the third of the economic order. The different organs of the three sectors are elected for two years. There are three key posts: the secretary of the Party, the president of the commune, and the president of the co-operative.

There is liaison between the three sectors, both at the organic and personal levels. The link between the commune and the co-operative is assured by the group for planning and statistics. On the other hand, the Party establishes personal links with the other two sectors. The chief of the militia alone is ex officio member of the Committee of the Party. There exists, however, a custom, almost institutionalized and applied at Hai Van, which consists in making the joint secretary of the Committee of the Party the president of the People's Committee, and yet another custom, according to which, the

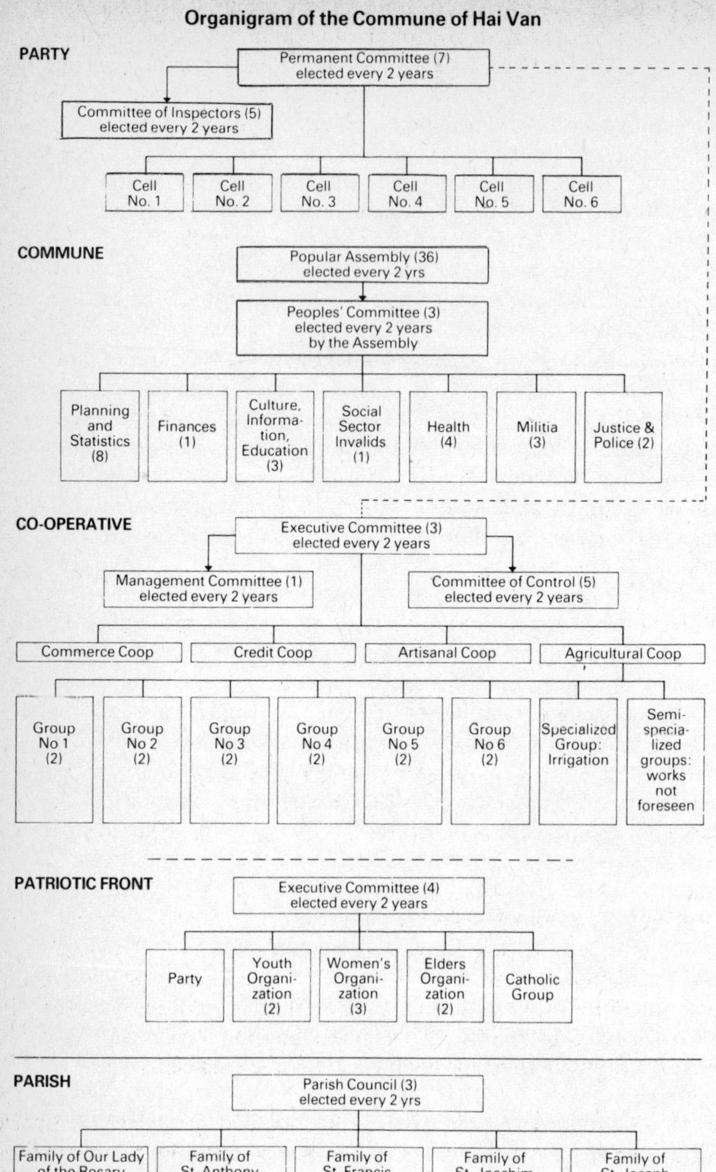
Organigram of the Commune of Hai Van
PARTY
Permanent Committee (7) elected every 2 years
Committee of Inspectors (5) elected every 2 years
Cell No. 1
Cell No. 2
Cell No. 3
Cell No. 4
Cell No. 5
Cell No. 6
COMMUNE
Popular Assembly (36) elected every 2 yrs
Peoples' Committee (3) elected every 2 years by the Assembly
Planning and Statistics (8)
Finances (1)
Culture, Information, Education (3)
Social Sector Invalids (1)
Health (4)
Militia (3)
Justice & Police (2)
CO-OPERATIVE
Executive Committee (3) elected every 2 years
Management Committee (1) elected every 2 years
Committee of Control (5) elected every 2 years
Commerce Coop
Credit Coop
Artisanal Coop
Agricultural Coop
Group No 1 (2)
Group No 2 (2)
Group No 3 (2)
Group No 4 (2)
Group No 5 (2)
Group No 6 (2)
Specialized Group: Irrigation
Semi-specialized groups: works not foreseen
PATRIOTIC FRONT
Executive Committee (4) elected every 2 years
Party
Youth Organization (2)
Women's Organization (3)
Elders Organization (2)
Catholic Group
PARISH
Parish Council (3) elected every 2 yrs
Family of Our Lady of the Rosary
Family of St. Anthony
Family of St. Francis
Family of St. Joachim
Family of St. Joseph

president of the co-operative is a member of the Committee of the Party, but these customs are not written laws or absolute norms.

Twice a year, at Hai Van, the members of the Party are subjected to criticism by non-members. This is done in the absence of the former and can finally be consigned to writing; a box is placed for this purpose and the complaints need not be signed. The Committee of the Party examines the grievances but no punishments may be meted out without reference to the echelon of the district. On the other hand, every other remedy may be applied on the spot. For the introduction of new members into the Party, a similar procedure is followed in order to have at hand the opinions of the whole of the population. The Committee of Inspection is entrusted with the function of examining every complaint concerning the members or the functioning of the commune and of the co-operative and of being watchful of all that happens concerning the observance of laws, and according to the orientation of the Party. The Patriotic Front is an organism which has no function of direct organization and it is for this reason that it is set apart in the organigram. It is meant to regroup the different social strata of the population and, at Hai Van, its function is not well developed. In the formal plan, the Front is charged with the task of composing the list of candidates for election to the commune.

As for the parish, there is a Parish Council composed of three lay people. At the level of the former villages, there exists what has been called a 'family', i.e. an organization of the laity who are occupied with all that concerns local religious life. In each of them there is a 'head of the family' and the families, in their turn, divided into groups of ten Catholic families, and each group has a person charged with responsibility. This organization was inherited from the Spanish missionaries, but, contrary to what happened in the past, the persons charged with responsibility are no longer appointed by the priest, but by election.

The Bureaucracy as a Social Process

The sociological phenomenon of the bureaucracy poses a problem to be met with in any transition to socialism: on the one hand, the process of transformation is intentional and therefore demands a well-developed executive apparatus; and, on the other, by reason of the still feeble state of the forces of production, points of reference have to be set up everywhere where local collective control cannot yet be placed in the hands of the people themselves. We will find again here the fundamental phenomenon of a sociology of transition, with the non-correspondences between the level of the forces of production and that of social relations. The more specific problem of the bureaucracy is institutionalization and that is a sociological process far more than a question of social psychology or of ethics. Once roles have been insituted, hierarchies are created, models of behaviour are set up, interests become vested, and it is very difficult to modify them. Further, they tend to reproduce themselves beyond the function for which they were instituted. A question worth posing is to ask to what degree this phenomenon exists at the level of the commune or of the co-operative and also what degree of awareness of this phenomenon the rural people might have.

An exploratory inquiry of modest proportions on this question has revealed that almost six out of ten persons believed that the problem of the bureaucracy does not arise at the level of the commune or of the co-operative. But it has also been established that this phenomenon, as a social process, under which aspect it is often denounced in the Party press and in the press of mass organizations, is perceived as such only by those with a level of education above the average, i.e. among the specialist cadres of the co-operative, among conscripts and among students of the higher grades. Among manual labourers, whether they are peasants or workers proper, the criticisms made were always concrete, for example, a hesitant or arrogant attitude among some leaders of the co-operatives, in the accounting departments, etc.

It must be said that at the level of the commune and of the co-operative of the kind found in Hai Van, there are scarcely grounds on which to build up an elaborate bureaucracy. It is evident in the higher echelons that this problem is of a general nature. The transition to production on a large scale is, doubtless, risky, when the levels of the permanent cadres are multiplied and the sociological basis of this phenomenon enlarged. This naturally leads us to a question which we only skimmed over in our study of the commune, namely conflicts of roles and the accumulation of monopolies of functions. The first aspect has been envisaged apropos of relations between those who fill the three key roles – the secretary of the Party, the president of the People's Committee, and the president of the co-operative. The range of operations of the president of the co-operative is easy to understand: it concerns economic functioning in its diverse dimensions. Economics is not outside the range required by the head of a commune. The plan deals with his attributes, and for this purpose he must remain in contact with the district for every operation of the drawing up of the plan and then for its implementation. The president declares it a complex problem, for management of the whole complex demands technical competence in different fields. For this purpose he receives a training for a year and a half and assists regularly at the meetings of the presidents of the communes at the district or province level. It is he, for example, who after having visited other communes, introduces a new variety of rice which gives better yields; and if things do not go according to plan in the economic sector, it is his duty to summon a meeting to discuss the problem.

As for the secretary of the Party, he himself defines his role thus: to gather together the forces of the commune on the basis of the orientation of the Party, to be an animator of the whole set up, and to assure general control over the activities of the commune and of the co-operative. He does not intervene directly in the fields of competence of others, but he can advise, suggest changes, and encourage them. It is evident, said the secretary, that if there is no unity of viewpoint between the different individuals charged with responsibility, conflicts will arise; sometimes there are very lively discussions. As the secretary of the Party has been in office since 1949, and the president of the co-operative re-elected for the seventh time, the existence of a tendency to co-optation or of monopolization of the roles could arise. We could not, within the limits of this research, verify this, but the very individuals charged with responsibility have in no way excluded this possibility. That the re-election of the president of the co-operative has been the genuine expression of the will of its members does not seem to have been contested by anyone. As for the secretary of the Party, he affirms that a change is desirable, but his desire notwithstanding, hardly any relief has been offered up to now. He recalls also that for 20 years the commune achieved real progress. He concluded: 'Democratic centralism is not the equivalent of a perfect democracy; it is democracy in the process of development, but if the Party attempts to impose solutions, the immediate reaction of the peasants would be non-participation. Hence, it is always necessary to have their approval.'

The problem of the accumulation of functions was also raised, notably, between the functions in the committee of the Party and in the command posts in the commune and in the co-operative. Those responsible, when questioned on this subject, admitted that the problem was a delicate one, but at the same time felt it was necessary, as far as possible, to assure unity of viewpoint in the policies to be followed. In other cases the situation is easily understood. Thus, the president of the Organization for Youth is the one responsible for the technical sector of the commune (for which he receives only 12 dongs a year), and further, as chief of the militia, he is a member of the Party. The Party, like the others composing the Front, designates candidates for the popular assembly. At Hai Van, of the 36 members, six are of the Party. Let us recall that there are 100 members of the Party in the commune, one third of whom are Catholic. The inclusions as well as the exclusions have been heatedly debated by the non-members. Between 1960 and 1979 nine members were excluded.

Reflections on the sociological devices revealed by the organization in its entirety, and what we have gathered on the functioning in the commune, make it clear that the intentional process of transition finds itself faced with exigencies which can, in fact, become contradictory: on the one hand, a precise orientation of transformations, and on the other, the popular consensus, which supposes participation. Precise orientations simultaneously concern the material base, with the establishment of new relations of production and the development of material techniques and of management, the sphere of the collective organization of the group and the whole of the system of representation. Since social reality is a unity, everything can contribute to favour or hinder the transition. This demands such a complexity of decisions that the last-mentioned process cannot be the object of the whims of each individual either in their elaboration or in their application. Further, an absence of consensus renders every process of change futile. There is, therefore, a delicate operation involved, to effect a combination of the two aspects. The inquiry made at Hai Van seems to indicate that a certain equilibrium can be found locally, in spite of the daunting difficulties at the outset. In fact productivity, both in the agricultural and in the handicrafts sectors, has constantly increased, and the inquiries on the participation, the aspirations and the cultural models indicate a real integration of the villagers into the processes of change. No doubt much depends on the quality of the social agents, for one can well imagine what results would ensue if the institutionalization of certain bureaucratic processes was bound up with personalities cast in too rigid a mould.

The Social Aspects of Leadership

In the course of the inquiry we were able to interview 41 cadres who explained to us the organization of the institutions for which they are responsible, and who gave us their opinions on the work accomplished by the different services. The indications which they furnished to us have been integrated into the different sections of this study. We will limit ourselves here to an analysis of the factors which will enable us to know who the present-day leaders are of the different institutions of the commune and of the co-operative. The cadres can be divided into several categories according to the functions they perform and according to the institutions in which they exercise them. Table 4.1 gives a detailed picture of this distribution.

Table 4.1
Distribution of the 41 Cadres Questioned According to Type of Institution and Function Exercised

Economic cadres:		
Higher cadres:	Vice-presidents	2
	Commission of Control of the co-operative	1
	Cadres of the co-operative	2
Lower cadres:	Heads of production groups	4
	Heads of group	2
	Former head of group	1
	Heads of sub-groups	3
Administrative Cadres		
President of the commune		1
Former president		1
Vice-president		1
Person responsible for programming		1
Person responsible for distribution		1
Other administrative cadres		3
Responsible for self-defence		1
Teacher		1

Overseer of crèche	1
Doctor	1
Political Cadres	
Secretary of the Party	1
Secretary of the Youth Organization	1
Vice-secretaries of Youth Organization	2
Members of the committee of Youth Organization	2
President of the Women's Organization	1
President of the Patriotic Front	1
Member of the committee of the Patriotic Front	1
Religious Cadres	
Parish priest	1
President of the Parish Council	1
Vice-president of the Parish Council	1
Head of a 'family' (groups of families of only one village)	1

As Table 4.1 indicates, the persons interviewed work in all the principal sectors of the organizations of the commune, of the co-operative and of the political and religious groups. Except, perhaps, for education (since the school was on vacation and the cadres were on leave), these persons perform important functions. Further, through an intermediary, we met members of their work teams, in the dispensary, in the pharmacy and in the maternity homes – as far as we could go in matters of health – and in the homes for elders, in the house for culture, etc.

Characteristics of the Cadres Questioned

The persons who were interviewed, constitute the majority of those chiefly charged with responsibility. One can, therefore, say that the observations suggested by Table 4.2 are valid for this group. It stands out, first of all, that local leadership remains, on the whole, very much in the hands of males. Women are present in certain well-defined sectors – health, education, organizations of youth and of women – but they are absent from the economic and administrative organizations of the commune and of the co-operative. It is clear also that the younger generation (less than 35 years) are scarcely represented, if one excludes their role as leaders in youth organizations.

The level of education of the cadres is clearly above average. It is sufficient to compare the figures with those found in the samplings of different research studies which will be analysed further. From the professional point of view it is interesting to note that only 15% exercise their function in the cadres under a definite title. They are, chiefly, those whose activities demand a specialized training such as doctors, teachers, overseers of crèches, etc. As for the cadres of the co-operative and of the commune, almost all have been elected within the group of cultivators on a temporary basis, and will return to agriculture

Table 4.2
Demographic and Socio-Cultural Characteristics of the Cadres Interviewed

	A		*B*			*C*					*D*		*E*				*F*			*G*
	1	*2*	*1*	*2*	*3*	*1*	*2*	*3*	*4*	*5*	*1*	*2*	*1*	*2*	*3*	*4*	*1*	*2*	*3*	*1*
Economic:																				
Superiors	5	–	–	3	2	1	3	–	–	1	3	2	2	2	–	–	4	–	1	5
Rankers	9	1	2	6	2	–	7	1	1	1	6	4	5	2	1	–	9	1	–	7
Administrative	11	2	5	4	4	1	5	3	–	2	5	8	6	1	1	1	6	1	6	9
Politics	6	3	6	1	2	1	6	–	–	1	5	4	6	–	–	1	7	1	1	9
Religion	4	–	–	–	4	1	1	1	–	1	4	–	4	–	–	–	3	–	1	–
Total	*35*	*6*	*13*	*14*	*14*	*4*	*22*	*5*	*1*	*6*	*23*	*18*	*23*	*5*	*2*	*2*	*29*	*3*	*9*	*30*
%	85.4	14.6	31.7	34.1	34.1	9.8	53.7	12.2	2.4	14.6	56.1	43.9	56.1	12.2	4.9	4.9	70.7	7.3	22.0	73.2

A = Sex
A1 = Male
A2 = Female

B = Age
B1 = less than 35 years
B2 = 35–49 years
B3 = 50 years and over

C = Education
C1 = Primary
C2 = Secondary
C3 = Tertiary
C4 = Literate
C5 = Cadre School

D = Religion
D1 = Catholic
D2 = Non-Catholic

E = Social Origin
E1 = Poor peasant
E2 = Middle peasants
E3 = Workers
E4 = Co-operators

F = Occupation
F1 = Agriculture
F2 = Workers
F3 = Cadres

G = Members of political party and organizations

at the end of their mandates. This procedure in the designation of cadres avoids the establishment of a cadre caste even though some of them are re-elected for several terms. This is doubtless possible only in co-operatives of average size, the management of which does not demand specialized technical skills beyond that acquired by experience and secondary school education, and completed by an intensive course at the level of the district or of the province. This, no doubt, is the reason why at the present juncture, those elected come from the 35+ age group. It will be noted, further, that all the cadres, except the priest, come from the village itself. (Among the teachers nominated by the province, are some from outside the village.) Most of them have their origins among the poor peasants, for whom the revolution was a revelation of the potentialities which are too often believed to be non-existent in class-ridden societies. It must be remembered, though, that it is in the co-operative that we meet the cadres who come from middle-class peasant backgrounds. Here is a sociological fact quite comprehensible if one considers that their own background and the background of their parents afford them the opportunity of a certain level of knowledge and experience of management.

Finally it should be emphasized that adherence to a religious faith is not, at present, a hindrance to access to leadership. The majority of the group encountered was in fact Catholic, although their proportion is less than that of the Catholic population in the village. Among the cadres of 40+, Catholics are almost nil. They have, therefore, been recruited during the first stage of the revolutionary regime, almost exclusively among the 15% of the non-Catholic population. It should not be forgotten that the Catholics were slower than the others to enter into the movement for the building up of socialism, on account of politico-religious events of which we will speak later, and by the very fact of being restrained for a long time by the local clergy from participating not only in the political organizations but also in the co-operative. Further, moral pressure was brought to bear on the parents to make them reject education for their children. Today, all these tendencies contrary to socialism have disappeared, and Catholics are present in all responsible positions, as the results of the inquiry show, both in the Party and in the mass organizations.

5. Education and Health Services

Even though our research may not have deepened our knowledge of the socio-cultural services, i.e. education, the library and health, we have gathered together some information which will serve as indicators of a certain number of social processes, which will acquire a certain sociological value with regard to the rest of the inquiry. If we speak of services as new foci for collectives it is because they fulfil tasks formerly undertaken by the very fundamental structure – the extended family, and eventually, the unit which was the village. Today these sectors of activity have become highly specialized and they form, therefore, new foci where collective activity is developed, and new roles take on shape and substance. And in consequence, new social relations are engendered within these institutions, and in the same way, new relations are forged between the population and those institutions. A further aspect worth reflecting upon is the correspondence, in a period of transition, between the existence of services and their utilization by the people.

The Educational Services

Education is one of the non-economic services which is an object of planning because of the importance of its double function. It is one of the key institutio for the socialization of the younger generations and for the inculcation of a knowledge of the development of the forces of production. Like every other institution the educational system is also in a state of transition. This means that it is being elaborated and constructed as much at the level of the extent to which it is being spread as with regard to the plan which determines the content of knowledge which it imparts and the pedagogical methods which it develops. We have not been able, within the limits of this work, to undertake an analysis of the content of the courses being dispensed today at Hai Van, in its primary and secondary schools. We will limit ourselves, therefore, to an analysis of the material constituting the programmes of the courses and of available educational statistics, and completing our inquiry with other observations we were able to make. Our perspective will be that of a study of a process of transition. Setting out from the situation as it existed before the revolution, we will attempt to extract the sociological significance of the structures which have been set up in order to be able to understand certain aspects of the present situation.

The Sociological Significance of the Introduction of a School System

At the time of the revolution in 1945, there existed at Hai Van a small primary school for the children of the litterati and of the mandarins. Its function was to teach the rudiments of the Chinese language and to enable the children to read and write. There was no provision made for the schooling of the other children. The statistics of the period 1945/46 reflect this situation. If one excludes from the population of the time (1,583) children under seven years and adults aged over 60 (179), the remainder may be categorized as in Table 5.1.

Table 5.1
Level of Education of the Population of Hai Van, 1945/46

		%
Illiterate	1,230	87.3
Able to read and write	75	5.3
Primary School education	7	0.5
Learning the alphabet	85	6.0
In primary school	11	0.8
In secondary school	1	0.07

During this time, then, 87% of the population of the village was denied every form of communication through reading and writing. Does this mean that the young generations were not 'educated'? Not at all. It is certain that the very reproduction of the society of the past demanded a socialization of the young to the current ways and customs, to the inculcation of a model of social and individual practices and to the very transmission of a know-how (agricultural techniques, domestic tasks, etc.) corresponding to the level of development of the forces of production. In every village this task of socialization devolved principally upon the family, but also on the rest of the village population in the measure in which it exercised social control over the members of the group. Add to this that in the Catholic villages, it belonged to the religious agent to see to it that the children were brought up in their religious beliefs, and in their religious and ethical practices. In a general way one may say, therefore, that if socialization was not systematic and was realized in a haphazard sort of way, it was nonetheless very real.

It is easy to understand that, if a process of social change is to be introduced into a society, the problem of education must be tackled. This principle is as valid for a transition to capitalism as it is to socialism. It is evident that we are faced here with a necessary condition, not merely a sufficient one. It is important to be able to socialize the young generations to a new system of values, to new forms of social practice and to impart to them a satisfactory knowledge of the exigencies of scientific development. This is why in all present day societies education is one of the sectors in the charge of, or at least controlled by, the public authority.

From a sociological point of view, the development of a school system implies, for the traditional rural family, the loss of one of its functions, while the reason for the change does not appear evident at all. In fact, in the measure in which the material conditions of peasant life have suffered scarcely any change, or if schooling offers only a few possibilities of climbing up the social ladder, peasants can scarcely be interested, or even consider it a waste of time to send the young to school, especially if they could otherwise work. For this reason the political authority generally makes schooling compulsory at the primary level at least, in order to ensure that children receive some basic education.

The educational policy during the first years after the revolution envisaged a plan for a simultaneous campaign of literacy for the whole population by the establishment of primary schools (a four year course) in every village and locality. In the small urban centres secondary schools were opened (a three year course) to serve the needs of the region. This policy which, at the same time, affected the education of youth and of adults, had the advantage of including the parents themselves in the struggle for the development of knowledge and also of making them discover, beyond the mere benefits of mastering the alphabet, the importance of schooling for children.

How this policy affected Hai Van some ten years later is shown in Table 5.2. The total population, excluding infants and those aged 60 or more, was 3,288.

Table 5.2
Level of Education of the Population of Hai Van, 1960

	Illiterate		*Persons having left school, or complementary course*		*Completion of course: in a school of general knowledge*		*in a complementary course for adults*	
		%		*%*		*%*		*%*
Mastery of the alphabet			568	19.7	–	–	846	29.4
Primary education complete or incomplete			700	24.3	327	11.4	212	7.4
Secondary education complete or incomplete			54	1.9	118	4.1	30	1.0
Three degree cycle			–	–	5	0.2	–	–
Total	*16*	*0.6*	*1322*	*45.9*	*450*	*15.7*	*1088*	*37.8*

Table 5.2 reveals the enormous effort made to teach the alphabet to adults; 1,414 adults of the village went through the complementary course teaching them to read and write. Further, 700 children and adults followed, if not entirely, at least partially, the classes of primary education; 327 children attended primary school and 212 adults followed this programme in a com-

plementary course.

If the population as a whole seemed to have responded to the campaign for mastery of the alphabet, there were observable differences between the participation of males and females, and consequently differences between the levels of education of the two sexes. A comparison is made in Table 5.3.

Table 5.3
Level of Education According to the Sexes, 1946 and 1960

	1946				*1960*			
	Men		*Women*		*Men*		*Women*	
		%		%		%		%
Illiterate	409	77.2	821	93.9	6	0.4	10	0.9
Mastery of Alphabet	106	20.0	49	5.6	379	26.6	735	63.6
Primary education complete or incomplete	14	2.6	4	0.5	884	62.0	355	30.7
Secondary education complete or incomplete	1	0.2	0	–	151	10.6	56	4.8
Three degree cycle	–	–	–	–	5	0.4	–	–
% in the total population		*48.3*		*51.7*		*48.5*		*51.5*

Both men and women followed the course for learning the alphabet, but only a few of the women pursued the complementary course at the primary level. Further, there were fewer girls than boys in the classes of the secondary schools. This is easy to understand if one reckons with the position which women occupied in the former context. In villages with a Catholic majority but with an ethos impregnated with Confucianism, the woman was considered the property of the father before she became that of the husband, and was excluded from all public functions, even in the dominant classes. Consecrated as it were to the performance of domestic chores and therefore with very little time at her disposal, it was very difficult for her, even after the revolution, to pursue complementary courses. Most of the young girls of an age when they should have been attending primary school, had to occupy themselves with the care of siblings while the adults worked in the fields. We must not forget that in 1960 the collectivization of the rural economy was far from what it is today.

Thus the difference between the levels of education of boys and girls may be explained partially by reference to the past, but there is also another cause. In fact, there were fewer girls than boys in the classes of general education even at the primary level. This situation was indicative of an ambiguous attitude in the parents to whom an identical offer was made for their children of either sex. To understand this one must take into account, first of all, that the collectivization of production was then far from being accomplished and this implied the persistence of former forms of division of labour. In this model, girls, even very young girls, had to undertake a part of the domestic work. Schoolgoing therefore appeared to the parents to be not only useless but also a complicating factor in the organization of daily life. On the other hand, the schooling of boys took on another significance in the measure in which in traditional society, schools reserved for the sons of the ruling classes were the privileged means of determining the social position. For those who were peasants before, it signified social promotion. Even today it is striking to see how the peasants who still remember the former social set-up measure the benefits of the revolution by comparing their present situation with that of the ruling classes before the revolution. This reference to their practices, notably symbolic, remains for many adult peasants the model of the people's success. The internal management of peasant houses is significant in this regard.

An analysis of the level of education of male adults of less than 40 years of age who participated in the inquiry, shows, among the oldest, a very short schooling period – two or three years at most. This phenomenon, peculiar to Catholics, is explained, according to those interviewed, by the fact that pressure was brought to bear on the parents by the religious agent who was opposed, at that time, to the schooling of children. It was the problem of a typical reaction of a social agent who persisted in retaining the monopoly of the socialization of youth outside the family milieu and for whom the school appeared to be a competing institution. The same phenomenon recurs elsewhere in capitalist societies, both in Europe and in Latin America.

The Present System of Education

It is interesting to measure the incidence of the fundamental transformation of the social relations on the level of education of the population during the last 20 years, and this despite the war. At the level of the commune of Hai Van, this change was translated concretely by the collectivization of the economy and by an institutional development corresponding to the specifications of the important social functions, undertaken in former times by the family. Such an evolution was evidently at the origin of the irreversible transformations in the practices of the social agents, the definition of roles, and the cultural models, as the whole of this research will reveal. Further, the fusion of the former villages has pushed the population up to 5,261 persons, from which figure we will exclude, for the purposes of this analysis, some 611 infants and people aged over 65.

If one considers only the population engaged in professional activity, it is clear that the majority is composed of those who belong to the category of the literate. Beyond that, nearly 30% have followed either partially or completely the first cycle (four years of primary education) and 16% have completed or partially followed the second cycle (three years); 15 persons have passed the level of the third cycle.

The distributions (into categories) taken up in the second table, including children at school and adults going through their complementary courses, enable us to forecast the categorization in the following year. One will notice a relative diminution of those barely literate, an increase of 23% at primary school level, and a relative increase of 45% at the secondary school

Table 5.4
Level of Education of the Population of Hai Van 1978/79

	Those who have terminated their studies		*Those who have terminated their studies or are in the course of education*					
			Men		*Women*		*Total*	
		%		%		%		%
Literate	1,799	53.9	875	36.4	904	40.3	1,779	38.3
1st cycle complete or incomplete	985	29.9	913	38.0	802	35.8	1,715	36.9
2nd cycle complete or incomplete	520	15.8	542	22.6	512	22.8	1,054	22.7
3rd cycle complete or incomplete	15	0.45	77	3.2	25	1.1	102	2.2

level. The tendency, therefore, is in the direction of a lengthening of the schooling period up to the end of the second cycle, i.e. up to the age of 14 or less.

But statistics also indicate a marked change in the education of girls. If only on account of the past, the proportion of women with bare knowledge of the alphabet is much higher than that of men, but there is an observable parity between the percentages of men and women who will have followed the second cycle. These figures are indicative of an evolution in the cultural model concerning female education – an evolution which corresponds to a change in the social position of the woman both in the economic and political sphères, and also in the family.

Table 5.5
Distribution of Schools, Staff and Students According to Study Cycles

	Number of schools	*Number of classes*	*Personnel*	*Students*	*%*	*Number of students pêr class*	*Number of students per teacher*
Nursery	2	18	36	429	24.7	24	12
General Knowledge							
1st cycle (4 years)	1	20	36	684	39.4	60	33
2nd cycle *(3 years)				510	29.4		
Complementary							
1st cycle		2		42	2.4		
2nd cycle	1	2	6	24	1.4	22	18
3rd cycle		1		45	2.6		
Total	*4*	*43*	*78*	*1,734*	*100.0*		

* Further, 38 youths are pursuing their 3-year cycle of studies outside the village.

Education in the commune is geared in three directions: nursery schools; general education of the 1st and 2nd cycles; and adult education. At present, schooling is compulsory for children aged between seven and 14. Nursery school courses for children between the ages of five and seven aim to prepare the children for primary school education and give them some grounding in the three Rs. Although attendance is not compulsory, children at nursery school constitute about a quarter of the schoolgoing population.

General education accounts for 1,200 students, i.e. 22.8% of the total population of the commune and 25.8% of the population between the ages of seven and 65. What then of their future? Since there are as many in the 1st cycle as in the 2nd, the population will remain relatively stable. In fact, the present average of students per year has risen to 139 at the nursery level, 171 in the first cycle and 170 in the second cycle; but one must also reckon with the non-obligatory character of attending school at the nursery level. The effort to furnish the schools ought to have a bearing on the overflow of the classes of the 2nd cycle and on the improvement of the local schools. It will also depend on the policies followed, concerning the eventual prolongation of the study courses at the level of the 3rd cycle.

At present, the strength of the last cycle is very low. According to the teachers, 15% of the students of the terminal class of the 2nd cycle are likely to pursue further studies. A partial explanation for the low percentage consists in the late-comers to school which some schools have accumulated during the course of the classes. But it is explained also by a certain lack of interest on the part of the family with regard to the schooling of children. The inquiry on the family, the detailed results of which are given in subsequent chapters, shows that parents devote, as a rule, very little time to their children, and that in the majority of cases the care of the children devolves upon the grandparents who guide them in their studies. Account being taken of the fact that the grandparents themselves have mastered literacy only recently, of perpetuating a cultural model which tends to denigrate the value of schooling for children is very real.

Table 5.6
Programme of Studies of 1st and 2nd Cycles of General Education in Course Periods by Year of Study (one course period = 50 mins)

Subjects	*1st year*	*2nd year*	*3rd year*	*4th year*	*Total*	*%*
Mother tongue:						
Literature	70	70	70	70	280	
Reading	350	350	350	70	1,120	
Orthography	70	70	210	70	420	
Writing	70	70	35	35	210	
Recitation	70	70	35	35	210	
Elocution	–	–	–	35	35	
Grammar	–	–	35	35	70	
Total					*2,345*	*48.3*

Mathematics	350	350	350	350	1,400	
Sciences	–	–	–	35	35	
Total					*1,435*	*29.6*
History	–	–	–	35	35	
Geography	–	–	–	35	35	
Total					*70*	*1.4*
Civics:						
Morals	35	35	35	35	140	
Discussion	35	35	35	35	140	
Social Activities	–	–	35	35	70	
Manual Work	–	35	35	35	105	
Total					*455*	*9.4*
Culture and Sport						
Gymnastics	35	35	35	35	140	
Painting	35	35	35	35	140	
Singing	35	35	35	35	140	
Total					*420*	*8.5*
Handicrafts	35	35	35	35	140	
Grand Total					*4,855*	*100.0*

Second Cycle

Subjects	*5th year*	*6th year*	*7th year*	*Total*	*%*
Literature	420	350	350	1,120	22.3
Sciences					
Mathematics	420	385	385	1,090	
Physics	–	60	210	270	
Chemistry	–	–	105	105	
Hygiene	35	–	–	35	
Biology	70	70	70	210	
Total				*1,710*	*34.0*
History	35	105	105	245	
Geography	120	105	105	330	
Total				*575*	*11.4*
Civics:					
Morals	35	35	35	105	
Politics	–	–	35	35	
Discussion	35	35	35	105	
Social Activities	70	70	70	210	
Manual Work	70	175	210	455	
Total				*910*	*18.1*
Culture and Sport:					
Gymnastics	70	70	70	210	

Painting	35	35	–	70	
Singing	35	35	–	70	
Total				*350*	*7.0*
Agricultural Techniques	105	105	105	315	
Handicrafts	17	17	17	51	
Total				*366*	*7.6*
Foreign Languages*	140	140	140	420	10.3
Grand total				*5,031*	*100.0*

* These courses are not being given today owing to lack of teachers.

The Library

A study of the programmes of the courses (Table 5.6) reveals an orientation of the 2nd cycle with a view to preparation for further studies. There is the risk that very little of what has been taught will abide once schooling is over. The statistics concerning the borrowing of books from the commune library reinforce this surmise. The library was opened in 1968 and comprised, in October 1978, 2,474 volumes and 17 collections of journals and periodicals. On the same date, and over a period of ten years, 244 persons had taken out membership cards, i.e. 4% of the population between seven and 60. It is clear that 77% of those who attend the library are schoolgoers or students. Of the remaining 23% the majority are young adults, or in a smaller proportion, those above 50 years of age. The library-using population between 31 and 50 years of age is almost non-existent. Further, only two women of 30+ have borrowed books from the library during its ten years of existence.

Over the course of ten years, 879 volumes constitute the sum total of the books borrowed by the users of the library. This represents 35.5% of the total number of books available. These statistics have been gathered from the individual membership cards, classified according to age. If we take account of all the books chosen by each user since he or she became a member of the library one will see the influence of the school. There is no doubt that many library users are influenced by the school to use the library when they are still schoolgoers, since 60% of the books have been borrowed by them. However, it also appears that the habit of reading lasts beyond the period of schooling between the ages of 15 and 30. On the other hand, mere literacy of adults does not seem to have developed in them a taste for further reading. This is a feature observable in all societies where adult literacy campaigns have been organized. It must be recognized that the acquisition of the reading habit at adult age does not make the practice easy. Besides, there is the fact that the reading habit is held in low esteem by manual workers, all the more so since the radio has been introduced simultaneously.

We have chosen this example to illustrate a sociological phenomenon which often goes unnoticed by promoters of social action, namely the fact that the mere setting up of an institution for social service is not automatically followed by an appreciation of its value and by the consequent use of it. This

Table 5.7
Distribution of Library Users According to Age, Sex and Occupation

Age		*Men*	*Women*	*School goers*	*Students*	*Farmers*	*Artisans*	*Employed*	*Cadres*	*Teachers*
7–14	141	77	64	141	–	–	–	–	–	–
15–30	79	51	28	–	45	13	–	2	11	8
31–50	6	4	2	–	–	–	–	1	2	3
51–60	16	16	–	–	–	2	1	–	–	3
Total	*242*	*148*	*94*	*141*	*45*	*15*	*1*	*3*	*13*	*14*
%		61.1	38.8	58.3	18.6	6.2	0.4	1.3	5.4	5.8

Table 5.8
Frequency and Type of Books Borrowed by Library Users (in %)

Age		*Socio-political*	*Technical scientific*	*Popular scientific*	*Science fiction*	*War*	*Bio-graphy*	*Detect-ive*	*Thrillers*	*Poetry*	*Total number of books*
7–14	Boys	–	–	–	14.5	24.8	20.3	31.5	3.5	5.5	313
	Girls	–	–	0.9	5.2	30.0	25.8	12.7	13.1	12.2	213
15–30	Men	4.2	2.1	0.5	5.2	26.6	6.8	25.5	21.9	7.3	192
	Women	1.1	2.2	7.6	2.2	30.4	6.5	13.0	30.4	5.4	92
31–50	Men	16.0	4.0	–	–	16.0	16.0	12.0	8.0	28.0	25
50 and over	Men	–	–	6.8	–	25.0	31.8	2.3	13.6	20.5	44
Total		*1.5*	*0.8*	*1.7*	*7.7*	*27.0*	*17.7*	*21.6*	*13.4*	*8.5*	*879*

demands a transformation of cultural models which influence the practices of the social agents – practices which fall foul of habits grown inveterate. It is certain that the need for change is not always evident and depends very often on transformation of other factors of social life, from which there results a time-lag, more or less long, according to the use of the means one does or does not make use of, to induce an acceleration of the process of change. In the case of formal education, for example, it is clear that legislation to make schoolgoing obligatory, applied rigorously, was one of the means to achieve the end. In the case of the use of the library or of other cultural institutions, other means must be used, for lack of which, one will run the risk of nullifying the purposes of those institutions regardless of the very real importance of the services they seek to render.

The Health Services

In traditional society, the preoccupation with health depended, evidently, on the level of development of the forces of production (i.e. the conquest of nature) and found expression in a search for protection against disease and by therapeutic practices. Even if one discovers today that certain therapeutic methods (the use of herbs etc.) have prophylactic properties well-known to the social agents of health (through empirical rather than not scientific knowledge), the prevention of disease was merely a matter of symbolism. This is why we prefer to use the word 'protection'. Face to face with nature still unmastered, the rural population attributed natural phenomena to supernatural forces, personified or not, which they conjured up by propitiatory practices. Within Catholicism, for example, there has been a development of popular religiosity which attributes to the saints a particular power to exorcize certain maladies. This is to be found no less in Vietnam than elsewhere. From the therapeutic point of view, there existed, as we have said, before, a practical knowledge, extracted from experience by observing the constancy of the beneficial effects of the use of plants or of other natural products for the cure of certain ills. This knowledge was in the hands of specialists (medicine men, sorcerers, or magicians) who integrated them into a system of curative practices strongly tainted by magic. In certain, very definite cases, Catholics went to priests to ask for their prayers or their blessings. In such a context it is clear that the mortality rate, especially, that of infants, was very high.

The Medical and Para-medical Set-up of the Commune

It was in 1965 that a modern medical service was set up in Hai Van. It was manned by a team of eight persons of whom three are doctors (two women and one man). The doctors have had a three year course of training at the provincial school of Nam Dinh. One of them is a specialist in traditional medicine. The team also has a midwife, a pharmacist and three medical attendants. This team is responsible for the medical services, consisting of a dispensary which is open every day, a maternity home and a pharmacy which produces the necessary medicines from plants cultivated on the spot. The responsibility for general hygiene devolves on the head doctor. Further, a nurse works half the time in each production team, and the other half is spent in work at the co-operative, as any other worker does. The remuneration for medical personnel is calculated in the same way as for other members of the co-operative, according to the days of work and points. Minor treatment is directly assured at the level of the production team. The local nurse is charged also with the responsibility of seeing to the prevention of disease at the same level. Patients more seriously affected are sent to the dispensary which treats, on an average, 300 patients a month. Cases which require hospitalization are sent to the district hospital some kilometres away.

Medical Practices and the Difficulties Met With

From the point of view of general curative medicine, illnesses of most frequent occurrence are diarrhoea, dysentery, fever, benign pulmonary conditions, gynaecological conditions, etc. which can be treated with medicines manufactured locally according to a programme being implemented by the Ministry of Health. According to the responsible head of the team there is a lack of vermifuges and antibiotics. Malaria, it should be remembered, is eradicable, if constant warfare is waged against mosquitoes.

The major difficulty, however, lies at the level of preventive medicine and concerns the problem of water and its use. Most of the families still use water from ponds for domestic purposes. Hence there is a campaign to persuade peasants to construct a well and a bathing place for every two families. The water should serve for the needs of the body and for some domestic purposes (washing crockery, etc.). At Hai Van the water is too brackish for consumption. To solve this problem families are urged to store water in concrete cisterns, hermetically sealed; it is a difficult task to have to persuade families to set aside a part of their revenues for this purpose. The fact is that the families are more concerned with building houses of durable materials and with improving them, rather than with the improvement of essential amenities. Once again one is confronted with cultural models in which expenses incurred on what is prestigious are a socio-economic status symbol. This rationale accords ill with an attitude which regards as superfluous expenditure, money spent for utilitarian purposes. It is difficult to make the peasant understand the logic of the casual connection between water and disease.

The second problem, no less daunting, concerns hygiene and infant malnutrition. Generally, children are less well cared for than young adults, and this is the cause of skin diseases and intestinal ailments. They also suffer from malnutrition from an overconsumption of carbohydrates (rice), from a lack of proteins, and especially, vitamins. Vegetables and fruits produced by the local economy increase revenues rather than improve the diet. The neglected health of the children, according to the medical team, is partially, at least, an indirect consequence of the collectivization of the economy and of women working at the co-operative. Of the time left over, the greater part of it is devoted to domestic production, household tasks, marketing, etc. (see

Chapter 6 concerning the woman and the family). Thus there has developed a new social practice during the last 50 years – that of entrusting the care and rearing of children to the aged members of the family. This is a practice with deleterious effects on the health of the child. That these guardians of children are utterly devoted to their charges is beyond discussion, but more often than not they are persons who are conduits for models of age old practices and sometimes these are in contradiction with the development efforts being made by the medical team. We have seen already that this situation is scarcely favourable from an educational point of view.

Family Planning

Family planning has been a major preoccupation of the state because of the importance of the birth rate when it is joined with a diminution of the mortality rate. The model of the ideal family is that of two children: but it is admitted, because of a wish to respect former cultural models in a time of transition, that a third child is often longed for when the first two are girls. The converse proposition, however, is not admissible. It is the medical team of the village which is responsible for educating the population in this matter, for nothing is obligatory in this sphere. The method initially proposed was that of Ogino, the application of which was found to be very difficult. And for this reason sterilization was also introduced, the choice of one or the other being left to personal preference. According to the medical team, the education of adults in these cases is a long process, although it has been facilitated by the lack of opposition from the clergy. At present the great majority of young women favour family planning.

As regards pre-natal medicine, every pregnant woman is obliged to submit herself to a medical check up at least twice during the course of her pregnancy. It is obligatory that the confinement takes place in the maternity home of the commune where the mother (and sometimes, also, the grandmother) is instructed in hygienic practices as regards the new born. All children of less than a year are given a medical check up once every three months. All these practices have had the effect of sharply reducing the infant mortality rate: in 1978, of 125 children born, only two deaths were recorded.

Conclusions

Generally speaking, one may say that the population has adopted, with relative ease, the new practices introduced by the health team in the field of therapeutic medicine, while it remains conservative in the field of preventive medicine. Why then this difference in the collective behaviour of one and the same population? Unlike in economics, and still more unlike in education, health is a vital sector of which the social agents have a relatively feeble grasp and for which they have to appeal to specialists whether they be the traditional medicine men or modern doctors. Further, it is a sphere where the art of the specialist produces immediate results, the benefits of which are measurable and do not compete with any other interest. In such cases the adoption of therapeutic medicine is relatively easy. It is quite otherwise with preventive medicine which calls for the intervention of social agents and their comprehension of the mechanisms involved may often leave much to be desired. Further still, the inquiry has disclosed to us that preventive medicine is not yet seen to be a collective responsibility. In this department of social life individualism is still the prevalent feature. One must, however, recall the road traversed in a generation and the conditions which prevailed in Hai Van before 1945.

6. The Family and Its Function

Since the end of the 12th Century the organization of the rural economy of Vietnam has been characterized by a feature that lasted up to the revolution of August 1945. From the modes of production sprang social relationships which were fundamentally tributary in nature. But the political authority could interfere at the level of the rural communes to grant to the 'notables' a part of the land, up to then possessed collectively, in a special form that was both private and hereditary. These 'notables' derived profit from their property by leasing it out. The system of devolution of these estates followed the customary rule of dividing their fruits among the proprietors' male descendants. The practice of making nominal gifts of land and their progressive fragmentation resulted in rendering them negotiable, and in fact, of encouraging their transfer to proprietors other than those to whom the original grants were made.

This kind of economic organization produced a type of family that was nuclear with regard to both unit of production and habitation. However. the nuclearization of the family did not imply the total disappearance of the social functions of the extended family. Groups related by blood and established, as a rule, in the same village, became the focuses of the effective life of the people, the means of establishing their privileged identity in the social ladder, and of tracing their common ancestral origins. Further, the extended family remained as a very striking instance of social control, particularly by the direct ancestors.

In the nuclear family the woman was not devoted solely to housekeeping – she played her part also in direct production such as transplanting rice and selling produce. Except for these mercantile activities women were excluded from social life and from local political associations (*giaps*) which flourished in the villages. This exclusion was the expression of a cultural model impregnated with Confucianism which considered the young girl the property of the father before she became the possession of her husband. This conception of the role of a woman in society, it may be hazarded, like all the corresponding social practices, was functional in this that it maintained the balance in matrimonial exchanges in a society where classes were defined by the private channels people had (or did not have) at their disposal for availing themselves of the means of production, i.e. land. Child marriages belong to the same social conception. Similar practices are observable also in other Asiatic but non-Confucian societies such as in Kerala, in India, where the Brahmin caste guarantees to its male members exclusive ownership of the means of production.

The formal object of this chapter is to study the importance of the family in the different social structures of traditional society. As in most of the Asiatic societies, ancient kingdoms, corresponding to the appearance of class-ridden societies, were, in fact, tributary in nature. This mode of production, qualified by Marx as Asiatic, is characterized by a network of social relationships built up on the obligations of peasant social groups to furnish either to their sovereign or to someone in the administrative hierarchy a 'tribute', corresponding to a predetermined portion of the harvest, in exchange for the guarantee of military protection.

In village-based social groups the organization giving access to common land preserved the model of societies based on lineage. The usufruct of a piece of land collectively owned was allotted periodically and in rotation to every male over 18 years of age. This particular form of land tenure produced a model for matrimonial exchange – the bride, from the time of marriage, integrating herself into the family of her in-laws and living under the authority of her husband's parents. Even French colonization did not alter this model totally.

It is well known that in order to consolidate the social basis of the colonial system the political device used was to make privileged land grants to members of the administration, thus reducing the peasant family to the state of 'landless peasants', i.e. mere agricultural workers. However, the family model was scarcely touched for the simple reason that other possibilities did not exist. Certainly none did that could effect a worthwhile migration of rural workers. The result was a constant increase in unemployment since the techniques of production were not keeping abreast of development.

After the revolution the agrarian reform had to allocate land to each family unit. The process of integrating the land into peasant co-operatives was gradual and its development passed through various phases (as was pointed out earlier), before arriving at the form of land tenure which we know today. This collectivization of the rural economy and the allocation of land to families for the purposes both of residence and domestic economy quickened the process of erosion of the family model of yesteryear by the very fact of the individualization of the workforce at the heart of collective enterprise and by the recognition given to the nuclear family as the social cell of private life. From all this one must expect a progressive alteration in the models of the roles family members play, especially the role of the woman, now become a 'peasant worker' and therefore subject to fixed norms of work on the one hand, and enjoying, on the other, equal rights with men. The prolonged war and the consequent mobilization of the larger part of the male labour force compelled women, in a certain measure, to undertake responsibilities in spheres from which they were normally excluded. Finally, the political demography of the Vietnamese government and the diffusion of family planning methods, even though the practice was not obligatory, must exercise some influence in the short run on the cultural models that concern human reproduction and therefore on the size of the family.

The presence of different factors making for change was at the origin of our inquiry into some of their consequences. It is certain that the existence of factors making for change does not necessarily connote the occurrence of change – all the more so when dealing with cultural practices the cohesion of which into social institutions goes back very far in time. If a change in the infrastructure supposes a transformation in the superstructure, the balance of the corresponding changes will not occur at the same time. Furthermore, social phenomena do not follow the laws of logic of linear and unequivocal causality. Here one is in the region of probability and multiple consequence. What then will be the overriding family model? It is hard to guess. That is what this inquiry is seeking to sketch the outlines of, even though things may be in a transitional phase.

This analysis comprises two principal parts. The first studies the structure of the family from a demographic point of view and considers it in the perspective of changes which could have affected it. The second will broach a series of themes which will serve as indicators and empirical foundations for reflection on the position of women and their role in the heart of the rural family of the commune studied.

Social Practices, Cultural Models and Demographic Structures

This inquiry was conducted among 99 women, all of them married, belonging to the same production group. Of the 535 persons in the group studied, the sampling represents one in every three families. Since the inquiry is seeking to determine the role in the family of the working woman, we have eliminated from our survey mothers of families where all the children have left home. With the exception of three persons over 50 years old, the age of the women questioned in the course of the inquiry was between 20 and 50; 95 of them were working in the co-operative, 72 in agriculture and 23 as labourers; four others were employed by the commune, as teachers or as members of the medical team.

In this part of the analysis the results of the sampling will be divided into three categories: women less than 30, those between 30 and 39, and those aged 40 or more. This distinction is justified by the fact that those of the first category, after 1949, have always lived in a socialist society. Those between 30 and 39 are characterized by their transit to socialism, while the oldest spent their youth in a colonial society. The husband is generally somewhat older than the wife, and the variations are never very significant. The war did not have a marked influence on this phenomenon.

Table 6.1 is interesting for two reasons: it shows, first of all, the progress made in the field of formal education in a rural region, particularly among women. Points to be noted are: a fall in the percentages for those

The Level of Education of the Married Partners

Table 6.1
Educational Level of Women and of their Husbands: Compared (%)

Women aged less than 30

	Primary		Secondary		
Husbands	*Incomplete*	*Complete*	*Incomplete*	*Complete*	*Total*
Primary					
incomplete	9.5	–	–	4.8	14.3
complete	4.8	7.1	–	–	11.9
Secondary					
incomplete	14.3	4.8	11.9	–	26.2
complete	2.4	23.8	4.8	11.9	42.9
3rd level	–	–	2.4	–	2.4
Total	*31.0*	*35.7*	*19.0*	*16.7*	*100.0*

Women aged 30-39

	Alphabetization	*Primary*		*Secondary*		
Husbands		*Incomplete*	*Complete*	*Incomplete*	*Complete*	*Total*
Alphabetization		6.3	3.1	3.1	–	12.5
Primary						
incomplete		18.8	–	–	–	18.8
complete		34.4	6.3	–	–	40.7
Secondary						
incomplete		9.4	–	–	–	9.4
complete		6.3	9.4	3.1	–	18.8
Total		*75.2*	*18.8*	*6.2*	–	*100.0*

Women aged 40 and over

	Alphabetization	*Primary*		*Secondary*		
Husbands		*Incomplete*	*Complete*	*Incomplete*	*Complete*	*Total*
Alphabetization		8.0	–	–	–	8.1
Primary						
incomplete	12.0	28.0	–	–	–	40.0
complete	4.0	28.0	–	–	–	32.0
Secondary						
incomplete	4.0	4.0	–	8.0	–	16.0
complete	–	4.0	–	–	–	4.0
Total	*20.0*	*72.0*	–	*8.0*	–	*100.0*

who did not terminate their primary school studies: 92% for women more than 40 years old; 75% for those between 30 and 39; no more than 31% for youths less than 30. This is a diminution of about 65%. On the other hand the percentage for young women who completed their secondary education reached

16.7%, while in former times the women did not complete their secondary education. Another aspect worth noting is the tendency for the level of education to influence the choice of partners. With the exception of two cases, it is clear that women who have followed a course of secondary education have married men of equivalent educational attainments. Further, a young man who has not pursued his studies beyond the primary level chooses a wife of the same educational level. There is therefore a certain gap founded on the education of marriage partners – a gap the consequences of which one must try to discern.

Occupations of the Marriage Partners

In the commune of Hai Van the two most important sections of employment are agriculture and non-agricultural manual labour (joinery, brick-making, maintenance of hydraulic and electical installations, jute processing, lace work, etc.). This last mentioned employs a labour force of workers who are similar in no way to the industrial working population; they are specialist workers in the co-operatives.

Table 6.2 reveals an unequal distribution of women in the two sections (73 in agriculture, 23 in other manual labour) whereas among males the distribution is almost equal (43 in agriculture, 45 in other worker activity, five employed). This difference corresponds better to the structure of rural employment, not only in Vietnam but in all south and south-east Asia.

Table 6.2 shows married couples in relation to the occupation of the partners. It is clear that of the 73 women employed in agriculture: 37 or 50.7% have husbands employed in agriculture; 26 or 35.6% have husbands who are non-agricultural workers; 4 or 5.5% have husbands employed in other functions; 6 or 9.2% have husbands of unknown occupation. Of the 23 women non-agricultural workers: 17 or 73.9% have husbands who are non-agricultural workers; 5 or 21.7% have husbands who are in agriculture; 1 or 4.4% have husbands who are employed in other functions.

Table 6.2
Distribution of Women According to Age, Occupation and that of their Husbands

Women	*Aged less than 30*			*30 to 39*			*40 and over*			
Men	*(a)*	*(b)*	*(c)*	*(a)*	*(b)*	*(c)*	*(a)*	*(b)*	*(c)*	*Total*
Agricultural workers	16	3	–	11	2	1	10	–	–	43
Non-agricultural workers	11	7	–	6	5	2	9	5	–	45
Others	3	1	–	–	–	–	1	–	–	5
?	1	–	–	5	–	–	–	–	–	6
Total	*31*	*11*		*22*	*7*	*3*	*20*	*5*	–	*99*

(a) agricultural workers; (b) non-agricultural workers; (c) others.

54 couples may therefore be called homogeneous, occupation-wise. In 37 cases the partners are agricultural householders and in 17 cases non-agricultural workers. It is evident then that there is a strong tendency for rural families to split up into three categories: families engaged in agriculture, worker families and those where the partners are occupied in other sectors. Further, women who are non-agricultural workers, whatever their age group may be, have a strong propensity to marry non-agricultural workers (74%). It is important, therefore, to inquire into the consequential social and cultural practices. Even if the worker proper (i.e. non-agricultural) is at the very heart of the co-operative, it is at least a workable hypothesis that his or her activities, which are not directly dependent on natural conditions and which demand a knowledge and use of technical skills, contribute to a more rapid development of the forces of production. And this could well imply another way of life, other conceptions of education of the children, etc. We shall try to verify this hypothesis in the course of this analysis.

Marriage, Children and the Family Structure

At Hai Van, as everywhere else in North Vietnam, it was the policy of the government to encourage family planning in order to limit the birth rate since a rise in births was to be expected after the war. To this end, child marriages were forbidden and the natural and mechanical (sterilizer) methods of birth control were explained to the people by health teams, without however making their use obligatory. One of our tasks is to try to discern the effects of this policy by the analysis of certain demographic statistics.

The focus of Table 6.3 is to be found in the 18 year age group (the highest frequency, i.e. 45). It is evident that from these observations one cannot generalize for the whole population of the Delta, even if the sampling were

Table 6.3
Distribution of Women According to Age at Marriage and Duration of the Marriage (years)

		Duration of marriage					
Age at marriage	*Number of women*	*0-5*	*6-10*	*11-15*	*16-20*	*21-25*	*26 and over*
14	3	–	–	1	1	–	1
15	4	–	–	–	2	1	1
16	8	–	–	1	2	2	3
17	19	2	2	5	4	5	1
18	45	13	11	9	3	3	6
19	5	1	2	–	1	–	1
20	7	3	1	2	–	–	1
21	2	2	–	–	–	–	–
22	2	–	1	–	1	–	–
23	2	–	1	1	–	–	–
25	1	–	–	1	–	–	–

Table 6.4
Duration of Marriage

	0-5	*6-10*	*11-15*	*16-20*	*21-25*	*26 and over*
% of persons married before 18 years of age	9.5	11.1	35.0	64.3	72.7	38.5

done in a more systematic manner. In the commune of Hai Van, it would appear that 18 years is the normal marriage age for girls. It is a question here therefore of a social practice, the model of which has been integrated into the local culture. The change is the result of a regressive evolution particularly marked during the decade 1964–74 but which has been pursued (even if the tendency is towards stabilization) since the end of the war. It is arguable that what is at stake here is not only a consequence of the war. It is evident therefore that the new legislation fixing the marriage age for girls at 18 has been applied in the commune and that its effects are measurable. It is certain however that this legalized prohibition has met with conditions favourable to its acceptance by the very fact of the fundamental transformation of the social relations of production. Child marriages in traditional societies among rural families served the double purpose of guaranteeing the balance of social relations without prejudice to the labour force. Today these constraints have disappeared. From the economic point of view the distribution of labour issues from the co-operative. Further, a working girl can make an appreciable contribution to the family exchequer while helping the mother of the family who also may be a worker. Her presence in the parental home thus takes on a significance quite other than what it was in the past. In such conditions the law advancing the marriage age has had the effect of accelerating the process of cultural erosion. Hence the fact that it has met with practically no resistance.

For the whole sampling, the average number of children per family is 3.5 while for women between the ages of 21 and 35 the average number of children is 2.6. Before interpreting these statistics we must consider a second aspect of the question – the influence exercised by the duration of marriage on the number of children.

Table 6.5 is of interest in the measure in which it indicates the periods during which human fecundity is at its highest. A relatively low figure for births during the first five years of marriage, roughly 1.2 per couple, may easily be noted. This average is going to increase by at least 92% during the next five years, i.e. among couples who count between five and ten years of married life. After this period the growth declines progressively, the average increasing by 43% between 11 and 15 years of married life, and by 33% between 16 and 20 years. If one keeps in mind the fact that the marriage age today is 18 years one may conclude that women between the ages of 18 and 23 tend to have the first child two or three years after marriage, whilst the birthrate is highest among women between the ages of 23 and 28. After this the birthrate declines up to the age of 35 and births become exceptional for women more than 35.

Table 6.5
Distribution of Women According to their Age and Number of Children

Number of children	*Age of women*						
	Less than 20	*21-25*	*26-30*	*31-35*	*36-40*	*Over 40*	*Total*
0	2 66.6	2 7.4	–	–	–	–	4 4.0
1	1 33.3	10 37.0	2 8.7	–	1 7.1	–	14 14.1
2	–	12 44.4	5 21.7	3 20.0	2 14.2	–	22 22.2
3	–	2 7.4	13 52.2	2 13.3	1 7.1	–	18 18.2
4	–	1 3.7	4 17.4	3 20.0	2 14.2	1 5.9	11 11.1
5	–	–	–	7 46.7	3 21.3	3 11.8	13 13.1
6	–	–	–	–	2 14.2	7 41.1	9 9.1
7	–	–	–	–	2 14.2	4 23.6	6 6.1
8	–	–	–	–	1 7.1	2 11.8	3 3.0
9	–	–	–	–	–	1 5.9	1 1.0
Average number of children	3	27	24	15	14	18	99
per woman	0.33	1.6	2.8	3.9	4.6	6.4	3.5

Table 6.6
Number of Children per Married Woman and the Duration of Marriage

Number of children	*Duration of Marriage (years)*					
	1-5	*6-10*	*11-15*	*16-20*	*21-25*	*26 and over*
0	4	–	–	–	–	–
1	10	4	2	1	–	–
2	7	8	3	1	–	–
3	1	4	3	2	–	1
4	–	3	3	3	2	–
5	–	–	4	5	1	3
6	–	–	–	3	1	4
7	–	–	–	–	2	4
8	–	–	–	–	2	1
9	–	–	–	–	1	–
Averge number of children per family	1.2	2.3	3.3	4.4	6.0	6.0

Things being so one may well wonder at the demographic future of the families studied. It is also evident that one can no longer reach the actual averages of the age groups of 36 years and more. Can one hope for a stabilization of the figures around the average for the 31-35 age groups, let us say, 3.9 children per family? For this result it would be necessary that all women alive today in the 21-25 age group would each have, on an average 2.3 children during the next ten years, which is highly improbable. One may deduce, therefore, that the decline in the birth rate observable today is not an accidental

Table 6.7
Size and Structure of Families of the Women Questioned

Women aged less than 30

Size of family	Total number of families	Nuclear families	Incomplete families	Families harbouring a parent	Extended families
2	5	1	4	–	–
3	15	14	1	–	–
4	13	10	1	–	2
5	7	4	–	2	1
6	2	1	–	–	1
Total	*42*	*30 (71.4%)*	*6 (14.3%)*	*3 (7.1%)*	*4 (9.5%)*

Women aged 30–39

Size of family	Total number of families	Nuclear families	Incomplete families	Families harbouring a parent	Extended families
3	2	1	1	–	–
4	2	2	–	–	–
5	7	5	–	2	–
6	6	3	–	1	2
7	11	6	–	3	2
8	2	–	–	2	–
9	2	–	–	2	–
Total	*32*	*17 (53.1%)*	*1 (3.1%)*	*10 (31.3%)*	*4 (12.5%)*

Women aged 40 and over

Size of family	Total number of families	Nuclear families	Incomplete families	Families harbouring a parent	Extended families
3	2	–	2	–	–
4	1	–	1	–	–
5	4	–	4	–	–
6	3	1	2	–	–
7	3	–	3	–	–
8	8	3	3	2	–
9	3	1	2	–	–
10	1	–	–	1	–
11	1	–	–	–	1
Total	*26*	*5*	*17*	*3*	*1*
Grand Total	*99*	*51*	*24*	*16*	*9*

phenomenon – it reflects the demographic policy based on the raising of the marriage age and on the planned spacing of births during the first years of marriage. These conclusions are evidently valid only for the small group of a hundred women whose practices we have studied.

The Size of the Families

In Table 6.7 we understand by nuclear family that which consists of a couple and their children; the incomplete family is a nuclear family of which a number of children no longer live with their parents either because they are married or because they are living with other people. The third category is that of nuclear families who are lodging a grandparent. The fourth class, the extended family, includes housewives who live with the parents of one of the partners.

Taken as a whole, 75 of the families are nuclear; in 51 of the cases parents and surviving children live together; in 24% of the cases some of the children do not live any longer under the paternal roof. It should be noted that in the case of 14% of young housewives the children do not live with their parents; 9% of the women questioned (9.5% of those less than 30 years of age and 12.5% of those between 30 and 40) still live in the midst of extended families.

The Position of Women and their Role in the Family

The collectivization of the rural economy and the development of specialized institutions to be responsible for the social functions in the spheres of education, health, and culture have had the effect of separating work-site from dwelling. Today all the workers, both male and female, practise their profession and have recourse to service facilities outside their house. In theory the repercussions of these changes ought to be felt in the family structure in matters that concern, among things, the organization of life in this group. This, at any rate, is the hypothesis we formulate without prejudice to the final shape which these forms may take. We have chosen, therefore, to explore this field of research – a privileged one – from the point of view of the persons involved – the woman, the mother of the family, the female worker in the cooperative – and also from the point of view of certain aspects of daily life. Under these headings we are going to study these aspects: the use of time by women, the distribution of daily tasks between the members of the family, and lastly, decision making in the family.

The Use of Time by Women

The concept of time in a tradition-bound rural family is something very peculiar, whether in Vietnam or in any other society. Depending as they did fundamentally upon nature, the peasant lived in unison with the rhythm of the seasons and the days; this influenced not only his material life but also his social and cultural activity. The peasant family had to till the soil and get the fields ready for sowing at the approach of the rainy season. The peasant had to give thought every day to the preparation of food and the raising of cattle. But all this was done according to a certain rhythm; with the result that city-dwellers came to look upon rural folk as those who always had time to spare.

It is quite otherwise today for a rural family in a commune such as Hai Van. Parents and children alike have fixed timetables for going to work and to school. One must not only be on time but also complete one's domestic tasks in short and strictly circumscribed intervals of time. We sought to learn how women organized their circumscribed time intervals by asking them to describe in minute detail the uses they made of their time during the two days immediately prior to our inquiry. Their replies have enabled the researchers to reconstruct, for each person interviewed, a typical working day, taking into account the fact that eight hours of work was done at the co-operative, for it was then the height of the season for transplanting rice.

One must not give these observations, interesting though they may be, too definitive a character. For methodological reasons, we have divided the day into three periods of eight hours each: eight hours of work at the co-operative (a constant for all women), eight hours sleep and eight hours of extra-curricular activity, these last two periods being variable and enabling us to determine the use made by women of time not subject to a strict timetable. Before coming to the analysis of these models we asked ourselves in what measure women were capable of recounting the uses they made of their time and of giving accurately the time-spans for each of their daily chores. Table 6.8 indicates the number of hours for which they could give no accurate account.

72% of the women questioned testified to their ability to give detailed reports of the time content of their working day, a couple of hours allowance being made for normal forgetfulness. This proportion reached 100% among young women of less than 30 years of age, 43.8% among those between 30

Table 6.8
Number of Hours in a Working Day for Which the Women Could Not Accurately Account

Age of women	*Number of hours* 0	1	2	3	4	5	6	7	8
Less than 30	12 (28.6%)	17 (40.5%)	13 (30.9%)	–	–	–	–	–	–
30–39	1 (3.1%)	2 (6.3%)	11 (34.4%)	8 (25.0%)	2 (6.3%)	2 (6.3%)	2 (6.3%)	1 (3.1%)	3 (9.4%)
40 and over	3 (12.0%)	3 (12.0%)	10 (40.0%)	3 (12.0%)	4 (16.0%)	1 (4.0%)	–	1 (4.0%)	–
Total	*16 (16.2%)*	*22 (22.2%)*	*34 (34.3%)*	*11 (11.1%)*	*6 (6.1%)*	*3 (3.0%)*	*2 (2.0%)*	*2 (2.0%)*	*3 (3.0%)*

Table 6.9
Use of Time by Women Aged Less than 30 (in hours:minutes)

Work at the co-operative	*Sleep*	*Domestic work*	*Care of children*	*Relaxation etc.*
8 hours : 13 persons	8 : 13	4 : 1	2 : 1	2 : 1
		5 : 11	2 : 2	1 : 2
		6 : 1	1 : 7	2 : 7
			0 : 7	3 : 2
			1 : 1	1 : 1
		4 : 1	0 : 1	5 : 1
			2 : 1	2 : 1
8 hours : 16 persons	7 : 16	5 : 8	1 : 6	3 : 6
			0 : 1	4 : 1
		6 : 7	2 : 1	0 : 1
			1 : 4	1 : 1
			0 : 2	2 : 2
		4 : 1	1 : 1	5 : 1
			2 : 1	3 : 1
8 hours : 13 persons	6 : 13	5 : 1	1 : 3	4 : 3
			0 : 1	5 : 1
		6 : 7	2 : 2	2 : 2
			1 : 4	3 : 4
			0 : 1	4 : 1

Average for the three categories (in hours)

	Sleep	*Work at the co-operative*	*Domestic work*	*Care of children*	*Relaxation etc.*
13 persons	8	8	5	1	2
16 persons	7	8	5.22	0.52	2.45
13 persons	6	8	5.28	1.04	3.38

and 39 years, and 52.7% among those of 40 years and above. This is not a question merely of memory, for memory functions only in the measure in which the rationale behind the activities themselves can be made to come alive again. One may therefore conclude that the curtailing of time devoted to domestic tasks has developed in these women, a rationalization of the use of time, i.e. a very real development of the forces of production. This conclusion seems to derive confirmation from the fact that persons who did not work at the co-operative and who had no fixed professional activity were those least able to recall their use of time.

What is the timetable of a woman of less than 30 years living in Hai Van? Let us recall that this sampling comprises only married women of nuclear families consisting of four or five persons, including young children.

Young women can be divided into three classes by the time given to sleep.

It is certain that some of them curtail sleep to have more time for activities other than those at the co-operative. This 'free' time is devoted principally to domestic work which divides itself into work devoted to domestic production (generally three hours of work in the garden or in cattle rearing), and time spent on household tasks which use up about two to two and a half hours a day. The care of infants requires, on an average, an hour on the part of the mother. Eight women, of the 42 questioned, spent about two hours a day on this, and eight others spent no time at all to care for their children either because (as in four cases) they had no children or because the children were being cared for by others. Lastly, the time given to minor chores and relaxation varied between two and three and a half hours. The curtailing, therefore, of the time for sleep – a maximum of two hours – does not imply a lengthening of working hours (a maximum of half an hour devoted to housekeeping). Women who sleep less spend more time on all their minor activities, which they do not consider as work.

For women aged between 30 and 40, we have reckoned with only 22 cases of women who could describe their working time for all hours. Here again the duration of sleep divides the persons into three categories. Since the method of calculating the average time is the same as that which was used for the group of younger women, we will not go into all the details again.

Table 6.10
Average Distribution of Time (in hours) for Women Aged 30-40

	Sleep	*Work at the co-operative*	*Domestic work*	*Care of children*	*Relaxation etc.*
6 persons	8	8	2.50	1	4.10
12 persons	7	8	4.30	1.05	3.25
4 persons	6	8	4.30	1	4.30

These persons have generally less work than young women (although their families are larger) because the mothers get help from their grown-up children or from an aged parent living with the family, both for work in the garden and for housekeeping – these women thus have more time for rest. On the other hand those who curtail sleeping time to six hours tend to prolong their relaxation and other activities which go up to as much as four and a half hours a day.

According to these figures the older have a tendency to sleep less than the younger. Not that they work less, but that they spend more time on their children and at least three hours on sundry activities.

These three analyses on the use of time highlight certain features concerning the tasks of women when work at the co-operative demands eight hours of production a day. In what concerns sleep, 69% of the women take seven hours or less of rest, a relatively low norm if one remembers that professional work is generally very heavy. Domestic work and the care of children must be

Table 6.11
Average Distribution of Time (in hours/minutes) for Women Aged 40 and Over

	Sleep	*Work at the co-operative*	*Domestic work*	*Care of children*	*Relaxation etc.*
2 persons	8	8	4	1	3
6 persons	7	8	4:30	1:20	3
9 persons	6	8	4	1:20	4:40

considered as work necessary for the natural increase of the labour-force. The time which is devoted to these tasks varies between six and a half hours and three hours 50 minutes, according to the evidence of women who did not always take into account some of the activities which are scarcely enumerable and are included in 'free time'. This work appears relatively heavy as it concerns domestic economy which is indispensable today for most families. In this connection it must be noted that, far more than middle-aged women, it is the young who have to clock fixed quotas of work in their various tasks. It may be said that most of them have to put in 12 hours of work for ends directly economic eight hours in the co-operative and three hours in the garden – to which must be added three hours at the very minimum, for so-called non-economic activity, even if they are necessary for the natural increase of the work-force.

In the case of young couples it is the wife (whose husband is often engaged in extra-professional activities such as politics) who sees to the gardening and the housekeeping. This is doubtless the reason for the lodging of children with their grandparents. Older women are better off in the measure in which they can depend on the help of older children and of the grandparents who live with the family, either because they have retired from active professional life or after widowhood. In this situation some young children suffer the consequences of having a father who cannot spare the time to attend to their education, or because they are entrusted to strangers. This is a serious problem in the light of the discoveries of child psychology according to which the potentialities of a child are determined before the age of four.

The Organization of Domestic Work

The analysis of the timetables of mothers of families has shown the importance of the time set apart by women in families for tasks necessary to ensure material survival. It was noticed however that there were variations in the amount of time given to those tasks in the daily timetable of women according to their age, the younger being more heavily loaded with work than the older.

The analysis of the timetable, however, treats only of one side of the question, that of time devoted to those domestic tasks. Hence we must deepen this knowledge by a study of the organization of this work in the family. We must analyse, therefore, the manner of the division of this work between the members of the family, keeping in mind the specific differences implied in the different tasks. For this purpose we divided the last mentioned into three classes: the management of the finances of housekeeping; production which involves domestic economy; and housekeeping. Further, in our hypothesis we made the age of the woman, a variable factor, the discriminating element because of a conglomeration of differences with regard to family demography, the level of education, etc.

Management of the Family Finances

The collectivization of the economy has had the effect of generalizing the salary scale of the whole labour force, but this does not imply unvarying family incomes, what with fluctuations in the time spent on work, which are the consequences of the agricultural character of the co-operative, even if today the production of three annual harvests imposes regular work quotas on the workers. Add to this the subjection of the domestic economy to the laws of the market, which also involves fluctuation in the family revenue. The material survival of the rural family supposes a rationalization in the use of financial means at the family's disposal. How does all this work out?

Table 6.12
Principal Agents in Management of the Family Budget, According to the Woman's Age

Agents of management	*Aged less than 30*	*Aged 30–39*	*Aged 40 and over*	*Total*
No indication	1 (2.4%)	– –	– –	1 (1.0%)
Wife alone	33 (78.6%)	28 (87.5%)	25(100%)	86 (86.9%)
Husband alone	– –	1 (3.1%)	– –	1 (1.0%)
Both wife and husband	8 (19.0%)	3 (9.4%)	– –	11 (11.1%)
Total	*42*	*32*	*25*	*99*

In 87% of the families, financial management is the responsibility of the woman. This endows her with a very real power since she controls the consumption habits of the members of the family. There is evident, however, in the younger generations, a tendency to collective budgeting by the couple itself.

Table 6.13 concerns the production task, namely, horticulture and small livestock farming. As far as horticulture is concerned, the sample taken as a whole shows that horticulture is the exclusive task of the wife in 28% of the families and of the husbands in 19% of the families; in 50% of the families horticulture is conducted by both husband and wife working together. What this means, therefore, is that 79% of the wives and 70% of the husbands are forced to supplement their work in the co-operative by horticultural tasks in order to live, or to live a little better.

Table 6.13
Agents Involved in Domestic Agricultural Production and Small Scale Cattle Rearing According to the Woman's Age

	Aged less than 30		*Aged 30-39*		*Aged 40 and over*	
Agents	*Cultivation*	*Cattle-Rearing*	*Cultivation*	*Cattle-Rearing*	*Cultivation*	*Cattle-Rearing*
Wife only	13 (31.0%)	26 (61.9%)	10 (31.3%)	20 (62.5%)	5 (20.0%)	14 (56.0%)
Husband only	9 (21.4%)	1 (2.4%)	4 (12.5%)	–	6 (24.0%)	3 (12.0%)
Both husband and wife	19 (45.2%)	13 (31.0%)	17 (53.2%)	12 (37.5%)	14 (56.0%)	6 (24.0%)
Others	1 (2.4%)	2 (4.8%)	–	–	–	1 (4.0%)
No problems	–	–	1 (3.0%)	–	–	1 (4.0%)
Total	*42*	*42*	*32*	*32*	*25*	*25*

All together

	Cultivation		*Cattle-Rearing*	
Wife only	28	(28.3%)	60	(60.6%)
Husband only	19	(19.2%)	4	(4.0%)
Both husband and wife	50	(50.5%)	31	(31.3%)
Others	1	(1.0%)	3	(3.0%)
No problems	1	(1.0%)	1	(1.0%)

Women have a proportionately larger share than men in livestock farming than in horticulture: 92% of the women devote a part of their working day to livestock farming while the percentage for men is 35. These figures have, however, significant variations according to the age of the woman. For instance, 31% of women under 40 undertake horticulture unaided, and 62% livestock farming. These percentages fall to 20 and 56 respectively for older women. On the other hand, 21 and 24% of the husbands take charge of this work in the younger and older households respectively. Though these percentages rise in middle-age households we may also observe that the joint achievements of these tasks by both husbands and wives tends to rise according to the age of the couple.

As we remarked earlier, all the families in the sample are not agricultural. The question to which we addressed ourselves therefore was whether non-agricultural worker families show a different type of rationality in the distribution of domestic production tasks between husband and wife, especially as non-agricultural worker families are relatively more numerous in the younger generations of families: Table 6.14 refers.

In the majority of non-agricultural worker families, productive domestic work is accomplished with both partners working together. Where this is

Table 6.14
Agents Intervening in Domestic Agricultural Production, According to Occupation of Married Partners

Agents	*Non-agricultural workers*		*Mixed: (husband non-agricultural worker)*		*Mixed: (wife non-agricultural worker)*		*Agricultural workers*	
	Horticulture	*Livestock*	*Horticulture*	*Livestock*	*Horticulture*	*Livestock*	*Horticulture*	*Livestock*
Wife only	6 (31.6%)	8 (42.1%)	12 (38.7%)	20 (64.5%)	–	2	10 (22.7%)	30 (68.2%)
Husband only	1 (5.3%)	–	4 (12.9%)	2 (6.5%)	2	–	12 (27.3%)	2 (4.5%)
Both husband and wife	12 (63.2%)	11 (57.9%)	14 (45.0%)	6 (19.4%)	2	2	22 (50.0%)	12 (27.3%)
Others	–	–	–	3 (9.7%)	1	–	–	–
No problems	–	–	1	–	–	1	–	–
Total	*19*	*19*	*31*	*31*	*5*	*5*	*44*	*44*

not the case, it is the woman who does it alone with no help from the husband. This is a partial reason why young women have a heavily loaded timetable, for it is among young housewives that one will find, relatively speaking, the largest number of homogeneous working class families.

On the other hand, in families given to agriculture, the ratio of work shared by the two married partners is just one to one, but the proportion of families where the husband is solely responsible for cultivating the garden comes very close to a third of the families of this category; this enables a large number of mothers to be occupied solely with housekeeping. Finally, in families where the wife is occupied with agriculture and the husband is a worker proper, the proportion of wives assuming sole responsibility for domestic production exceeds by far what is observed in homogeneous families.

One may say, then, that on the whole, the share of work which falls on wives in this respect depends largely on what the husband is ready or not to accept as his share of the burden. That the cultural model varies according to whether we are dealing with workers proper or peasants can be seen in Table 6.15

Table 6.15
Domestic Agricultural Work Done by Husbands, According to Job Category

	Of 100 non-agricultural worker husbands	*Of 100 husbands in agriculture*
Those assuming sole responsibility for cultivating garden	10	29
Those sharing the work with their wives	52	49
Those doing no work	38	22

The worker proper, more than the cultivator, has the tendency to leave the task of cultivating the garden to his wife and is much less inclined to assume sole responsibility for those tasks, the fruit of which accounts for something like 45% of the family revenue. On average, in 100 families, the domestic revenue is the product of the contributions of wife and husband in the ratio of 65:35 where the husband is a worker proper, and of 60:40 where the husband is a cultivator. This situation is partially explained by the influence which has dissimilar effects on the worker family and the rural family. Let us now examine the rate of male participation in cultivating the garden.

It is clear from the figures in Table 6.16 that among cultivators, male participation in domestic production is hardly influenced by the husband's educational level. Among workers proper the situation is quite otherwise. Those who have not completed their primary education have a tendency to leave these production tasks to their wives whatever may be the level of education reached by the latter. As for workers proper who have completed their secondary education, practices seem to vary according to the educational

Table 6.16
Quantum of Husbands' Participation in Domestic Agricultural Production, According to Education and Job Category

	Families where husband is a worker proper	*Families where husband is a cultivator*
Where both parties have completed their secondary education	1.5	1.2
Husband has completed secondary education, and wife primary	0.84	1.1
Husband primary and wife secondary	0.20	–
Both husband and wife primary	0.68	1.1
Average	0.70	1.1

standards of the wives who, if they have pursued secondary school studies leave the greater share of cultivating to their husbands. But if the wife is of primary school level, and especially if she works in the agricultural sector of the co-operative, it is she who does most of the work in cultivating the garden.

These findings are indicative of groups in the process of climbing up the social ladder. One may well imagine that the profession of worker proper is a source of social prestige in a society which emphasizes technical development and this could produce among workers a certain snobbishness as regards agricultural work, at least among those whose level of education is rather low and are thus less likely to rationalize their practices. This is only a hypothesis to explain a situation which reveals quite clearly the process of transition in the social scale, by which rural families rise.

The Distribution of the Tasks of Housekeeping

We now come to the last category of this analysis of the distribution of domestic work, the tasks of housekeeping which, in traditional society, devolved entirely on the wife. At this time, even when women worked in the fields during the season for transplanting rice and helping with the harvest, the level of production was limited to one crop a year. In such a situation the division of labour was very clear cut, the men being occupied with agriculture and the women with domestic activities.

How do things stand in the family where all the female members do outdoor work or are engaged in studies? Let us build up this analysis by reckoning with the size of the family, for it is evident that a large family allows more scope for the distribution of tasks, all the more so, as we have seen above, because large families today are to be found especially among the generation of parents who have reached the age of 40 and whose children are

Table 6.17
Agents Responsible for Household Tasks, According to Task and Size of Family

Small families (2 or 3 persons) = 23 families

	Mother only	*Father only*	*Children only*	*Couple*	*Children and mother*	*Grand-parents*
Light Tasks:						
Done entirely by one person	12	–	–	–	–	–
Work Divided:						
Kitchen work	2	–	–	9	–	–
Crockery	5	–	1	5	–	–
Laundry	6	–	–	3	2	–
Cleaning	3	–	7	1	–	–
Total	*16*	–	*8*	*18*	*2*	–
	(36.4%)		*(18.2%)*	*(40.9%)*	*(4.5%)*	
Heavy Work:						
Drawing water	12	3	5	2	–	1
	(52.2%)	(13.0%)	(21.7%)	(8.7%)		(4.3%)

Average families (4 or 5 persons) = 33 families

	Mother only	*Father only*	*Children only*	*Couple*	*Children and mother*	*Grand-parents*
Light Tasks:						
Done entirely by one person	18	–	–	–	–	–
Work Divided:						
Kitchen work	6	–	2	7	–	–
Crockery	7	–	2	6	–	–
Laundry	7	–	–	8	–	–
Cleaning	4	–	9	2	–	–
Total	*24*	–	*13*	*23*	–	–
	(40.0%)		*(21.7%)*	*(38.3%)*		
Heavy Work:						
Drawing water	17	3	10	3	–	–
	(51.5%)	(9.1%)	(30.3%)	(9.1%)		

Large families (6 to 11 persons) = 43 families

	Mother only	*Father only*	*Children only*	*Couple*	*Children and mother*	*Grand-parents*
Light Tasks:						
Done entirely by one person	9	–	–	–	–	–

Work divided:						
Kitchen work	9	1	3	9	11	–
Crockery	6	–	6	16	6	–
Laundry	12	2	4	11	5	–
Cleaning	11	–	13	9	–	1
Total	*38*	*3*	*26*	*45*	*22*	*1*
	(28.1%)	*(2.2%)*	*(19.3%)*	*(33.3%)*	*(16.3%)*	*(0.7%)*
Heavy Work:						
Drawing water	11	7	17	8	–	–
	(25.6%)	(16.3%)	(39.5%)	(18.6%)		

Total = 99 families		
Tasks		
Done entirely by the mother	39	39.4% of the families
Shared between the members of the family	60	60.6% of the families

generally adolescents.

Tables 6.17 and 6.18 suggest certain features. It is clear in the first place that the traditional model, which corresponded to a form of division of labour according to which women undertook all the household tasks, persists in 39.4% of the families questioned. Further investigation reveals that this feature is common to worker families (36% of them) and rural families (42% of them). This is not a feature peculiar to women with a low level of education since 50% of the 39 women interviewed had completed their secondary education as against 37.6% of those who had not completed their primary education. Lastly, this feature is more marked in the younger generations. One may ask whether it is a case of some sort of cultural remnant of a past model, or whether it is a feature caused by the fact that in some families the time at the disposal of the spouses is taken up by extra-professional activities outside the home, such as participation in politics. It is not easy to give an answer. What is certain is that for a significant number of young wives – and of them 50% are well educated – any kind of participation in political, social and cultural activity becomes a problem simply because of lack of time.

In 60 other families the tasks of housekeeping are shared. But once again it stands out that the work-load of the wife is rather heavy in the small and medium sized families, i.e. those where the mothers are generally less than 40 years old. In all households the fathers of families appear less capable of assuming sole responsibility for even part of the tasks, though this does not hinder them from coming to the help of their wives in performing certain tasks. In 47 families the mother is helped by her adolescent children, particularly for drawing water or for work that does not occur daily, such as house-cleaning.

It may be concluded, therefore, that on the whole, the most important part of housekeeping – be it production or housekeeping proper – is done by women. In other words, they undertake the largest share of the work necessary

Table 6.18
Work Sharing in Relation to Members of the Family (%)

	Total	*Cooking*	*Light Tasks* *Crockery*	*Laundry*	*Cleaning*	*Heavy Tasks Drawing Water*
Mother only	55.4	56.6	57.6	64.6	57.6	40.4
Father only	0.6	1.0	–	2.0	–	13.1
Children only	17.2	6.1	9.1	4.0	29.3	32.3
Couple	20.0	25.3	27.3	22.2	12.1	13.1
Children and mother	4.8	11.1	6.1	7.1	–	–
Grandparents	0.4	–	–	–	1.0	1.0

for the natural increase of the work-force in addition to their efforts in direct production. In concrete terms, this means heavily loaded timetables of work compared with those of men. In these circumstances one can scarcely imagine their doing more, and so, one can readily understand female absenteeism – which was underscored earlier – with regard to participation in meetings of the co-operative or their very weak connection with mass movements. We have also said that this state of affairs deprives the woman of all possibility of enlarging her social horizon and confines her generally to the level of her production group. Further, we have noted a certain negligence in the care and education of children. This is consequent upon an excess of work, the long term effects of which could be very damaging to the younger generation. Thus, one runs the risk of effecting inequality between the sexes, particularly, in the cultural sphere, and at the political level, even if the political intentions are the very opposite of these effects.

It is clear that though the transformation of the relations brought about by productive activity have hastened the nuclearization of the family – a process which is indubitably beneficial to women in so far as new social responsibilities are created for them – they have also been the cause of unintentional effects characteristic of societies in transition. One may hope, however, that this state of affairs will be mitigated in the course of the transition to large-scale production and mechanization of agriculture and that, in consequence, the work-load of women will be lightened chiefly in the field of economic production.

Decision-Making in the Family

Having studied how the women of Hai Van rationalize their use of time, and after our analysis of the time given by mothers of families to extra-professional activities, and the way in which families are organized to accomplish domestic tasks, we are going to enter into one of the central aspects of family life – decision making. We are dealing now with a privileged indicator for the study of changes which affect families and, in consequence, the role played by women in the family.

It is well known that in traditional families, women have very little say in the taking of decisions which affect the family group. Whatever may have been her position in the structure of the extended family, her role was limited to submissive execution of the decisions taken by males; if the women in question were young they had to submit themselves further to the authority of the mother-in-law, who was chiefly responsible for the execution of the will of the head of the family. The cultural model which underlies these practices was marked by a certain rigidity resulting from the influence of Confucianism on the ethos, which was to be found even in the popular syncretistic religions, both Buddhist and Christian. This was the result of the cultural imperialism of the dominating classes and was assimilated by the inferior classes – a typical case of class hegemony. One of the social functions of Confucianism was to ensure the reproduction of the patriarchal family model by developing an ideology which tended to make a woman the 'property' of her father until she became the possession of her husband; from this followed the unconditional obedience she owed to them, a privilege inherited by the eldest son in case the mother became a widow.

Since the revolution, however, socialist ideology has sought to promote equality of the sexes in all spheres of social life. The aim is to destroy the cultural model of the past in favour of female participation at all levels. Our interest therefore is centred round the influence of this new ideology in a group which was strongly characterized by the cultural model of the past. For this purpose, the inquiry presented to the women questioned a series of activities about which it was supposed a decision would have to be taken, and they were asked to indicate who, in their households, would take a decision about their execution. These activities were divided into three categories: those referring to the basic, bread-and-butter issues of day-to-day life; those having long-term effects on family life; and those pertaining to the social and cultural aspects of life.

Decision-Making at the Basic Level

Here we include activities which are to be found necessarily in all families: food and clothing for daily needs, and other urgent needs involving either financial investment or other important long-term consequences. Here again we shall analyse the answers given according to the ages of the wives.

If one goes by the total number of decisions taken for the population studied as a whole, it will be evident that it is the couple which decides by common consent in almost half the cases (48.5%). This percentage is slightly lower in the case of young housewives, and slightly higher in the case of middle-aged housewives. Women decide alone in 29% of the cases but the percentage is much higher for older women. The woman decides, on her own, in matters regarding daily life, such as the purchase of food and clothing. The husband, acting on his own, takes relatively few decisions (14%); but it must be noted that his intervention tends to increase in the case of young house-

Table 6.19
Agents Responsible for Basic Decision-Making

Women aged less than 30 (42 families)

Material activities	*Women only*	*Husbands only*	*Couple*	*In-laws*	*Couple and in-laws*	*?*
Food	31 (73.8%)	–	10 (23.8%)	1 (2.4%)	–	–
Clothing	24 (57.1%)	2 (4.8%)	15 (35.7%)	1 (2.4%)	–	–
Purchase of a bicycle, radio, etc.	2 (4.8%)	5 (11.9%)	23 (54.8%)	1 (2.4%)	2 (4.8%)	9 (21.4%)
Savings	1 (2.4%)	1 (2.4%)	34 (81.0%)	–	–	6 (14.2%)
Internal management of the house	7 (16.7%)	21 (50.0%)	12 (28.6%)	1 (2.4%)	–	1 (2.4%)
Type of production (domestic economy)	4 (9.5%)	16 (38.1%)	19 (45.2)	3 (7.1%)	–	–
Total	*69 (26.7%)*	*45 (17.4%)*	*119 (46.1%)*	*7 (2.7%)*	*2 (0.8%)*	*16 (6.2%)*

Women aged 30–39 (32 families)

Material activities	*Women only*	*Husbands only*	*Couple*	*In-laws*	*Couple and in-laws*	*?*
Food	22 (68.8%)	–	5 (16.0%)	–	–	5 (15.6%)
Clothing	16 (50.0%)	–	16 (50.0%)	–	–	–
Purchase of a bicycle, radio, etc.	–	2 (6.3%)	25 (78.1%)	–	4 (12.5%)	1 (3.1%)
Savings	3 (9.4%)	–	26 (81.3%)	–	–	3 (9.4%)
Internal management of the house	4 (12.5%)	16 (50.0%)	10 (31.3%)	1 (3.1%)	–	1 (3.1%)
Type of production (domestic economy)	4 (12.5%)	8 (25.0%)	17 (53.1%)	–	1 (3.1%)	2 (6.3%)
Total	*49 (25.5%)*	*26 (13.5%)*	*99 (51.6%)*	*1 (0.5%)*	*5 (2.6%)*	*12 (6.3%)*

Women aged 40 and over (25 families)

Material activities	*Women only*	*Husbands only*	*Couple*	*In-laws*	*Couple and in-laws*	*?*
Food	21 (84.0%)	–	4 (16.0%)	–	–	–
Clothing	20 (80.0%)	–	4 (16.0%)	–	1 (4.0%)	–
Purchase of a bicycle, radio, etc.	3 (12.0%)	2 (8.0%)	17 (68.0%)	1 (4.0%)	–	2 (8.0%)
Savings	2 (8.0%)	2 (8.0%)	18 (72.0%)	–	–	3 (12.0%)
Internal management of the house	3 (12.0%)	7 (28.0%)	14 (56.0%)	–	1 (4.0%)	–
Type of production (domestic economy)	4 (16.0%)	4 (16.0%)	16 (64.0%)	–	1 (4.0%)	–
Total	*53 (35.3%)*	*15 (10.0%)*	*73 (48.7%)*	*1 (0.7%)*	*3 (2.0%)*	*5 (3.3%)*
Sample as a whole	171 (28.5%)	86 (14.3%)	291 (48.5%)	9 (1.5%)	10 (1.7%)	33 (5.5%)

wives, when it is a question of extraordinary expenses or activities. The internal management of the house is a male preserve, which is not strange if one keeps in mind the symbolic significance which the family house has in traditional culture. Pre-socialist ideology centred on the cult of family ancestors – this system of beliefs and cultural practices fulfilled the double function of guaranteeing the identity of the extended family and of assuring its protection. In this context the family house was, above all else, the dwelling place of the guardian-ancestors, and only subsequently the house of the living. In this structure, the head of the family was the necessary intermediary between the world of the ancestors and that of the living. It was he, who by virtue of his position, assured the protection of all the members of the extended family, provided that the ritual integrating the whole organization of the space limited by the house and garden was duly performed. Hence the whole tradition of the rural milieu of Vietnam is shot through with the aspiration of families centred wholly on the betterment of the home which had to be constructed according to a host of architectural minutiae and internal dispositions, all of them deeply impregnated with religious overtones. Even in Catholic families where the altar of saints replaces that of the ancestors the significance of the house was not very different. One can see, therefore, why the father of the family was the sole repository of all responsibility.

Today, although the religious overtones of a house have disappeared or are on the way to disappearing, the primary ambition of a family in the current economic situation (which is much better than in the past) still remains the construction of a house and the arranging of its interior according to a fashion identical with that flaunted by mandarin families of pre-revolutionary days. Further, there also persists, at least in some important families, the role of the father as the sole repository of all decision-making concerning the house. It should be noted that this cultural model is still vigorous in young families and even more so than in the older ones. One hypothesis is that this situation is a consequence of the war which obliged the mother of the family to stand in for the father in a certain number of cases.

Decision-Making at the Level of Cultural and Socio-Political Activity

These activities, for the most part, constitute an ensemble of practices which developed in the villages together with socialism, i.e. they have no reference to models of the past, particularly with regards those who have to make the decisions.

Table 6.20 reveals quite another dispersion of agents in decision-making not only when the data are compared with those which related to the basic, bread-and-butter issues of family life, but also when one reckons with the different

Table 6.20
Repositories of Decision-Making in Cultural and Socio-Political Activities

Women aged less than 30 (42 families)

Activities	*Women only*	*Husbands only*	*Couple*	*In-laws*	*?*
Cultural:					
Children's education	2 (4.8%)	5 (11.9%)	1 (2.4%)	3 (7.1%)	31 (73.8%)
Choice of newspaper	1 (2.4%)	5 (11.9%)	36 (85.7%)	–	–
Choice of radio programme	7 (16.7%)	6 (14.3%)	23 (54.8%)	6 (14.3%)	–
Cinema show	18 (42.9%)	5 (11.9%)	9 (21.4%)	10 (23.8%)	–
Socio-political activity					
Visits to friends	26 (61.9%)	12 (28.6%)	3 (7.1%)	1 (2.4%)	–
Political meetings	7 (16.7%)	35 (83.3%)	–	–	–
Women's meetings	38 (90.5%)	4 (9.5%)	–	–	–
Religious:					
Attendance at mass	40 (95.2%)	2 (4.8%)	–	–	–
Family demography:					
Number of children	–	–	38 (90.5%)	–	4 (9.6%)

Women aged 30-39 (32 families)

Activities	*Women only*	*Husbands only*	*Couples*	*In-laws*	*?*
Children's education	4 (12.5%)	5 (15.6%)	1 (3.1%)	15 (46.9%)	7 (21.9%)
Choice of newspaper	2 (6.2%)	6 (18.8%)	22 (63.8%)	1 (3.1%)	1 (3.1%)

Choice of radio programme	3 (9.4%)	2 (6.2%)	22 (63.8%)	5 (15.6%)	–
Cinema show	5 (15.6%)	10 (31.2%)	10 (31.3%)	7 (21.9%)	–
Socio-political activity:					
Visits to friends	20 (62.5%)	11 (34.4%)	–	–	1(3.1%)
Political meetings	1 (3.1%)	30 (93.8%)	–	–	1(3.1%)
Women's meetings	32 (100.0%)	–	–	–	–
Religious:					
Attendance at mass	28 (87.5%)	3 (9.4%)	–	–	–
Family demography:					
Number of children	10 (31.2%)	2 (6.2%)	14 (43.6%)	–	6(18.8%)

Women aged 40 and over (25 families)

Activities	*Women only*	*Husbands only*	*Couple*	*In-laws*	*?*
Cultural:					
Children's education	4 (16.0%)	4 (16.0%)	–	14 (56.0%)	3(12.0%)
Choice of newspaper	2 (8.0%)	2 (8.0%)	16 (64.0%)	1 (4.0%)	4(16.0%)
Choice of radio programme	7 (28.0%)	1 (4.0%)	16 (64.0%)	1 (4.0%)	–
Cinema show	1 (4.0%)	10 (40.0%)	–	2 (8.0%)	12(48.0%)
Socio-political activity					
Visits to friends	14 (56.0%)	11 (44.0%)	–	–	–
Political meetings	3 (12.0%)	22 (88.0%)	–	–	–
Women's meetings	23 (92.0%)	2 (8.0%)	–	–	–
Religious:					
Attendance at mass	20 (80.0%)	5 (20.0%)	–	–	–
Family demography:					
Number of children	10 (40.0%)	–	6 (24.0%)	–	9(36.0%)

types of activities which we have regrouped here.

From the point of view of cultural activities it is clear that the choice and control of the studies of children is, principally, the affair of the grandparents. This absenteeism complements what we said previously, in this sense that the grandparents intervene not only to nurture the children in their infancy but also throughout their period of study and adolescence. If one excludes the young families whose children are not yet attending school, it stands out that in 29 out of 47 families (61.7%) which have school-going children the decision concerning them rests with the grandparents. This means – without wishing to prejudice the manner in which the grandparents acquit themselves of their task – that one of the most important phases of the lives of the children is of relatively little interest to the parents. This seems to be the reason behind the abandonment of schooling at a relatively early age and of sending the young ones to work as soon as possible. This practice could be explained by the possibility of the economic development of rural families consequent upon the novel organization of its economy and by the hope of a better life with the increase in revenue as the principal aim. The more workers there are in a family the more will its revenue increase. This would be a very normal reaction among peasants who are just being introduced to a welfare economy after a period of long-standing poverty.

The choice of a newspaper or of a radio programme is decided principally by the couple, and even by the aged parents, doubtless because it has to do with activities which interest the whole family. As for cinema shows, it all depends on who is interested. Young wives – the inquiry on leisure has revealed already their fondness for cinema shows – decide in only 43% of the cases, in the other families it is the husband who takes the decision.

As for visiting friends, it is the wife who decides most often, perhaps because it is an activity which does not occur in the precincts of the family home. On the other hand, participation in political activities is something that belongs to the husband, except women's meetings where the mother alone decides. They also decide on the days on which to assist at mass (Saturday or Sunday), the decision being influenced by the organization of domestic work.

In brief, this analysis of the organization of domestic work and of decision-making in the peasant families of today permits us to conclude that the former cultural model where the role of the wife was determined both by the very structure of the extended family and by the religious character of the ethos is definitely on its way out.

To this architectonic of the peasant class there corresponded a very specific symbolic system of the religious type, the essential function of which was to assure protection of the individual through the intermediary of the village and the family. In conditions where the level of productive forces was rudimentary the villages produced cultural forms invoking the protection of the presiding spirits, and the families produced the cult of ancestors with analogous functions. These religious forms have always been in need of intermediaries capable of reproducing, without any deviation, propitiatory cultural practices. In the extended family with a patri-linear structure, this function devolved on the head of the family, who was the keystone of the system. He was also endowed with a symbolic power, the devolution of which followed the same law of blood relationship which regulated the relations of the parent. The woman's position was determined both by the structural factors – she did not belong to it by natural kinship but was integrated into the family by the marriage alliance – and also symbolically by the fact of religious taboos attached to her sex. Both confined her role as a social agent without power. This model, forged by age-old circumstances, acquired an autonomy sufficient to perdure even in social entities which adopted Christianity.

Even on the religious plane, Christianity tended in the direction of the submission of the wife to her husband, though this was not to ensure the symbolic protection of the family as was the case in traditional religion. This latter role devolved on the clergy.

With the introduction of new social relationships brought about by production, the cohesion of the nuclear family gained in strength. At the symbolical level, one witnesses the disappearance of a need for protection of the religious type. The introduction of new agricultural techniques, the development of institutions, e.g. for sanitation and education, are all so many elements which raise directly or indirectly the level of the forces of production. These exogenou changes affected the family model and, consequently, the definition of the roles of intra-family relationships.

The Transformation of Social Relationships

The extended family in the social organization of the traditional village was a privileged group of affective equilibrium for its members, the fundamental element of the transmission of the culture values, the meeting point of the past and the present, effected through the cult of ancestors, central also to assure protection to the group. We have seen already how the collectivization of the economy entailed transformation in intra-family relationships, even at the level of opinions concerning accommodation and management of living quarters. We propose now to analyse its effects on the extra-family relationships. One may well gamble on the hypothesis that at the very least one will notice a decline in the primacy of natural relationships with a corresponding rise in social relationships. This does not mean, however, that change is automatic – one can still observe today the persistence of social practices bound to a model of social organization belonging to the past. This is what we are seeking to verify.

The Social Relationships of Friendship

Working together in a single work-team constitutes a possible basis for the enlargement of social relations. Likewise, new institutions (schools, crèches, cultural centres, mass associations) created at the community level multiply occasions for meeting persons outside their native village. In what measure is such intercourse at the origin of the development of a network of new social relationships?

Taking the population studied as a whole, 17.8% said that they have no friends, their relationships being with the family. The remainder is divided into equal parts (42.5%), according to whether their friends are companions in their work places, or others. It will be noted that for 22% of the sampling, friendly relationships with the workers of the work-team stretch outside the milieu of work into the family, while for 17% such relationships are limited to professional life. The distributions according to the characteristics of the population studied indicate some interesting features. Significant differences between women and men may be noticed: for women, the fact that they work outside their home is a very important means for effecting their social integration at a level which goes beyond that of the family. For 57% of them, extra-family relationships are with women with whom they work, relationships established between families in more than 38% of the cases.

Table 6.21
Social Relationships, According to Age, Sex, Occupation and Political Activity

Social relationships	*Total population*	*Men*	*Women*	*Less than 35*	*Ages 35–49*	*50 and over*	*Occupations* Agriculture	*Workers*	*Others*	*Political Affiliation* Party and mass association	*Non-members*
With members of the extended family only	13 (17.8%)	8 (17.0%)	5 (19.2%)	9 (34.6%)	1 (3.3%)	3 (17.6%)	13 (22.0%)	– –	– –	5 (15.6%)	8 (19.5%)
With friends met at work only	13 (17.8%)	8 (17.0%)	5 (19.2%)	3 (11.5%)	7 (23.3%)	3 (17.6%)	10 (16.9%)	3 (37.5%)	– –	4 (12.5%)	9 (22.0%)
With worker friends met also outside work	16 (24.7%)	6 (12.8%)	10 (38.5%)	4 (15.4%)	11 (36.7%)	1 (5.6%)	13 (22.0%)	2 (25.0%)	1	8 (25.0%)	8 (19.5%)
With friends outside the work milieu	31 (42.5%)	25 (53.2%)	6 (23.1%)	10 (38.5%)	11 (36.7%)	10 (58.9%)	23 (39.0%)	3 (37.5%)	5	15 (46.9%)	16 (39.0%)
Total	*73*	*47*	*26*	*26*	*30*	*17*	*59*	*8*	*6*	*32*	*41*

Men, on the other hand, develop more extra-professional relationships, probably because they have more free time which allows them opportunities for greater participation in other activities.

Considered according to age groups, it is clear that those less than 35 years (let us recall that they are all responsible members of their families) establish relationships especially with members of the extended family or with persons they have met outside their work places. Those older (35–49 years) are, on the contrary, much more integrated into the network of social relationships. Outside the family circle, for 60% of the cases these relationships are with persons outside the work place. Finally, it may be observed, that membership of the party or mass association is a factor that enlarges social relationships.

In brief, one may say that the collectivization of work has been for many an agent of social cohesion, particularly for women, confined as they were in former times to the precincts of the family. It is clear that participation in extra-professional activities enlarges social space, for the man at any rate. As for women, members of mass associations establish, relatively more than the others, friendly relationships in their working milieus, but scarcely go beyond the limits of the production team. The dimension of the commune is a newly constituted social dimension, for the great majority of women a significant sociological reality. This finding must be placed side by side with the observation made earlier concerning the low participation of women at the level of the organs of management in the co-operative.

Relations with Institutions and New Social Agents

The transition to socialism has created a string of new institutions in the village, which have been established in the spheres of economy and administration, and it is of interest to discover what use people make of these services, particularly when they are faced with new difficulties. We have limited ourselves, intentionally, to difficulties which may crop up in the daily lives of a nuclear family, as it is question of a structure in which each individual must find a place of affective equilibrium, and, in the case of adults, exercise responsibility and take decisions both at the level of the bread-and-butter issues of daily life as well as the education of children, looking after ageing parents, etc. For this purpose we presented to the persons interviewed a series of situations asking them to resolve the implied difficulties. The institutions or social agents mentioned in Table 6.22 were mentioned spontaneously by those interviewed. We have intentionally chosen situations related to the day-to-day life of a family, concerned with economic life, internal relationshops, education of children, etc. We considered it a workable hypothesis that the phenomenon of women working outside the family circle, that of having to lodge, in certain cases, aged parents, and the heterogeneity of the neighbourhood, could pose novel problems which the family would have to face. But these various circumstances do not affect all families in the same way. That is why we have retained in Table 6.23 the questions which concern at least 20% of the families studied, taking account of the ages of couples.

Problems of the health of children and financial difficulties are common

Table 6.22
Institutions or Social Agents to Whom Recourse is made by Villagers in Difficulties:Outline of Population Studied

Situations	*No problems*	*Doctor, Infirmary*	*Priest*	*Parents' family*	*Neighbours*	*Advisory councils*	*Directors of Co-operatives*	*No one*
Children's illnesses	17 (23.6%)	50 (69.4%)	1 (1.4%)	–	–	–	–	5 (6.9%)
Financial difficulties	17 (23.6%)	–	–	9 (12.5%)	9. (12.5%)	–	13 (18.1%)	15 (20.8%)
Difficulties with neighbours	57 (78.1%)	–	–	4 (5.5%)	2 (2.7%)	–	–	10 (13.7%)
Education of children	52 (71.2%)	–	–	4 (5.5%)	4 (5.4%)	2 (2.7%)	–	11 (15.1%)
Relations with aged parents	61 (83.6%)	–	–	3 (4.1%)	–	–	–	9 (12.3%)
Difficulties of married children	67 (91.8%)	–	–	–	–	–	–	8 (8.2%)
Relations with production team	63 (85.3%)	–	–	–	–	–	7 (9.6%)	3 (4.1%)
Marriage difficulties	65 (89.0%)	–	–	1 (1.4%)	–	–	–	7 (9.6%)
By sex (%)								
Children's illnesses:								
Male	23.4	72.3	–	–	–	–	–	4.3
Female	23.1	61.5	3.8	–	–	–	–	11.5
Financial problems:								
Male	23.4	–	–	17.0	14.0	–	21.3	23.4
Female	19.2	–	–	30.8	30.8	–	7.7	11.5

Neighbours:								
Male	70.2	–	–	4.3	4.3	–	–	21.3
Female	92.3	–	–	7.7	–	–	–	–
Education of children:								
Male	59.6	–	–	8.5	4.3	4.3	–	23.4
Female	92.3	–	–	–	7.7	–	–	–
Aged parents:								
Male	78.7	–	–	2.1	–	–	–	19.4
Female	88.4	–	–	7.7	–	–	–	3.8
Married children:								
Male	87.2	–	–	–	–	–	–	12.8
Female	100.0	–	–	–	–	–	–	–
Members of the production team:								
Male	83.0	–	–	–	–	–	10.6	6.4
Female	92.4	–	–	–	–	–	7.6	–
Marriage difficulties:								
Male	87.2	–	–	–	–	–	–	12.8
Female	92.3	–	–	3.8	–	–	–	3.8
By age (%)								
Children's illnesses:								
Less than 35	30.8	61.6	–	–	–	–	–	7.7
35–49	26.7	60.0	3.3	–	–	–	–	10.0
50 and over	–	100.0	–	–	–	–	–	–

Finances:								
Less than 35	23.1	–	–	34.6	23.1	–	7.7	11.5
35–49	19.4	–	–	19.4	19.4	–	19.4	22.6
50 and over	25.0	–	–	6.3	18.8	–	25.0	25.0
Neighbours:								
Less than 35	80.8	–	–	11.5	–	–	–	7.7
35–49	77.4	–	–	6.5	3.2	–	–	12.9
50 and over	75.0	–	–	–	–	–	–	25.0
Education of children:								
Less than 35	92.3	–	–	3.8	–	–	–	3.8
35–49	60.0	–	–	13.3	13.3	6.7	–	36.7
50 and over	58.8	–	–	5.9	–	5.9	–	29.7
Aged parents:								
Less than 35	84.6	–	–	3.8	–	–	–	11.5
35–49	90.0	–	–	6.7	–	–	–	3.3
50 and over	64.7	–	–	–	–	–	–	35.3
Married children:								
Less than 35	100.0	–	–	–	–	–	–	–
35–49	96.7	–	–	–	–	–	–	3.3
50 and over	76.5	–	–	–	–	–	–	23.5
Production group:								
Less than 35	89.5	–	–	–	–	–	7.7	7.7
35–49	86.7	–	–	–	–	–	10.0	3.3
50 and over	76.5	–	–	–	–	–	5.9	11.8
Marriage difficulties:								
Less than 35	84.6	–	–	3.8	–	–	–	3.8
35–49	90.0	–	–	–	–	–	–	10.0
50 and over	82.4	–	–	–	–	–	–	17.6

Table 6.23
Difficulties Confronting at Least 15% of Families, According to Age of Wives

Difficulties encountered	*Young wives*	*Middle-aged wives*	*Older wives*
Children's health	b	b	–
Education of children	–	b	b
Relations with married children	–	–	b
Marriage	c	–	c
Aged parents	c	–	b
Financial	a	a	a
Relations with neighbours	b	b	b
Work	–	c	b

Key: a: The difficulty affects more than 75% of the families
b: The difficulty affects at least 20% of the families
c: The difficulty affects between 15 and 20% of the families

to the majority of families, but the other problems make their appearance only in a limited number of cases. It is also to be noted that women generally are very sensitive to the material difficulties that crop up in daily life while men seem to be much more preoccupied with questions of education and human relationships. It should also be noted that older wives seem to have more problems than others, with regard to both family relationships as well as with their work and with their neighbours.

How do these families try to solve their problems? It is of interest to know in what measure they do or do not have recourse to the traditional groups or to the new institutions. Taking the doctor and dispensary, the conciliation board and the directors of the co-operative as new institutions or agents associated with new institutions; and taking the priest, the family and the neighbours as the traditional agents, one can make a synthesis as in Table 6.24.

Table 6.24 brings out an interesting phenomenon: the recourse to new institutions is associated with their speciality; it is not a case of agents with a plurality of functions, like the family or the religious intermediary of the institutions of traditional society, to which recourse could be had in all the needs of daily life. It is also apparent that traditional agents, particularly the family, do not have the ability to resolve new problems, be they problems such as the education of the young, the generation gap or problems between the married partners themselves. This, in the large part, is the explanation for the relatively high percentage of replies expressing a certain reserve.

In the commune of Hai Van, therefore (and no doubt in the greater part of the rural areas) there is developing a new social phenomenon characterized by functional and therefore, specific, social relationships. This observation becomes more marked still when one analyses the type of relationship which is established with the officials of the different institutions as shown in Table 6.25

Table 6.24
Institutions or Persons to Whom Recourse is made in Case of Difficulties (%)

Difficulties	*New Institutions*	*Traditional Agents*	*Persons*
Health of children	89.3	1.8	8.9
Education of children	9.5	38.1	52.4
Relations with married children	–	–	100.0
Marriage	–	12.5	87.5
Aged parents	–	25.0	75.0
Financial	28.3	39.1	32.6
Relations with neighbours	–	37.5	62.5
Relations at work	70.0	–	30.0

Table 6.25
Type of Relationships Established with Certain Officials (%)

	Doctors	*Party secretaries*	*Heads of production groups*	*Teachers*	*Priests*
Functional meetings in the institutions	79.5	75.3	63.0	67.1	86.3
'Let them come to us but we will not go to them'	11.0	1.4	2.7	9.6	9.6
'Let us go to them but let them not come to us'	2.8	2.7	9.6	8.2	1.4
'We are friends'	6.8	20.5	20.5	13.7	1.4

If one excludes relationships with priests (strongly influenced by the fact that they have often been in conflict with their parishioners), it becomes clear that in more than 60% of the cases the relations with the institution are solely functional – and this increases when the responsibility of the institution rests at the level of the commune (doctor, secretary of the party).

The development of the functional relations which derive from the separation of the various sectors of social life, and from the specific nature of their institutions is generally the hallmark of an urban milieu or of an industrialized area where the work-place is separate from the home. To this spatial separation there corresponds an entirely different organization of work, both with regard to the times of work and the integration of workers into the production teams, and also with regard to remuneration. Such dissociation demands a whole network of services (education, health, distribution of the goods produced) – tasks which were done in former times by rural families. It is clear, therefore, that the collectivization of the rural economy produces effects very similar to those produced by industrialization. The rationalization introduced into the organization of the collective life produces effects which are proportional to the unity prevailing in large social groups in which primary social relations are pushed to the background of small groups such as families and work-teams.

7. Cultural Transformation

In this part of our inquiry we will try to isolate and identify the incidence of change introduced by the new mode of social organization and by the values which they presuppose. This will be done with reference to certain aspects of the culture of the village population. By culture we understand here the whole system of symbols, i.e. representations, of values (collective aims), and of norms controlling practices. In a transitional phase from one mode of production to another it would be unwise to count on the total correspondence between culture and the new social relations of production. Our interest will therefore be to identify certain cultural elements that have persisted, or certain elements of the prior system which continue to be transmitted by different social groups, within a given population. In chapter 6 we looked at certain aspects of this; we will examine these in greater detail in this chapter.

One must beware of falling into the trap of too simplistic a scheme which would conceive culture as a simple superstructural appendix, in total dependence on a material base as tight and narrow as a strait-jacket. Reality shows us that on the one hand, the relation between the modes of production and culture are dialectical, and that on the other, the rhythms of transformation of each of these elements are possessed of a certain autonomy. Further, we must not forget that the distinction between the infrastructure and the superstructure is not equivalent to that between matter and idea. The idea part of the infrastructure is fundamental, no less than the material aspects of the superstructure. It is the manner in which people organize their lives which forms the base, and this already supposes the existence of a 'culture'. This work, however, is only a very partial approach. We are dealing here with only two indicators – the conception of the home on the one hand, and the utilization of free time on the other.

The management of territory, and the type of home constitute, from the sociological point of view, the expression of social relations in so far as they contribute to their reproduction. Further, every form of organization of physical space required for social life, by the very fact of its temporal stability, preserves characteristics of the past. They indicate a persistence of, and the integration of, elements of prior modes of social organization into the present social formation.

Even at the level of a village such as Hai Van, the disposition of the home expresses at once a particular tradition and the new mode of organization of the rural milieu in Vietnamese society. The commune is, in fact, the product of the fusion of five villages of former times. Each one of them is today a satellite of a community centre with which it is connected by an interior route and by one of the principal canals of the irrigation system. This centre, which is eminently functional for the system as a whole, regroups the collective equipment of the commune (community house, cultural centre, sanitary equipment, maternity home, chief dispensary, pharmacy, secondary school, library) and of the co-operative (administrative centre, workshop for craftsmen, emporium, etc.). It is in the hamlet that one can observe the meeting of the past with the present. At the level of collective equipment, buildings of former times are still being used for their former purposes, e.g. the church, which continues to remain as a place reserved for the cult of a population, the majority of whom are Catholic, or the temples dedicated to the spirits. Other buildings have lost their former functions – the houses of the mandarins of former times are now converted into crèches, or into places for production groups. More recently constructed buildings express the present organization of the economy for the population of the hamlets, which constitute today the different production teams of the co-operative. It is also at the level of the hamlets that the home is situated. If the home no longer symbolizes, as in the past, class differences, it remains, in the prevailing form, relatively similar to the models of former times, except for the use of more durable material for its construction. Of the part of the economy left to private production (the product of which represents, on an average, 40 to 45% of the family income), the home remains the property of a single family. Each family has at its disposal a piece of land, the extent of which varies, and is divided between the house, the garden and the pond. This form of single family home, corresponding to a specific economic model, was a stabilizing factor during the period of transition from rural economy to collectivization. On the one hand, it respected, at least partially, the rural tradition, and on the other, the reservation for private use of the garden and of the pond brought in revenue to complement that of the collective economy, the contributions of which were far below the present levels.

In the near future, however, the demands of production on a large scale, joined to the consequences of population growth, will make the problem of the redisposition of the rural habitation a compelling one. It was from this point of view that we introduced into this study of the commune an inquiry into opinions concerning the home. Setting out from this last consideration concerning the possible forms of habitation, one has to discover the cultural references which would affect the different sections of the peasantry with regard to the acceptance or refusal of various proposals. Since such models can be either restraints on, or spurs to, the driving forces of change, it is important to reckon with them in the plan as a whole, at least to lay down a policy of education for the masses which will permit the integration of the peasants into the system as the principal historical agents in the process of change. We will find here a good indicator of such a transition.

This inquiry was conducted by interviews; the questionnaire was very short and comprised, in addition to the questions of the identification of those interviewed, a series of concrete propositions concerning the home – some corresponding to situations that have been lived through (the single family home, the extended family circle), others corresponding to the new forms from the modernization of the present day home to the collective habitation. Those interviewed were asked to reply to each of the propositions either for or against and justify the answer given.

The aim of the analysis of the opinions thus expressed was, firstly, to disclose the occurrence of objective factors influencing the choice made, (sex, age, level of education, political participation, adherence to a religious faith, size of the family interviewed, etc.). In the second place, by the study of motivations, we tried to find the cultural frameworks which underlie these choices, frameworks which, in the last analysis, are revealed to be indicators of more fundamental attitudes, difficult to perceive in the first place, in so far as the social agents themselves are unaware of them. The inquiry was conducted on 93 persons.

The Home: Present and Future Forms

Table 7.1 is a resume of the opinions expressed concerning the present form of the rural habitation for all the persons questioned according to their regrouping into different categories, determined by sex, age, political participation (membership of the Party or a mass organization), adherence to a religious faith and the size of the family.

85% of the replies were in favour of maintaining the present form of the home. This preponderant majority, however, is only a mean, covering up and concealing deviations rather strongly marked between the positions of certain categories. And so it is that, in the final reckoning, only 42% of those less than 35 years of age were in favour of maintaining the status quo, while the figure reached 97% for those above 50 or those interviewed whose educational level did not go beyond the primary school. The correlations calculated for each of the categories, according to sex, age, political participation, etc. (the Cramer Test) enable certain observations to be made. Age (i.e. here the cleavage between the under 35s and the over 35s) is the most influential factor regarding opinions, more so even than the level of education (the rift between those who have not completed their primary education and those who have attended secondary school) and political participation. Adherence to a religion plays only a secondary role, even though there is a stronger resistance to change among Catholics than among non-Catholics. Sex and the size of the family were not significant as factors influencing the opinions expressed.

In other words, one can affirm – at least regarding the eventual possibility of a change in the form of the home within the limits of the representativeness of this sampling – that the most dynamic group, i.e. the most open to change is to be found among those under 35 who have pursued their studies up to

Table 7.1
Opinions For and Against Maintaining the Single Family Home with Garden and Pond

	Opinions				
	Favourable		*Unfavourable*		
		%		%	
All those interviewed	79	84.9	14	15.1	
Sex:					
Men	61	84.7	11	15.3	
Women	18	85.7	3	14.3	*r* = –0.01
Age:					
less than 35	8	42.1	11	57.9	
35-49	35	94.6	2	5.4	*r* = + 0.60
50 and over	36	97.3	1	2.7	
Political participation:					
Party members	8	66.7	4	33.3	
Members of organizations	5	45.5	6	54.5	*r* = + 0.45
Non-members	66	94.3	4	5.7	
Education:					
Literate only	16	94.1	1	5.9	
Primary	43	97.7	1	2.3	*r* = – 0.46
Secondary	20	62.5	12	37.5	
Religion:					
Catholics	61	92.4	5	7.6	
Non-Catholics	18	66.7	9	33.3	*r* = –0.36
Size of family:					
1-3	11	84.6	2	15.4	
4-5	28	73.7	10	26.3	*r* = + 0.26
6 and more	40	95.2	2	4.8	

secondary school level and who are members of youth organizations. The least dynamic, but also the most numerous, are to be found in the 35+ age group; among those who have not completed their education, who are not members of any political organization and are Catholics. This is, evidently, only a first approximation which we will try to make more accurate in the course of the analysis.

The questions relative to motivations being 'open', those interrogated could express their opinions in language which was familiar to them and without restraint. In the analysis, we have regrouped them into categories. And so, we will find, that for motives justifying the maintenance of the present form of the home, there are four principal points of reference, viz., the safeguarding of the autonomy of the family, respect for tradition, economic necessity, and, finally, the assurance of suitable environmental features (cleanliness of the locations of the houses, hygiene, etc.). Motives given by those not favouring retention of the present form of home can be divided into two categories: family isolation, and private economy as a hindrance to the development of the collective economy.

Taken as a whole, 57% of those in favour of maintaining the status quo were motivated by economic necessity. This is understandable if one reckons with the fact that 40-45% of their revenue comes from the pond and the private garden. This position is by no means evidence of a spirit of individualism. It is clear that collectivization of private gardens would augment the land of the co-operative by only 5% and that the increase of collective production which resulted therefrom, at least for the present, would not come anywhere near compensating for the loss of 40-45% of the family revenue. This point of view is largely shared by the young generation (75% of the less than 35s), the Party members and those of mass organizations (61%), those whose schooling was prolonged up to the second grade (60%) and the heads of large families.

The second motivation, in descending order, was the safeguarding of the physical conditions of the environment: 47% of those interviewed deemed the single family home, surrounded by a garden, with a private reservoir of water at their disposal to be necessary conditions for the maintenance of family health. The fact that 47% of the persons questioned expressed such an opinion has relevance for the belief that at Hai Van, the collective dimension of preventive medicine is, perhaps, not sufficiently appreciated. In other words, one may surmise that preventive health and hygiene do not appear yet as collective tasks for which the families are mutually responsible, for preventive health has always been considered a part of the cultural representation pertaining to individual initiative. This is particularly true of women (61%).

The respect for tradition is the third reason which underlies the position of the status quo, among some of those interviewed – a reason given by 29%, and of more frequent occurrence in those of the 50+ age group, especially where the head of the household was a male and where the old couple lived alone. The last of the reasons advanced revealed a desire for safeguarding the autonomy of the family (27% in favour of the single family home in its present form). They are those most actively engaged in politics (38.4%), and those who have had a secondary school education (40%) and who are very solicitous of total separation between public and private life.

40 persons, i.e. 15% of the total, were not in favour of an individualized form of the home. Among them, four considered this an obstacle to social integration of the family and six others maintained that partial privatization of the economy was inimical to the development of collective production; four others advanced both reasons. These are a minority, but it is interesting to note that some persons at the level of the commune see a link between the home and production – this is the type of analysis which would enable the peasants to understand the implications of a transition to a new technical dimension of production, provided one does not push this conclusion to the extreme limit of brutally destroying the cultural models and habits of the past.

Table 7.2
Motives of Persons Favouring Retention of Present Form of Home (%)

Motivations	*Total*	*Sex*		*Age*			*Political participation*		*Education*		*Religion*		*Family size*		
		Men (61)	*Women* (18)	*Less than 35* (8)	*35-49* (35)	*50 and over*	*Party and organizations* (13)	*Non-members* (66)	*Primary* (43)	*Secondary* (20)	*Catholic* (60)	*Non-Catholic* (19)	*1-3* (11)	*4-5* (28)	*6 and over* (40)
Family autonomy	26.6	27.9	22.2	62.5	34.3	11.1	38.4	24.2	18.6	40.0	23.0	36.8	–	32.1	30.0
Tradition	27.8	31.1	16.7	–	22.9	39.9	7.7	31.8	41.9	20.0	28.3	26.3	54.5	32.1	17.5
Economy	57.0	57.4	55.6	75.0	60.0	50.0	61.5	56.0	44.2	60.0	59.0	63.0	18.2	64.0	62.0
Physical conditions of the environment	46.8	42.6	61.0	25.0	40.0	58.3	61.5	43.9	37.2	40.0	59.0	26.3	54.5	42.9	47.4

Attitudes Towards Modernization of the Home

Two questions sought to gauge the openmindedness of the population to the problem of the modernization of housing, with due respect to the single family house surrounded by a garden. While maintaining this last factor unchanged (respect for the single family house), the first of the two forms proposed sought the construction of houses with separate rooms for resting and working; the other proposal, aware of the present limits of the built-up zone, was for the construction of two storey houses.

Table 7.3
Opinions in Favour of House with Several Rooms, and in Favour of Two Storey Building

	Opinions for and against							
	House with several rooms				*Single family two storey house*			
	For		*Against*		*For*		*Against*	
	No.	*(%)*	*No.*	*(%)*	*No.*	*(%)*	*No.*	*(%)*
Total	40	43.0	53	57.0	47	50.5	46	49.5
Sex:								
Male	31	43.1	41	56.9	39	54.2	33	45.8
Female	9	42.9	12	57.1	8	38.1	13	61.9
Age:								
Less than 35	13	68.4	6	31.6	12	63.2	7	36.8
35-49	13	35.1	24	64.2	19	51.4	18	48.6
50 and over	14	37.8	23	62.2	16	43.2	21	56.8
Political participation:								
Party and organizations	14	60.9	9	39.1	13	56.5	10	43.5
Non-members	26	37.1	44	62.9	34	48.6	36	51.4
Education:								
Literate only	4	23.5	13	76.5	6	35.3	11	64.7
Primary	16	36.4	28	63.6	22	50.0	22	50.0
Secondary	20	62.5	12	37.5	19	59.4	13	40.6
Religion:								
Catholic	26	39.4	40	60.6	31	46.3	36	53.7
Non-Catholic	14	51.9	13	48.1	16	61.5	10	38.5
Family size:								
1-3	5	38.5	8	61.5	6	46.2	7	53.8
4-5	18	47.4	20	52.6	22	57.9	16	42.1
6 and over	17	40.5	25	59.5	19	45.2	23	54.8

The proposal to transform the present home by increasing the number of rooms was rejected by a majority. Only those categories of the less than 35s, with a secondary education and membership in the Party or youth organizations constituted a strong majority in favour of a restructuring of the form of the home, which would imply extension of the block of buildings. The proposal for a two storey house was more favourably received by the population as a whole, and also by a larger number of categories of people, namely men, the young and the middle-aged, participants in political activities, persons with schooling, non-Catholics and medium sized families. Opposed to it were women, the aged who, most often had had no formal education. These were the categories most resistant to modernization in any form whatsoever.

The analysis of the motivations advanced in favour of the one position or the other brings out a series of factors about which it is difficult to say whether they constitute a restraint on, or a spur to, change.

Table 7.4
Motivations Justifying Opinions For and Against an Extension of the Present Home

	Opinions for (40 pers)			*Opinions against* (53 pers)	
Improvement of living conditions	20	50.0%	Satisfied with the present situation	31	58.5%
Tradition	16	40.0%	Tradition	19	35.8%
Economy: possibilities of storage	8	20.0%	Economy: priority given to the garden	9	17.0%
			Lack of financial means	7	13.2%
Harmony in family relationships	5	12.5%			

The principal criterion involved was an estimate of the living conditions: 20 persons would have liked to see their living conditions improve, while 31 others felt quite satisfied. The second element, viz., the respect for tradition, is ambivalent in its influence, according to the aspect of tradition which one wishes to safeguard. Persons in favour of extending the home think that the separation of the house into rooms would permit them to offer more hospitality to their passing guests, as custom would have it. The others reject this type of construction in order to be able to have at their disposal a large room where all the members of the family can gather on the occasion of a feast or of a reunion.

The reference to economy is also ambivalent: for some several rooms would enable them to reserve one for the storing of rice; others consider that the extension of the home would perforce reduce the extent of land reserved for their private economy, or even that they do not have at their disposal the financial resources needed to extend the building. It should be noted, however, that the economic factor comes into the reckoning for only 24 persons, i.e. 26% of those questioned. Five persons cited family harmony as a reason to justify a structural modification of the habitat. It is important to know,

Table 7.5
Motivations Justifying Opinions For and Against General Extension of Homes

	Total sample	*Opinions in favour of extension of the home for: 1) Improvement of living conditions*	*%*	*Opinions against extension of the home for: 1) Satisfaction with living conditions*	*%*	*%*
Sex:						
Male	72	15	20.8	23	31.9	52.7
Female	21	5	23.8	8	38.1	61.9
Age:						
Less than 35	19	6	31.6	3	15.8	47.4
25-49	37	8	21.6	15	40.5	62.1
50 and over	37	6	16.2	13	35.1	51.3
Political participation:						
Party and organizations	23	6	26.1	7	30.4	56.5
Non-members	70	14	20.0	24	34.3	54.3
Education:						
Literate only	17	4	23.5	7	41.2	64.5
Primary	44	9	20.5	17	38.6	59.1
Secondary	32	7	21.9	7	21.9	43.8
Religion:						
Catholic	66	15	22.7	20	30.3	52.9
Non-Catholic	27	5	18.5	11	40.7	59.2
Family Size:						
1-3	13	–	–	9	69.2	69.2
4-5	38	11	28.9	11	28.9	57.8
6 and over	42	9	21.4	11	26.2	47.6

	Total sample	*2) Tradition: better hospitality*		*2) Tradition: large room for family reunions*		
Sex:						
Male	72	13	18.1	15	20.8	38.8
Female	21	3	14.3	4	19.0	33.3
Age:						
Less than 35	19	5	26.3	1	5.3	31.6
35-49	37	6	16.2	8	21.6	37.8
50 and over	37	5	13.5	10	27.0	40.5
Political participation:						
Party and organizations	23	5	21.7	1	4.3	26.0

Hai Van

Non-members	70	11	15.7	18	25.7	41.4
Education:						
Literate only	17	2	11.8	2	11.8	23.6
Primary	44	6	13.6	11	25.0	38.6
Secondary	32	8	25.0	6	18.8	43.8
Religion:						
Catholic	66	10	15.2	18	27.3	42.5
Non-Catholic	27	6	22.2	1	3.7	25.9
Family size:						
1-3	13	4	30.8	4	30.8	61.6
4-5	38	6	15.8	6	15.8	31.6
6 and over	42	6	14.3	9	21.4	35.7

	Total sample	*3) Economic: storing rice*		*3) diminution of garden size*		*lack of finances*		
Sex:								
Male	72	5	6.9	6	8.3	7	9.7	24.9
Female	21	3	14.3	3	14.3	3	14.3	42.9
Age:								
Less than 35	19	–	–	–	–	–	–	–
35-49	37	3	8.1	4	10.8	4	10.8	23.7
50 and over	37	5	13.5	5	13.5	3	8.1	33.1
Political participation:								
Party and organizations	23	2	8.7	1	4.3	–	–	13.0
Non-members	70	6	8.6	9	12.9	7	10.0	31.5
Education:								
Literate only	17	4	23.5	5	29.4	–	–	52.9
Primary	44	3	6.8	4	9.1	6	13.6	29.5
Secondary	32	1	3.1	–	–	1	3.1	6.2
Religion:								
Catholic	66	8	12.1	7	10.6	7	10.6	33.7
Non-Catholic	27	–	–	2	7.4	–	–	7.4
Family size:								
1-3	13	–	–	–	–	–	–	–
4-5	38	4	10.5	2	5.3	3	7.9	23.7
6 and over	42	4	9.5	7	16.7	4	9.5	35.7

		4) Family Harmony	
Sex:			
Male	72	5	6.9
Female	21	–	–
Age:			
Less than 35	19	4	21.1
35-49	37	–	–
50 and over	37	1	2.7

Political participation:			
Party and organizations	23	4	17.4
Non-members	70	1	4.3
Education:			
Literate only	17	–	–
Primary	44	–	–
Secondary	32	5	15.6
Religion:			
Catholic	66	2	3.0
Non-Catholic	27	3	11.1
Family Size:			
1-3	13	2	15.4
4-5	38	3	7.9
6 and over	42	–	–

however, whether the different characteristics of the persons questioned (age, sex, education, etc.) had any connection with the reasons given to justify the positions taken.

It is interesting to see to what points of reference the social agents spontaneously appeal in order to justify their opinion (for or against). The comparison with the totals for each of the motives and for the whole of the population studied enable us to draw up Table 7.6.

The Two Storey Single Family House

The two storey construction is an alternative which allows for the modernization of the home with due regard to the spatial reallocation of the plot of land which the family owns. Slightly over half those questioned were in favour of it; as Table 7.6 indicates, the strongest supporters of this type of lodging were the less than 35s who had received a secondary education and were non-Catholics. Women, the aged (particularly couples living alone and those who had had no formal education) were against the innovation.

The motivations justifying the positions taken have been divided into themes according to the frames of reference they express. Thus it is evident that affirmative opinions have been based on three principal types of arguments: the desire to improve living conditions; the acceptance of a form of modernization which represents the distribution of land and the part left to private economy; and finally, the search for the improvement of family relations. The rejection of this form of modernization is justified by: satisfaction with the prevailing conditions; the harking back to tradition; recoil from physical difficulties; and the fear that this type of house will not withstand the ravages of nature (storms, typhoons, etc.). Table 7.9 indicates the priority accorded to the improvement of living conditions, for those who favour the introduction of this type of habitat, and the harking back to tradition for the others. The analysis of the motives advanced by the different categories of persons questioned (Table 7.10) brings out clearly the relative emphasis of the differences. This is expressed in Table 7.7.

Table 7.6
Social References of the Persons Questioned

References	*Categories of persons most preoccupied by:*	*Categories of persons least preoccupied by:*
Living conditions	women those aged 35-49 those who have not been to school small families of 1-3 persons	those aged less than 35 those with secondary education families of 6 persons and over
Tradition	families of 1-3 persons	members of the Party and organizations those without schooling non-Catholics
Family economy	women those without schooling	those aged less than 35 those with secondary education non-Catholics families of 1-3 persons
Family harmony	those aged less than 35 members of the Party those with secondary education families of 1-3 persons	women those aged 35–49 those literate and with primary education families of 6 persons and over

Table 7.7
Motivations Underlying Opinions For and Against Construction of Single Family Two Storey Houses

	Opinions for (47)	%		*Opinions Against* (46)	%
Improvement of material living conditions	30	63.8	Satisfaction with material living conditions	7	15.2
Respect for private economy	6	12.8	Tradition	26	56.5
Improvement of family relations	6	12.8	Physical difficulties	8	17.4
Other reasons	14	29.8	Fear of nature	7	15.2

Table 7.8
Motivations Underlying Opinions For and Against Construction of Two Storey Houses, According to Characteristics of Sample (%)

	Sex		Age			Political participation		Education			Religion		Family size		
	Men (72)	*Women* (21)	*Less than 35* (19)	*35-49* (37)	*50 and over* (37)	*Party and organizations* (23)	*Non-members* (70)	*Literate only* (17)	*Primary* (44)	*Secondary* (32)	*Catholics* (67)	*Non-Catholics* (26)	*1-3* (13)	*4-5* (38)	*6 and over* (42)
Opinions for:															
Better living conditions	41.7	23.8	57.9	37.8	13.5	26.1	34.3	35.3	27.3	34.1	25.4	50.0	23.1	39.5	28.6
Private economy	7.1	4.8	5.3	2.7	5.4	13.0	4.3	5.9	2.3	12.5	6.0	7.7	7.7	7.9	4.8
Family harmony	8.3	—	—	10.8	5.4	—	8.6	11.8	9.1	—	9.0	—	—	7.9	7.1
Various	19.4	9.5	15.8	10.8	26.9	13.0	15.7	17.6	13.6	12.5	17.9	19.2	7.7	23.7	9.5
Opinions against:															
Satisfied with living conditions	8.3	4.8	5.3	10.8	5.4	8.7	7.1	—	9.1	6.8	9.0	3.8	7.7	5.3	9.5
Tradition	27.7	15.9	21.1	32.4	27.0	26.1	28.6	47.1	25.0	25.0	29.9	23.1	15.4	26.3	33.3
Physical difficulties	5.6	19.0	5.3	5.4	13.5	4.3	10.0	17.6	6.8	6.3	9.0	7.7	23.1	5.3	9.5
Fear (nature of)	6.9	9.5	10.5	2.7	8.1	8.7	7.1	11.8	4.5	9.3	7.5	7.7	15.4	5.3	7.1

Table 7.9
Types of Motivation Advanced

	Categories of persons most preoccupied by:	*Categories of persons least preoccupied by:*
Living conditions	men those aged less than 50 non-Catholics	those aged 50 and over
Family economy	Party members those educated to secondary level	those aged 35-49 those educated to primary level
Family harmony	those aged from 35-49 without formal education	women those aged less than 35 Party members and of organizations educated at secondary level non-Catholics small families of 1-3 persons
Tradition	those without formal education	women small families of 1-3 persons
Physical difficulties	women those without formal education small families of 1-3 persons	Party members
Fear of nature	those aged less than 35 without formal education families of 1-3 persons	those aged 35-49 those with primary education

Considered in Table 7.9 are the categories whose percentages are higher or lower than the average, increased or diminished by the value of the typical difference. For the population studied as a whole, and with regard to the two propositions for modernization of the present habitat, it will be observed that it is where innovation is greatest (the construction of a two storey house) that one finds the proposition most welcome.

The Urbanization of the Rural Habitat

A third proposition envisaged a solution much more radical – the introduction into the village of an urban form of habitation and collective equipment, i.e. the construction of high-rise buildings in concentric circles around a centre, which would regroup the commercial and cultural centres, (library, cinema, etc.) schools, the crèche, and the medical services. In this case it is necessary to bear in mind that each family dwelling would have running water and

Table 7.10
Opinions Concerning Urbanization of the Villages

	Opinions for	%	*Opinions against*	%
Total	63	66.7	31	33.3
Sex:				
men	52	72.2	20	27.8
women	10	47.6	11	52.4
Age:				
Less than 35	16	84.2	3	15.8
35-49	23	62.2	14	37.8
50 and over	23	62.2	14	37.8
Political affiliation:				
Party and organizations	18	78.3	5	21.7
Non-members	44	62.9	26	37.1
Education:				
Literate only	12	63.1	7	36.9
Primary	24	55.8	19	44.2
Secondary	26	83.9	5	16.1
Religion:				
Catholic.	39	59.1	27	40.9
Non-Catholic	23	85.2	4	14.8
Family size:				
1-3	8	61.5	5	38.5
4-5	26	68.4	12	31.6
6 and over	28	66.7	14	33.3

electricity.

Of the whole of the population studied here, 67% favoured this mode of housing and the management of the land. The percentage of opinion favourable to this proposition exceeded by far the average among the less than 35s, those with a secondary education, Party and mass organization members, and non-Catholics (84.2%, 83.9%, 78.3% and 85.2% respectively). Women were more against than for the proposition. The favourable opinions presuppose four types of innovation. In the first place, are those who express the desire for better living conditions (40.9%); then comes the possibility of broader cultural development (14%); followed by the opportunities for a better education for the young (9.7%); and finally, for 11.8% this type of housing represented 'the dream of their lives'.

The unfavourable opinions are justified in the first place by the alleged futility of those changes: 20.4% believed in the adage 'what will be will be'; 7.5% rejected change because they wished to stick to tradition; and 4.3% because the collective character of the dwellings would be harmful to family liberty.

As in the cases of the two other propositions, the reasons advanced for

Table 7.11
Motivations Underlying Opinions For and Against Urbanization of the Rural Habitat (%)

Opinions for		*Opinions against*	
Improvement of living conditions	40.9	No necessity	20.4
Possibility of cultural development	14.0	Respect for tradition	7.5
Possibility of better education for youth	9.7	Lack of liberty for the family	4.3
Hopes for the future	11.8		

justifying an opinion either for or against vary very much according to the categories of persons questioned. The search for an improvement of living conditions, for example, presented extremes going from 52.6% among the less than 35s to 23.8% among women. Greater still was the variation when it was a question of considering the environment in function of the cultural possibilities which it offered: 2.7% of the 50+ group and 42% of the youth were worried by the question.

The Motivations and their Sociological Significance

We will base our conclusions on Table 7.14 which synthesizes the prevailing positions and the chief motives advanced by each of the categories of persons questioned. Two aspects of the question stand out: one concerns the concrete forms of the home, and the other deals with the subtle differences in attitude of the categories of the rural population when confronted by change.

When compared, the positions in favour of the three forms of housing proposed (4/15 responses favourable to the improvement of the present form; 7/15 favourable to a single family house with two storeys; and 14/15 favourable to a flat in a building in a semi-urbanized environment, as Table 7.14 shows) one will observe a gradual growth in favourable opinions in the measure in which the form proposed deviates from the present model. One may surmise that never having lived in an apartment building explains the enthusiasm for the propositions in almost all the groups. However, the analysis of the reasons advanced gives ground for believing that it has a more solid foundation than that.What does the apparent contradiction between the satisfaction with the present day living conditions and the desire to improve the material conditions of the home reveal?

The first solution proposed for improving the home (the division of the house into rooms) would imply more often than not, a spatial extension of the family house (and therefore a diminution of the size of the garden for domestic economy). This idea provokes, according to all the evidence available, a conflict of interests between the economic needs of the family, met in part by domestic production, and an aspiration for more comfort. At present, the economic needs have priority, and the living conditions which the house

Table 7.12
Motivations Underlying Opinions For and Against Urbanization, According to Characteristics of Sample (%)

	Sex		Age			Political participation		Education			Religion		Family size		
	Men (72)	*Women (21)*	*Less than 35 (19)*	*35-49 (37)*	*50 and over (37)*	*Party and organizations (23)*	*Non-members (70)*	*Literate only (19)*	*Primary (43)*	*Secondary (31)*	*Catholics (66)*	*Non-Catholics (27)*	*1-3 (13)*	*4-5 (38)*	*6 and over (42)*
Opinions for:															
Improvement of living conditions (41.3)	45.8	23.8	52.6	35.1	40.5	39.1	41.4	36.8	34.9	51.6	39.4	44.4	46.1	47.3	33.3
Culture (14.0)	15.3	9.5	42.1	10.8	2.7	30.4	8.6	5.3	4.7	32.3	9.1	25.9	15.4	21.1	7.1
Education of youth (9.8)	8.3	14.3	–	10.8	13.5	13.0	8.6	31.6	4.7	3.2	12.1	3.7	–	7.8	14.2
Aspirations (12.0)	13.9	4.8	5.3	24.3	13.5	4.3	14.3	5.3	18.6	6.4	16.7	–	–	5.2	21.4
Opinions against:															
Futility (20.7)	19.4	23.8	–	21.6	29.7	4.3	25.7	21.2	25.6	12.8	25.8	7.4	15.4	18.4	23.8
Tradition (7.6)	1.3	19.0	–	10.2	8.1	13.0	5.7	10.6	7.0	6.4	3.0	18.5	7.7	7.8	7.1
Lack of liberty (4.3)	2.8	9.5	10.5	5.4	–	–	5.7	5.3	7.0	–	6.1	–	15.4	–	4.7

Table 7.13
Types of Socio-Economic and Cultural Preoccupations in Function of the Home

	Categories of persons least preoccupied by:	*Categories of persons most preoccupied by:*
An improvement in living conditions	women	those aged less than 35 those with secondary education
Cultural possibilities	those aged 50 and over those with primary education	those aged less than 35 Party and organizations members those with secondary education
The possibilities of education for youth	those aged less than 35 families of 1-3 persons	those with no formal education
Tradition	men those aged less than 35	women non-Catholics
The absence of liberty for the family	those aged 50 and over Party members those educated to secondary level families of 4-5 persons	women those aged less than 35 families of 1-3 persons
	Categories of persons least satisfied by:	*Categories of persons most satisfied by:*
Present day living conditions	Party members those aged less than 35 non-Catholics	those aged 50 and over

offers are accepted, not for any real benefits they may bring, but perforce. This is why the radical solution proposed in the matter of housing, and finally, in the matter of equality of life, betrays a general aspiration for more material comfort and more facilities in the organization of daily life. One may conjecture that the construction of small sized 'agro-villas' (agrarian towns), as in Cuba, would scarcely overcome the cultural obstacles among the peasants of the commune. From this one may also conclude that the supposed deep attachment of the rural population to the family home, and more still, to the private garden, is more relative than appears on the surface. The garden, like the pond, is of concern only to the extent that it serves the family economy or makes life easier, providing, for instance, a source of water closer to the home. This is at least the implicit logic of the responses we have analysed, regardless of the level of the consciousness of this logic in the persons interviewed.

In Table 7.14 a position for or against is said to be predominant when it is expressed by 51% or more of the persons of the category. Only those

Table 7.14
Positions and Predominant Justifications with Regard to Changes in Housing

	Proposals for Change:		
	Division of the present house into rooms	*Single family house with two storeys*	*Apartment building*
Sex: Men	*Against* Satisified with living conditions	*For* Improvement in living conditions	*For* Improvement in living conditions
Women	*Against* Satisfied with living conditions	*Against* Physical difficulties (19%)	*Against* Futile (23.8%)
Age: Less than 35	*For* Improvement of living conditions	*For* Improvement of living conditions	*For* Improvement in living conditions: cultural possibilities
35-49	*Against* Satisified with living conditions	*For* Improvement of living conditions	*For* Improvement of living conditions
50 and over	*Against* Satisified with living conditions	*Against* Tradition (27%)	*For* Improvement of living conditions
Political Participation Party and Organizations	*For* Improvement in living conditions (26%)	*For* Improvement in living conditions (26%)	*For* Improvement in living conditions: cultural possibilities
Non-members	*Against* Satisified with living conditions	*Against* Tradition (28.6%)	*For* Improvement in living conditions
Education: Literate Literate only	*Against* Satisified with living conditions	*Against* Tradition	*For* Improvement in living conditions: education of youth
Primary	*Against* Satisified with living conditions		*For* Improvement in living conditions: cultural possibilities

Secondary	*For* Tradition: better hospitality (25%)	*For* Improvement in living conditions	*For* Improvement in living conditions: cultural possibilities
Religion: Catholic	*Against* Satisified with living conditions	*Against* Tradition	*For* Improvement in living conditions
Non-Catholic	*For* Satisified with living conditions	*For* Improvement in living conditions	*For* Improvement in living conditions
Family Size: 1-3	*Against* Satisified with living conditions	*Against* Physical difficulties (23.6%)	*For* Improvement in living conditions
4-5	*Against* Economy (26.2%)	*For* Improvement in living conditions	*For* Improvement in living conditions
6 and over	*Against* Tradition (21.4%); satisfied (21.4%)	*Against* Tradition	*For* Improvement in living conditions

justifications have been reconsidered which have been advanced by 30% or more of the persons interrogated, except in the cases where the highest percentage is indicated in parentheses.

An inquiry such as this is not only interesting by reason of the indication which it furnishes concerning the opinions and wishes of the peasants in the matter of lodging: it furnishes further an analytical study of the level of openness to change of the village population, in terms of the different categories which constitute that population. All these questions constitute, in fact, a sequence of indications enabling us to identify four levels of openness: 1) The groups open to change (the less than 35s, the members of the Party and of mass organizations, the secondary school leavers, and non-Catholics); 2) The groups relatively closed to change (women) and two intermediary levels, according to which they manifest a more positive tendency towards change than towards maintaining the status quo; 3) Men, those between 35 and 49; and 4) The 50+ group, non-members of mass organizations, those who have received no formal education, and Catholics.

Among the groups most open to change, it is evident that the young generation forms the most dynamic elements. It is true that, according to our inquiry, they have several characteristics, which favour openness to change (secondary education completed or partial: 18/19; Party members: 5/19; members of mass organizations: 7/19; adherence to religion plays no part in their case, Catholics and non-Catholics alike revealing the same proportions). The category most closed to change in this sampling, viz., women, are generally the over 50s (11/12); the less educated (literate 11/21); and those scarcely belonging to any mass organizations (5/21).

The analysis of the motivations underlying these opinions seems to show that the age factor and the level of education are the determining elements, more than adherence to the Party and mass organizations. The persons who have had a secondary education are those most favourable to change, and they justify their positions with well reasoned arguments, regardless of their adherence or non-adherence to political organizations or to a religion. Among the members of political organizations and even of the Party, the attitude is more passive when the level of education is low. The most educated are more inclined to individualism, adherence to a religious faith is not in itself a restraint on change: Catholics are found as much among persons open to change as among others by the very fact of a higher percentage of Christians in the population studied.

A final remark concerns the incidence of progress realized by the social and economic transformation on the dynamics of the opinions of the rural population. For the older groups the present situation in the rural milieu constitutes an extraordinary acquisition when compared with the past – an acquisition which makes them satisfied, and turns them away from the projects of the future. This would probably explain a relatively half-hearted recourse to tradition, when we compare them to other rural populations of other Asiatic societies. These conclusions incline us to think that in the future, the development of education in the new generation whose only framework of reference will be the present situation, will provoke, inevitably, a new dynamic at village level. These groups run the risk, however, of being more critical than those of the past, and in any case, more demanding with regards the quality of life, both cultural and material.

The Use of Free Time

The second indicator was chosen because of the novelty of the very concept of free time for the rural population. It implies, in fact, the possibility of establishing objectively a dissociation between the time spent on professional work, and the so-called 'free' time, even if a part of this time is used for activities which serve to reproduce the work-force. Today the organization of work by the co-operative and the dissociation which it produces between the places of work and of residence, the times of work and of leisure, oblige the peasant to plan the use of time at his or her disposal for extra-professional activities, and to make choices which implicitly refer to values which determine his or her priorities. Further, socialist policy is not limited to the reorganization of the social relations engendered by production. It seeks conjointly to develop the productive forces not only at the level of practical economics, but also against the backdrop of health and of education. At this level the education of adults has effected the eradication of illiteracy (even among the aged), thus giving them access to new activities which would be promoted in the villages by the cultural commissions: an occasional cinema show, the use of the radio, of the library, a visit to a theatre, etc. This inquiry aimed, therefore, at studying the reactions of different sections of the rural population when confronted by new possibilities.

Apart from their professional and domestic activities and their time for rest, the peasants of Hai Van have at their disposal some hours of leisure every day, to which must be added the weekly holiday and the feast days. The question was what activities they preferred to indulge in during their leisure time. In concrete terms, the persons questioned were asked to select from a list of 11 activities which they preferred, liked a little, or not at all. These opinions and the choices made do not imply a total correspondence with their actual practices. Our interest was not to determine the use of free time, but to analyse the selections and rejections made by the interviewees. This study was centred, therefore, on three specific aspects: the capacity to choose; the hierarchy of choices relative to the type of activity; and the values underlying these choices. The inquiry was conducted on 74 persons: 47 men and 27 women of 20+, all married, all Catholics, and all working in the co-operative – 71 in agriculture and three workers proper.

The Capacity to Make Choices

Before embarking on the analysis of the selections made by the different categories of persons questioned we wished to know in what measure they could do this. It was a question of expressing an opinion, be it favourable or not, on each of the 11 activities proposed. It is evident that most of those activities introduced recently into the villages demand a certain level of personal development. It was to be expected, therefore, that the persons questioned would not be equally likely to make the selections demanded. Table 7.15 presents several distributions of the population studied in function of the number of activities which were evaluated favourably or not according to sex, age, level of education, etc. An examination of this table will enable us to put forward several observations.

The average number of activities for the whole group was 6.1, i.e. a little more than half (Median = 5.5), theoretically, at least, of the activities proposed. The averages calculated by categories show no important deviations: they vary within the limits of 5.5 (families of 4-5 persons) and of 6.9 (the less than 35s).

For the whole population, it will be noted that 45.8% of those questioned were able to evaluate between 0 and 5 of the activities proposed, and 54.2%, six or more activities. If one compares the distribution by categories one will see clearly that women, the literate, and the members of small families are the groups, least able, as a whole, to make a choice. As opposed to them, members of the Party and of organizations, the youth and those with a secondary school education (especially the last two categories), testify to a capacity to make clear choices, well above the average. Further, if the

Table 7.15
Capacity to Choose Among Free Time Activities (%)

Number of activities	Sex				Age					
	Men (47)		Women (37)		Less than 35 (27)		35–49 (28)		50 and over (20)	
0	2.1	–	–	–	–	–	3.6	–	–	–
1	–	–	–	–	–	–	–	–	–	–
2	4.3	6.4	14.8	14.8	11.1	11.1	7.1	10.7	10.0	10.0
3	19.1	–	11.1	–	3.7	–	25.0	–	15.0	–
4	6.4	–	7.4	–	3.7	–	3.6	–	20.0	–
5	12.8	38.3	14.8	33.3	14.8	25.2	14.3	42.9	5.0	40.0
6	6.4	–	11.1	–	3.7	–	3.6	–	10.0	–
7	19.1	–	–	–	14.8	–	14.3	–	10.0	–
8	8.5	34.0	3.7	–	7.4	25.9	3.6	21.5	10.0	30.0
9	4.3	–	7.4	–	7.4	–	3.6	–	10.0	–
10	6.4	–	22.2	–	18.5	–	10.7	–	5.0	–
11	10.6	21.3	7.4	37.0	14.8	40.7	10.7	25.0	5.0	20.0
Average number of activities	6.8		6.3		6.9		5.8		5.7	

Number of activities	Political participation				Education					
	Party (31)		Non-members (43)		Literate only (29)		Primary (28)		Secondary (17)	
0	–	–	2.3	–	–	–	3.4	–	–	–
1	–	–	–	–	–	–	–	–	–	–
2	6.4	6.4	11.4	13.7	13.8	13.8	6.9	13.3	5.9	5.9
3	6.4	–	20.5	–	13.8	–	13.8	–	17.6	–
4	9.7	–	6.8	–	10.3	–	10.3	–	–	–

5	12.9	29.0	11.4	38.7	10.3	34.4	10.3	34.4	17.6	35.2
6	9.7	–	2.3	–	6.9	–	3.4	–	5.9	–
7	19.4	–	9.1	–	10.3	–	17.2	–	11.8	–
8	9.7	38.8	4.5	15.9	3.4	20.6	13.8	35.4	–	17.7
9	12.9	–	2.3	–	–	–	6.9	–	17.6	–
10	9.7	–	13.6	–	13.8	–	10.3	–	11.8	–
11	3.2	25.8	15.9	31.8	17.2	31.0	3.4	20.6	11.8	41.2
Average number of activities	6.5		6.1		6.3		6.2		6.0	

Number of activities	*Family size*							
	1-3 persons (10)		*4-5 persons* (26)		*6 persons and over* (38)		*Total* (74)	
0	–	–	–	–	2.6	–	1.3	–
1	–	–	–	–	–	–	–	–
2	–	–	15.4	15.4	7.7	10.3	8.1	9.4
3	40.0	–	3.8	–	15.4	–	16.1	–
4	–	–	11.5	–	7.7	–	6.8	–
5	10.0	50.0	15.4	30.7	10.3	33.4	13.5	36.4
6	10.0	–	3.8	–	5.1	–	8.1	–
7	20.0	–	11.5	–	12.8	–	12.2	–
8	–	30.0	11.5	26.8	5.1	23.0	6.8	27.1
9	10.0	–	7.7	–	5.1	–	5.4	–
10	10.0	–	7.7	–	15.4	–	12.2	–
11	–	20.0	11.5	26.9	12.8	33.3	9.5	27.1
Average number of activities	5.6		5.5		6.4		6.1	

Table 7.16
Opinions on the Different Uses of Free Time, According to Sex and Age (%)

	Men			Women			Total			Aged less than 35			Aged 35-49			Aged 50 and over		
	a	*b*	*c*	*a*	*b*	*c*	*a*	*b*	*c*	*a*	*b*	*c*	*a*	*b*	*c*	*a*	*b*	*c*
Cinema	66.0	6.4	27.6	85.2	3.7	11.1	73.0	5.4	21.6	85.2	–	14.8	74.1	14.8	11.1	55.0	5.0	40.0
Radio	68.1	8.5	23.4	77.8	7.4	14.8	71.6	8.1	20.3	81.5	–	18.5	66.7	11.1	22.2	65.0	15.0	20.0
Reading (newspapers and journals)	59.6	10.6	29.8	51.9	3.7	44.4	56.8	9.1	35.1	63.0	3.7	33.3	66.7	7.4	25.9	35.0	15.0	50.0
Political activity	25.5	19.1	55.4	22.2	18.5	59.3	24.3	18.9	56.8	22.2	22.2	55.6	29.6	18.5	51.9	20.0	15.0	65.0
Sport	31.9	17.0	51.1	14.8	22.2	63.0	25.7	8.1	66.2	18.5	29.6	51.9	33.3	33.3	33.4	25.0	10.0	65.0
Handicrafts	48.9	4.3	46.8	25.9	18.5	55.6	40.5	9.5	50.0	37.0	22.2	40.6	25.9	3.7	70.4	65.0	–	35.0
Gardening	72.3	2.1	25.6	70.4	–	29.6	71.6	1.4	27.0	81.5	–	18.5	59.3	–	40.7	75.0	5.0	20.0
Theatre	57.4	6.4	36.2	77.8	–	22.2	64.9	4.0	31.1	77.8	–	22.2	74.1	7.4	18.5	35.0	5.0	60.0
Library	34.0	21.3	44.7	33.3	14.8	51.9	29.7	17.6	53.7	44.4	18.5	37.1	33.3	14.8	51.9	20.0	20.0	60.0
Parish choir	23.4	14.9	61.7	48.1	14.8	37.1	32.4	14.4	53.2	55.6	18.5	25.9	18.5	14.8	66.7	20.0	10.0	70.0
Visiting friends	48.9	12.8	38.3	40.7	7.4	51.9	45.9	10.8	43.3	59.3	7.4	33.3	40.6	11.1	48.3	35.0	15.0	50.0

(a) activities favoured; (b) activities rejected; (c) don't know.

percentages of those who have expressed an opinion on at least nine of the 11 activities proposed are considered, it will be observed that the development of the critical spirit is correlated to the access they had to secondary education.

Table 7.16 enables us to specify once more those observations where a particular phenomenon is revealed. When one examines the distribution of opinions expressed by those questioned, on each of the leisure activities proposed, one will see that the percentages are relatively low when they express the rejection of one or another activity. The fact is that the population studied is capable of expressing its preferences, but is rather hesitant about what it does not fancy, preferring rather to express no opinion at all. We are limited here to a presentation of opinions which take account of the sex and age of those interrogated, for the results were very similar, whatever the criterion of categorization (education, adherence to politics, etc.).

This attitude is not peculiar to the population of Hai Van, for a similar phenomenon may be observed in studies made of the practices and opinions of the rural populations of South India, Sri Lanka and Thailand. Our surmise is that it is a question here of a cultural trait peculiar to Asiatic societies, which could be an expression of a particular form of the logic of thought. This finding justifies our having limited our analysis solely to the preferences expressed.

Selection and Social Categories

This analysis has to do with a comparison of hierarchies of choice in the utilization of free time, according to the different social and demographic categories into which the population is divided. Those hierarchies were determined from the point of view of the individual, reckoning in this case with the strength of the preference, by awarding two points or one point according to whether the one interviewed liked much or moderately the one or the other of the activities proposed. The sum total of the contributions of the persons belonging to each of the categories was then reduced to 100 in order to facilitate comparisons. A careful reading of Table 7.17 permits us to make certain observations: from the point of view of the *purpose of an activity*, three activities may be clearly separated from the others: gardening; the cinema; and the radio.

Even if it is supposed that some people enjoy working in the garden, it is not hard to surmise that because domestic production makes an important contribution to family revenue, some have opted for gardening by force of economic necessity rather than on account of any real love of it. However, this does not exclude their having made selections also from other activities. At the bottom of the scale we find sports, participation in the parish choir, and in the activities of mass organizations. When one knows that 42% of those questioned are members of mass organizations, it will readily be granted that they do not wish political activities to encroach upon their leisure time.

If 75/100 is taken as the '*limen sensationis*' of a solid preference for a determinate category of persons, then the cinema is the preference of the larges number of categories, viz., women, those aged between 35 and 50, those with

Table 7.17
Choice of Free Time Activities, According to Characteristics of Sample (scale from 0-100)

	Cinema	*Radio*	*Reading (journals)*	*Reading (library books)*	*Theatre*	*Handi-crafts*	*Garden-ing*	*Sport*	*Visiting friends*	*Parish choir*	*Mass organi-zations*
Sex:											
Men	60	60	51	30	52	47	67	26	34	19	22
Women	79	74	42	26	74	26	68	14	35	24	20
Age:											
Less than 35	67	76	56	35	72	37	78	19	50	28	22
35-49	76	61	54	28	68	22	65	24	31	17	26
50 and over	50	55	30	20	32	65	75	25	25	20	15
Political participation:											
Party and organizations	68	75	47	33	50	43	72	17	48	30	25
Non-members	61	58	49	23	59	36	67	26	32	16	19
Education:											
Literate only	37	50	26	13	18	55	53	13	32	16	11
Primary	77	53	42	19	71	37	73	29	32	18	19
Secondary	75	94	75	47	66	25	69	19	41	25	50
Family size:											
1-3	82	82	55	45	55	36	45	18	27	23	27
4-5	56	58	42	31	62	46	85	23	40	23	19
6 and over	57	57	36	20	57	35	62	24	32	22	19
Average	65	65	48	28	55	39	68	22	36	22	22

primary and secondary education and small families of one to three members. The radio is well patronized by the young, the members of the Party, those with secondary school education and small families; gardening finds its enthusiasts among the less than 35s, the over 50s and average sized families. Reading of papers and magazines is appreciated by those with a secondary school education. Preferences for the theatre do not reach the '*limen sensationis* of 75/100. However, three categories – women, youth and those with a primary school education – come close to the threshold. What is one to make of these selections expressed by the different categories? Their respective scales indicative of the hierarchy of choices permits us to arrive at the conclusions shown in Table 7.18.

Table 7.18
Selections of Free Time Activities by Categories of Population

	Activities favoured	*Activities less favoured*
Men	–	Parish choir
Women	Cinema	Sports
Aged less than 35	Gardening Radio	Sports
Aged 35-49	Cinema	Parish choir
Aged 50 and over	Gardening	Mass activities
Party and organizations	Radio	Sports
Non-members	–	Music
Literate only	–	Mass activities
Primary education	Cinema	Music
Secondary education	Radio Cinema Reading	Sports
Small families	Cinema Radio	Sports
Average families	Gardening	Mass activities
Large families	–	Mass activities

One will notice, first of all, that there is no significant majority among men, the non-members of political organizations, the literate only and members of large families. The reasons for these are various. It could be that these are the categories, which, from the cultural point of view, have no homogeneity. Such would be the case, we think, of men and of non-members of political organizations. But it could also be that we are dealing with groups of persons who possess, less than others, the objective possibility of making a selection from among the several activities for free time, either because of narrowness of outlook or because they are burdened with domestic work in large families

Whatever the reasons, it is clear that the cinema and the radio have become popular pastimes, tending to supplement the more traditional activities such as the meetings of groups and of friends, and also the theatre, which was much appreciated in former times. It is certain that the introduction of new techniques in the cultural sphere ought to have an effect on the practices and aspirations of the rural population in so far as it is accompanied by a will to develop the forces of production not only against the background of production but also at the level of formal education. The mass media are, in fact, creating new practices and becoming powerful factors for the homogenization of culture.

Attitudes and Values Revealed by the Choice of Free Time Activities

We now have to examine attitudes and underlying values as these emerge from our investigations into the hierarchy of choices made for the use of free time. These categories of activities are the result of a regrouping according to certain criteria. For the first individual and collective series we will consider as individual an activity which does not demand a specific local organization, and which, for that very reason, can be realized at will by an individual or by a small group of people. Examples are the radio, handicrafts, reading newspapers, etc. Contrariwise, collective leisure demands permanent equipment or at least an initiative that is directed at all the members of the commune. Examples are cinema, the library, activities organized by mass organizations, choral music, etc. Active occupations are those where a person or a group of persons intervenes as creative agent, e.g., in handicrafts, gardening, reading, political meetings, etc., as opposed to those passive pastimes which demand little intervention from the agents – the cinema, the radio, the theatre etc.

The four subdivisions of aptitudes in Table 7.19 refer to aptitudes for manual and intellectual work, physical aptitudes (sport) or sociability. These categories are exclusive only in the measure where one considers them in a series. This means that the same activity is found reappearing in the three series.

On the whole, it is clear that preferences in general are for forms of activity which do not demand organization or local equipment, activities which can be indulged in by oneself at times of one's own choosing. Secondly, there is a preference for passive pastimes where little creativity is called for. These choices are more or less equally distributed between manual and intellectual activities.

If one uses averages as parameters, one will observe that the strongest discriminations are age, the level of education and the size of the family group. The less than 35s differ from their older brethren by the fact of their greater facility to keep themselves occupied, which does not exclude them any more than the others from collective activity. More also than the others, they have a tendency to make their choices bear on passive pastimes (radio, cinema) but in a manner predominantly intellectual; they are scarcely attracted by physical culture. These characteristics are explained in part, at least, and for men only, by the development of the schooling habit. The same tendencies stand out in greater relief among those who have completed their secondary

Table 7.19
Characteristics of Preferred Activities, According to Categories of the Sample

	Characteristics					*Aptitudes developed*		
	Individual (100)	*Collective (100)*	*Active (100)*	*Passive (100)*	*Manual (100)*	*Intellectual (100)*	*Physical (100)*	*Social (100)*
Sex:								
Men	56	35	38	56	58	50	28	26
Women	55	36	35	64	54	53	23	25
Age:								
Less than 35	62	43	39	78	57	64	19	32
35–49	47	37	32	64	46	54	27	24
50 and over	59	23	35	39	71	36	24	16
Political participation:								
Party and organizations	59	39	39	64	58	55	17	34
Non-members	53	34	34	59	52	50	26	22
Education:								
Literate only	46	20	27	35	54	29	13	20
Primary	60	38	34	67	55	52	29	23
Secondary	66	35	44	78	47	71	19	39
Family size:								
1–3	55	40	35	73	41	64	26	35
4–5	58	36	41	59	36	66	23	27
6 and over	48	33	31	57	49	45	24	24
Average	55	36	36	62	54	53	22	27

school course. The choice of members of small families also comes close to this model, a phenomenon due much more to the level of education than to age. In 60% of the cases the persons questioned have followed the secondary school course. One will note also that it is in these same categories that one finds the highest statistical figures for activities that concern social finality, i.e., those which are oriented less towards relaxation or cultural development of the person who indulges in them, but rather on a project which transcends it.

To sum up, these observations permit some conclusions. In the first place, it appears that the duality of economic production, (collective production/ domestic production) is a handicap for the development of extra-economic activities. Much more, top priority is given to production as an end, and this purpose is translated into practice by an increase in the time given to work. In the long run, this situation could beget, in the cultural background, a devaluing of non-economic activities as time lost. With regards activities indulged in during free time properly so-called, the introduction into the villages of an occasional cinema show and of the radio has met with enthusiastic support, particularly among the young. On the other hand, the almost total eradication of illiteracy has had no perceptible effect on the development of a taste for reading. Even in villages furnished with libraries, the chief users of the library during the last ten years have been school children and undergraduates. Very few adults (only four of them women) borrow books and the books borrowed are, for the most part, spy thrillers and science fiction works.

Our inquiry has shown us that at least a secondary school education is necessary for one to be able to appreciate the more intellectual forms of leisure. At this level primary education is insufficient, and by primary education is meant the termination of schooling soon after childhood. But this also enables us to understand the tendency which we have noted earlier concerning the passive character of the leisure activities; this is a possible indication of the difficulty experienced in utilizing free time.

8. Transformation of Religion

The population of Hai Van is overwhelmingly Catholic; this is something exceptional for Vietnam which has always been by and large, a Buddhist country, though the greater part of the rural population practices a religion which is a mixture of cultic rites and practices derived from several sources: animism, spiritism, Taoism, Confucianism, and Buddhism. For a sociology of religion more evocative of the cultural substratum of Vietnam, one must evidently do research studies on groups other than the Catholics.

Catholicism in this part of Vietnam was planted by Spanish missionaries over a period of three centuries, in rural settlements which were the poorest, not only economically and politically, but also culturally, i.e. areas where there were relatively few possibilities for endogenous renewal even after the replacement of foreigners by the native clergy. Besides, as has happened with most of the Christian minorities in Asia, the Catholic group was utilized by the colonial power which was looking for a local stepping-stone, particularly during the attempt to reconquer the former colony after the Second World War. The tactic adopted was to mobilize the religious faith of the peasant population and get them to oppose, even by violence, the new government with its socialistic orientation. Such a·policy necessarily erupted in this Catholic village into bloody conflicts between a nationalist section directed by the Communist Party and a majority mobilized for a religious 'crusade', even though the purpose of this 'crusade' was, in the last analysis, political. This explains the exodus to the South of half the population of Hai Van in 1954, after the Geneva Accords. As a sequel to this an important part of the local clergy used its power to obstruct the development of the new socialist structures, both at the economic and educational levels. It is thus through the gradual discovery of the changes in living conditions, that the rural population integrated itself into the co-operative system and into the newly organized forms of collective life. From the religious point of view, however, the division of the country cut off the Catholics of the North from the springtime of post-conciliar Catholicism from the 1960s. But let us examine all this in a little more detail.

The Evolution of the Catholic Group during the Period of Transition

To begin with, let us situate the Catholic group of Hai Van within the district of Hai Hau and in the diocese of Bui Chu. There are, in the district, 44 parishes and 156 churches – i.e. 3.5 places of worship on average for each parish. At Hai Van there are five churches of respectable dimensions, corresponding to the five former villages: Our Lady of the Rosary, the seat of the parish; St. Joachim; St. Anthony; St. Francis; and St. Joseph. The first, according to tradition, was propagated by the Dominicans, who, up to the time of the revolution, supplied the missionaries for the region; St. Joachim is, according to tradition, the father of Mary, while St. Joseph is the putative father of Jesus. St. Anthony is especially popular among Christians; he is an Italian saint who lived at Padua and was very close to the people. As for St. Francis of Assisi, he is universally known. There is nothing, therefore, very special about these patron saints of the different hamlets – they are like any others found throughout the Christian world.

While there were in the district nearly a hundred priests before the exodus of 1954, there are now only eight to serve 44 parishes. Each priest is responsible, on average, for 5.5 parishes and 19.5 places of worship. This means that Sunday mass can scarcely be assured each week in each of the places of worship, and that certain parishes have to take their turn with others for Sunday mass. The masses are celebrated on Saturday afternoons and on Sundays, the same priest celebrating in several places of worship. It must be added that several priests are very old, some of them over 80, the reason for this being, first of all, the exodus of the clergy in 1954, which took away about 75% of them, and also because at the time when this study was being conducted, the recruitment and training of new priests was not being systematically organized.[1]

The diocese of Bui Chu, which exceeds the limits of the district, has 31 priests for 143 parishes, i.e., an average of 4.6 parishes per priest; as there are around 350,000 Catholics it works out at roughly 2,450 Catholics per parish and 11,290 Catholics per priest. In 1963, 29 priests were ordained but as these ordinations were carried out without consultation with the authorities and since among those ordained many came from families considered by those same authorities as having played a negative role in the process of political change, several of them had to wait for quite some time to be given permission to exercise their parochial ministries. In 1979 some seminarists were studying at the Metropolitan See of Hanoi.

The Catholics of Hai Van Before the Revolution

Catholics appear to have been present in Hai Van since the foundation of the five villages which constitute the present commune. These five villages were built upon alluvial soil more than two centuries ago. Two churches date back to the 19th Century, and the principal church, Our Lady of the Rosary, was built after the architectural style of the famous Cathedral of Phat Diem.

In the historical context of its formation, the Catholic group formed a minority in the society of the Tongkin peninsula. This was the incentive they had to form themselves into homogeneous villages which became the sources and origins of their identity and the guarantee of their security. Converted as a consequence of the religious labours of foreign missionaries, they became an alien group in the society in which they lived, and they organized themselves socially into a ghetto which was a particularly marked feature of their existence during certain periods of history, e.g., under the Nguyen when they were subjected to violent persecution.

As for their beliefs and practices, the village was a mirror of the situation now become classical among populations both poor and – particularly under the French colonialists – oppressed. This is what the elders of Hai Van describe when they speak of the superstitions and of the existence of sorcerers and fortune-tellers who served both Catholics and others alike. This state of affairs was the logical consequence of the low level of the forces of production and the absence of control over the social mechanisms. The social and cultural context of their religious life was such as to be fraught with a multiplicity of functions, which fulfilled effectively a large part of the world of representations.

When confronted by the existential situation of the rural masses, one of the prerequisites for the penetration of the great and well-established religious systems, such as Buddhism and Christianity, is a reliance on a historical founder and on the great intellectual and philosophical traditions which enter into relationship with popular beliefs. These are systematized, according to the laws of sociology, by different devices, such as doctrinal tolerance, which admits a double system of beliefs, or of a double interpretation of the same beliefs, according to whether it is a question of intellectuals (and especially religious agents) or of common folk. There could even be a certain assimilation of the beliefs of people under the control of religious agents. Most often the three devices coexist according to the subject matter, the social agents and the places.

In such conditions, a religious institution plays a very important role: it furnishes the organizational cadre needed by the minority group. Its agents fulfil functions which go beyond the saying of prayers and the performing of religious rites, and they become the leaders of the group. Thus inserted into the social context, the religious institution also becomes a base for material organization. As such it has a triple function: first of all, there are the lands belonging to the diocese, to the religious congregations and to the parishes. This was the case at Hai Van where the parish possessed rice fields which came, for the most part, from legacies or donations from Catholic peasants[2] and were leased to peasants who cultivated them and thus found themselves in a situation similar to their dependence on landlords. Consequently, a tithe was collected from the revenues of the peasants, a sort of collective tax, proportional to the financial state of each taxpayer. Finally, certain religious functions carried with them the payment of a financial contribution, such as marriages, funerals and blessings, e.g. a papal blessing was valued at 300 to 500 piastres, but this was available only to the 'notables' and proprietary landlords. 'All this was accepted by the peasants', said an old rural Catholic worker of Hai Van, 'because in their minds, life on earth was only provisional, and it was necessary to ensure eternal life.'

But today, the perspectives are somewhat different and it is with a critical eye that the past is analysed. Hence the same peasant concluded by saying, 'The Christian is characterized by the fact that he loves his neighbour, but how could one live out such a precept in the situation which prevailed before the revolution?'

The Catholics During the Revolutionary Struggle

Right from the beginning of the struggle, the local landed proprietors were allied with the forces of reaction and later, with the French. In the five villages these proprietors were all Catholics and they were also, for the most part, members of the parish council. In 1946 the government of Ho Chi Minh put into effect the first measures of agrarian reform: the reduction of rent and of interest, resulting in the diminution of the economic power of the landlords, and a more equitable redistribution of land held in common. This removed the props of the economic base and the prestige of the 'notables'. The resistance put up by the landed proprietors was ferocious and the peasants had to struggle to obtain their rights, and this was true of the Catholic peasants as well. Thus, in the commune of Hai Xuan, next to that of Hai Van, in 1946, a demonstration mounted by poor Catholic peasants against a 'notable' named Thuong Oanh, a proprietary landlord, owning more than 3,000 *maus* of land, and himself a Catholic, ended in bloodshed. The son of the landed proprietor killed a peasant; the family emigrated to Hanoi and their property was administered by Mgr. Le Huu Tu, the archbishop of Phat Diem.

At Hai Van, in the villages which constitute the commune of today, the 'notables' contrived to introduce their men into the local administration in order to prevent the realization of the measures taken to implement the land reform. As a result of this, there ensued a very arduous political struggle by which the peasants were finally able to put into effect the law on the redistribution of land held in common on a more equitable basis. Even the women were able to receive their share of it – the first instance of such a happening in the life of Vietnamese villages. The material conditions of the peasants began to improve thereafter.

From 1947, scarcely two years after the proclamation of independence, the struggle was renewed with the French. The landlords and the 'notables' attempted to reconquer the land lost and avenged themselves against certain peasants. The present president of the Patriotic Front of Hai Van, a Catholic peasant, nearly 70 years old, was at this time one of the leaders of the peasant movement. But at the same time, the armed, Catholic militia, formed from the young Catholic anti-Communists, were organized in the region, by two priests, the Revds Khan and Bao. The local priest of the time led the group in the parish.

From 1947-49, the French occupied the Delta while guerrillas organized and strengthened themselves constantly. In 1949 the great offensive of the French was launched, which attempted to regain control of the Red River Delta, a veritable rice granary. A parachute operation was launched at Phat Diem and from there they attempted to gain mastery of the whole region to the south of the principal tributary of the river. On 15 October they penetrated to Phat Diem (25 km. from Hai Van) in order, they said, to protect Mgr. Le Huu Tu, who was in hiding with the Catholic militia. The diocese of Phat Diem stands next to that of Bui Chu, to which the parish of Hai Van belongs juridically, but the influence of Mgr. Le Huu Tu was felt far and wide throughout the whole region and there is no denying that he was ferociously anti-Communist and had organized the armed struggle of the Catholic militia. In fact, as the representative of the emperor Bao Dai, he had set up an autonomous Catholic zone which lasted for two years and four months, up to the moment when undermined by guerrillas, he lost control of it. It was the bishop who administered the zone, named functionaries, organized the army and directed the priests in military action. Several autonomous administrative zones were created and their administration entrusted to Vietnamese priests. The see of the bishop of Bui Chu became an autonomous province, a close copy of the ecclesiastical division, and this was done at the demand of the bishops themselves.

It was thus that a military outpost was established on the territory of Hai Van. With the aid of the local priest of the time, protected by a group of 12 bodyguards, the young Catholics were organized into a militia; they received 120 rifles; the priest organized a village administrative system with the collaboration of the landed proprietors. The village had, among other things, to contribute to feeding the French expeditionary corps. From this military outpost, operations were launched against the villages which had passed over to the Viet Minh, and which were often of a non-Catholic majority. Thus it attempted to maintain military control over the territory of the autonomous zones. Between 1949 and 1951 one of the churches of the village was converted into a prison and was guarded by Catholic militiamen. Pressure was exerted on the prisoners to convert the non-Catholics among them to Catholicism; their goods were confiscated and their houses destroyed. Some of them were tortured and put to death. The repression was so fierce in the neighbouring outpost that the entire revolutionary nucleus was practically eliminated. The present president of the Patriotic Front was imprisoned in the church for 12 months; he and his companions in prison succeeded in escaping when guerrilla activity was resumed in the region. His house was confiscated, and in 1954 he was compensated with a house abandoned by a family that had left for the South.

From 1951 the struggle was resumed against the French who controlled the region, but with ever growing difficulty, despite their alliance with the Catholic militia. One must not forget that the Catholics do not form a homogeneous group and that a section of them joined the anti-colonial struggle. The popular revolt, starting from Bui Chu, spread so far that the administration of the village set up by the French had to yield to the rebels.

A local priest, Revd Duan, whom they tried to force to reorganize and set up a new administration, refused to comply and was imprisoned. The struggle went on, especially against the 'seek and destroy' policy carried out by the Franco-Vietnamese battalions stationed in the region. All this provoked acute tension between the Catholics and non-Catholics, for, though not all the Catholics were allied with the French in what they considered a 'crusade' against atheistic Communism, the local militia, fighting on the side of the French, was composed entirely of Catholics, and most of the time commanded by priests. One of them, for instance, was stationed in a nearby village in charge of a fortified military station, with a rank equivalent to that of an officer in the French army; he was captured by the troops of the Viet Minh, condemned to death and then pardoned by Ho Chi Minh.

One may well ask why a large part of the Catholic group ended up by rallying round the former French colonizers against the Vietnamese patriots, when their real interests in no way demanded this of them, since they were poor peasants, and sometimes, even wretched and miserable. What did they have to lose? All one can say is that they acted under pressure. And here a sociological reflection is called for.

In fact, in their minds it was the identity of the group that was at stake. The liberation movement under the leadership of the Communist Party, could, according to them, only bring about the annihilation of Catholicism and of all religions. Since their collective identity was based upon their adherence to their religious faith, this signified for them a fate worse than the death of the individual. It must be said, in addition, that the clergy, who were the social leaders of the group, wielded a double authority – that of elder or head of the village, responsible, in consequence, for the identity of the group and its social reproduction, and that of religious agent, who, as such, was the guarantor of life beyond the grave. The fact that most of the bishops and priests were opposed to the Viet Minh and finally accepted French military aid, could not but induce the Catholic peasantry to follow suit at the political level.

But the majority of the clergy was also allied socially to a small group of 'notables' and Catholic landlords, and this had its repercussion on some peasants more politically aware than others. One may well imagine what the internal struggle must have been for them in their effort to dissociate in their minds the political role of the priest from his religious role. However, they were able to join up with some of the priests who did not follow the majority and who, in spite of the penalties of excommunication, were solidly behind the Viet Minh and the struggle for national independence.

It must also be recalled that the Catholics, evangelized in this region by Spanish missionaries, had been trained to a very strong group discipline. Apart from the fact that the type of Catholicism transmitted to them was of a very rigid nature, such discipline was the very condition of their survival as a group. This, perhaps, is the explanation why such discipline is still a live force, but now, within the new social and economic organization.

One finds oneself, therefore, face to face with a sociological process where the superstructure takes pride of place over the infrastructure. It is their adherence to Catholicism and not to economic interests which explains the attitude of the peasants. The institutionalization of cultural models and of group organization has been, perhaps, oriented towards social practices which can, objectively, be in contradiction with the economic, social, political and cultural liberation of the group. This is a mechanism so powerful that the group fears that its very existence will be at stake in the future; an argument which was made much of during this period of the history of Vietnam. This, then, is a typical case of the relative autonomy of the superstructure, which, it is important to note, from the point of view of a sociology of transition, but which is not without interest on the practical level as well. For the present, let us approach the circumstances of the group structure as they are to be found in the new situation which has arisen.

In 1954, the Geneva Accords put an end to the French war, but not without some ambiguities. To avoid the worst, the government of Hanoi accepted the provisional partition of the country, according to a cease-fire line drawn along the 17th parallel. Some months were allowed the inhabitants of the two zones to choose which zone they wished to live in. The peasants of Hai Van who had taken refuge elsewhere, either because they had supported the Viet Minh or because they had fled from the zones of fighting, returned to their village. The Catholics who had formed part of the armed militia were in a quandary: most of them wished to remain and accept, with some misgivings, the new situation. They were afraid of repression and the landlords feared it still more. Intense propaganda, both civil and religious, was carried on to encourage them to quit the North.

First the French, and then, the Americans, put ships at the disposal of the refugees, with small craft coming alongside larger ones to join them on the high seas. At Hai Van it was only at the last moment that the departure was organized, but then there was panic. In a night or less, 190 families consisting of 673 persons, took to the small crafts which led them to the French ships, and they set sail for the South, on what they thought was only a temporary exodus. On the other hand, several families returned from the South to settle down in the villages of the present commune; some of them had worked in the French rubber plantations.

Catholic Resistance to Agrarian Reform and the First Co-operatives

It was from 1955 that the agrarian reform, decreed already in 1953, in its new form, began to take concrete effect in Hai Van. Even though a large part of the former 'notables' and landed proprietors had left the village, some of them remained. But the long drawn out civil war was not going to subside in a day or two. It was impossible then to find among the Catholics who constituted the majority all the necessary personnel for the new economic, social and political organizations. They had therefore to be recruited from the small non-Catholic minority of Hai Van. The agrarian reform implied the division of the landowners into different categories: large, medium and small. This was the occasion for paying off grudges which, in their turn, provoked reactions.

The fifth phase of the agrarian reform was implemented in a manner very brutal and uncontrolled. The amalgam of landed proprietors, rich peasants, and middle peasants of a higher level made use of many subterfuges to find pretexts to settle local scores. Directives concerning the suppression of social categories were put into practice, sometimes, by physical elimination, pure and simple, under the direction of the people's courts. The structure of the former exploitation and the ferocity of the social struggle of the peasants, to which was added the colonial repression built on a part of the class of 'notables' and landed proprietors, will enable one to understand the dialectical process from which such abuses emanated. Nonetheless, they were morally and politically unjustifiable. It must also be noted that the suppression of some rich and even middle peasants deprived agriculture of valuable expertise. Several proprietors who had collaborated with the French and were, in varying degrees, responsible for the repression which was directed against the partisans of the Viet Minh, were put to death. It became easy to blame this on the anti-religious policies of the Party. Again, the sense of identity of the Catholic group was at stake, and a certain number of peasants perished for the part they played in the revolt against the agrarian reform. Confusion reigned once again and serious trouble ensued, obliging the political authorities to take drastic measures. It will be recalled that President Ho Chi Minh dismissed the man responsible for agrarian reform.

This retrograde step gave new vigour to some representatives of the former ruling class, and among them, in the region studied, were Catholic 'notables'. They attempted anew to recover their lost lands. In some cases Catholic peasants who had participated in the struggle for agrarian reform had to endure in public, sometimes, before the altar in their churches, the shame of confessing their crimes and of being ostracized from society.

It must be added that the new, locally recruited cadres had scarcely any competence in the management of the new economic structures, and this compounded the difficulties. Some of them in the region of Hai Van could not resist the temptation to pay off personal and family grudges. Later they were, in their turn, judged and condemned by the competent authorities. In short, during the period 1955–56 the situation was very confused.

It was at this juncture that a new parish priest was put in charge of Hai Van, together with several other neighbouring parishes. Just out of prison, after playing an active part in the anti-Communist struggle, he was hardly convinced of the good intentions behind the new measures of reform. After his captivity and before being reintegrated into the pastoral ministry, he had spent a few months with the bishop of Bui Chu. When the first co-operatives were set up in 1959, 61.6% of the Catholics supported them. But the priest was persuaded that this was a form of economic organization opposed to the doctrine of the Church, in that it was the first step taken towards collectivization, before making way for the ideological brain-washing of Catholics; he used his influence to cause the co-operative method to founder. Not only did he introduce trusted Catholics into the co-operatives to sabotage the initiative, but he also suggested to the Catholic members of the co-operative that they continue to cultivate their individual rice fields. Thus the system of private property was upheld. After two years, only phantom co-operatives existed in Hai Van: the process was made more easy because the rice fields were relatively neglected, while there was much individual cultivation of bananas and tea.

But this is not the whole story. The clergy at Hai Van, as in many other parishes, used all the authority they could muster and advised Catholic youths against joining the army, on the ground that it contradicted the Fifth Commandment, 'Thou shalt not kill'. They brought pressure to bear on parents not to send their children to school beyond the first year, i.e. after they had learnt to read and write, on the ground that their faith would be endangered. All this was part of their general reaction of this time, and is not meant to point an accusing finger at a single person. Similarly, there were attached to each church, *quans* or lay catechists. They also were mobilized to transmit these ideas and suggest these attitudes. The government intervened and prevented them thenceforth from teaching catechism to children. Further, at this time there existed in the village different religious associations and they counted, in all, more than a thousand members. These religious associations also played a role, under the inspiration of the clergy, in opposing the new measures.

There is no doubt that all these are the reactions of a religious group which was afraid of losing its identity in the new economic, social and political organizations. On the one hand, the consequences of the colonial war were not erased; and on the other, the atheism of the Party created a fear that a policy of eliminating religious groups would follow. Further, the revolution created a number of new roles which appeared in quick succession within the local community as rivals in the field of leadership, which was formerly exclusively the preserve of the priest, not only at the religious level, but also on the social plane. This is a classic situation which keeps reappearing in the transitional stages of all pre-capitalist societies where Catholicism has been firmly planted. It must be added that the privileged situation of the ecclesiastical institution is again called into question and the material goods of the Church are threatened. By confounding his two roles the priest becomes very definite in his mind that loss of social functions automatically signifies the loss of his religious functions as well, and this results in reaction. But the peasants themselves often know how to make the distinction. One of them, a fervent Christian, said: 'Once upon a time the priest was listened to without discussion; today we use our judgement.'

The Transition Within Catholicism

During the last 30 years the situation has definitely improved. Production on a collective basis has begun to yield better results and the Catholics now see that there is no obstacle to their practising their religion or having their children educated in it. The American bombing attacks mobilized all the energies of patriotism and large numbers of young Catholics joined the army. The hour had struck, if one may so speak, for rallying round the government. Catholics no longer hesitated to enter into the co-operatives – no more than the others at any rate. Further, they sent their children to school as usual, and new cadres were also beginning to be chosen from their ranks. Today the majority of cadres less than 40 years old is Catholic and a large number of them are members of the Party, one third of whom are Catholics.

This is how the peasant quoted above put it: 'In former times superstitions were prolific. Now they are disappearing.' The celebrations of religious feasts were burdensome and funerals cost a lot. Today all this is organized collectively and it is the whole group which meets the expenses. While in the past the priest was paid from 300 to 1000 piastres, according to each case, today his stipend has been raised to six dongs; the poor have nothing to pay for religious ceremonies. Further, an agreement has been entered into between the commune and the principal religious groups, the Catholics, of course, being the principal group. It dates from 21 September 1978 and is part of a tradition of *huong voc* (agreements of the community) which, at the level of the traditional *lång* (former village or present hamlet) has put the official seal on social and cultural unity. Couched in popular style by the community official responsible for juridical affairs, discussed and then approved by the popular assembly of the commune (in which the Catholics are in the majority) it was signed, first of all by the president of the commune (a Catholic) in his capacity as president of the 'committee for the promotion of a new mode of life' and then by the members of the committee, i.e. the secretary of the Party, a member of the committee of the commune, the parish priest and two others. This was a matter for local initiative, based, however, on government directives and those of the presidency of the Republic, about the guarantees for freedom of religion.

The agreement enunciates, first of all, the general principles, and then applies them to the three different religions of the region, namely, Catholicism, Buddhism and the cult of 'genies'. We will deal with the last two later. The general principles are three in number. First of all there is the guarantee of freedom to believe or not to believe, together with the elimination at one stroke, of what the document calls 'superstitions' and thus purifying the practice of religion. The second concerns the religious activities of believers and of the official agents: their freedom must be guaranteed with respect to laws. The third and final principle stipulates that religious activities ought not to jeopardize productive work, the progress of the co-operative, the building up and the defence of the fatherland, and the security and the right order of the Republic, and that they cannot be allowed to be the cause of waste of time and money.

What concerns Catholicism is the way in which this new orientation is to be made concrete and practical. And in this regard the first concern is with the arrangement of cultic practices. And here, it is stated quite clearly at what times the church bells should be rung; the times are 4 a.m. and 6 p.m. in summer and autumn respectively, and 4.30 a.m. and 5.30 p.m. in winter and spring. The time taken for celebrating mass should not exceed one hour on working days, and an hour and a half on Sundays. The feasts of the patron saints of each hamlet should be celebrated in their respective churches, and the celebration should not exceed 24 hours. The feast day is, in fact, a holiday for the inhabitants of the hamlet. Anything in a cultic practice that could be the cause of extravagant expenses or harmful to productive work must be avoided. No discrimination is permitted in the holding of functions such as marriages and funerals ('neither rank nor class in the performance of rites') between families of different financial statuses. Catholics no longer have incentives to incur heavy expenses on such occasions (clothing, decoration) for wasting money on such occasions would incur the risk of creating disunity in the village. As for prayers etc. the choice remains with the family or with the church but are not to be said in turn in different houses. As for the meetings of the members of extended families on the occasion of the anniversary of a deceased member, for the saying of common prayers, the heads of the respective production groups must be warned in time to enable them to rearrange the workers' timetable, and further, these prayer meetings should not last later than 9 p.m.

It is also stipulated that reception of sacraments is free and that no one may force another to receive them, neither the husband the wife, nor the parents their children, nor vice versa. Catechism for first communion has to be organized during school holidays so that the general education of the children will not suffer thereby. It has to be carried out over a period of two weeks and must not last more than two hours a day. The catechists are appointed by the Catholic group, but as citizens, they have to receive the approval of the popular committee of the commune, who must also be forewarned of the place of catechizing and the number of children to be catechized, in order that the commune may make a contribution for all that is well done. Finally, religious books with a negative content (e.g. superstition) are to be eliminated as well as passages or phrases which go counter to the building up of socialism (e.g. the defence of private ownership of the means of production, which is contrary to the principle of co-operative socialism).

As for the local ecclesiastical organization, its functions may be exercised by the laity, provided that, in so far as they are citizens, they will have to be approved by the popular committee of the commune (by a certificate of good conduct and moral integrity). These particular organizations must have a legal status in order to function properly, and they may not be harmful to the general interests. It is not permitted to organize religious feasts to celebrate personal events as was done during the old regime.

The final directives concern the priest. He must respect the laws of the state and the right of the 'collective authority' of the people, i.e. local democracy. He is free to preach provided his sermons show due respect for the laws of the land and are clear and without equivocation. The real point at issue is that the priest should not make use of religion to incite Catholics to act against the laws and general policies of the country, for instance, by going against the liberty to believe or not to believe, against the citizens' patriotic duties, or against participation of Catholics in national organizations. The priest must also be watchful and see to it that religious acts and rites are conformable 'to the way of life that is civilized and progressive' as the text of the decree says. This means he will be opposed to all superstitions, especially, to so-called apparitions of Our Lady, to curative rites using sand, the leaves of trees, banana roots or blessed water, in the guise of medicaments. Finally, in case of grave illness or if someone is dying, he should notify the administration of the commune to visit the patient or dying person.

All this is entrenched in the heart of a sociology of transition; when one is confronted by a progressive and very real transformation of the level of productive forces, what is called for is the curtailment of practices which reproduce ideal models that are an obstacle to their progress, and therefore, to seek to reconcile the religious representations with the new forces of production. If the previous religious forms are not dissolved rapidly and spontaneously, conditions must be created to accelerate the process. These measures do not produce their effects automatically, and depend, for their effectiveness, on a variety of factors such as the real means of meeting the needs expressed by these types of representations, resistance, more or less strong, from former cultural models, and the possibilities that religious systems possess in themselves of bringing about the necessary transformation. Further, the transformation of social relations brought about by production is not less real, and consequently, everything that would be a symbolic expression of the former relationships, including religious beliefs, must be discouraged. This is the case, for example, of the relationships based on class differences, reproduced symbolically in the differences in marriage and funeral rites. One could also add to this, though the document analysed makes no allusion to it, processions, both Catholic and those indicative of their social position.

In short, faced with the dissolution of previous cultic forms bound to aministic practices on the one hand, and to representations of the pre-revolutionary social structure on the other, there remain three choices: Buddhist beliefs, Catholic beliefs, and non-belief. As far as the content of Catholicism is concerned, the repercussions are felt on the most fundamental demands of the content of the faith, of ritual practices, and of ethics. At the level of organization, a greater responsibility rests with the laity. In the given circumstances, the state, represented by the commune, guarantees the liberty of indulging in these religious activities and practices, provided it reserves to itself the right to regulate what pertains to public order, and to exercise close control over the religious organization in everything that could imply the political uses of religion.

In the reading of all these arrangements with regard to religion, one should recall the history of the Catholic group. The point at issue was definitely to terminate the past and it was for this reason that the priest was called upon to sign the document. Further, we must not forget that the different assemblies of the commune have Catholic majorities in them, and that if there is a real desire on the part of the authorities of the commune to channel their religious activities so as to avoid prostituting them for political purposes, there exist also, in the heads of the Catholic villages (which have discussed and have approved the agreement), an equally real desire to guarantee the identity of their group as believers, and the reproduction of that same group with the lapse of time. It is a dialectic which is being resolved here at the level of the cummune, between the state (which is anxious to see to the growth of the forces of production and consequently, to develop a more rational mentality, while guaranteeing at the same time, the new social relations issuing from the new forms of production), and the group of believers.

The state wants to prevent religion being made a pretext for the carrying on of anti-national and anti-socialist activities, or any other activity that is inimical to public order. At the same time it wishes to guarantee respect for the freedom of religion in order that believers too will bear their share of the cost of this national effort, provided their national identity is safeguarded. But the delicate balancing of interests which has been arrived at and which, in Hai Van, is expressed in the 'agreement' has been the result of a long dialectical process, in each of its phases. And the end of the way has not yet been reached, since dialectical relationships are always changing. It is necessary, however, to analyse them in their concrete reality, as relations between human groups, and not in abstract ideologies, for, at this latter level, there is no dialectic, there is simply contradiction (atheism vs belief). It is only from the former point of view that one will be able to understand why a state whose basic doctrinal inspiration is atheistic inclines towards freedom of religion, and why, on the other hand, believers participate actively in the operations of the state.

Changes in the Religious Life of the non-Christian Minority

It is quite paradoxical to speak of a non-Christian minority in Vietnam: still, this is the case in Hai Van since the non-Christians there constitute only 15% of the population. It has been established also in our inquiry that the people always speak of 'non-Christians' and not of Buddhists (*luong*). It is rather difficult to describe exactly the nature of the religious faith of this minority. Further, we have been unable to conduct real research into this subject, and thus can only make a few rudimentary reflections on it.

At Hanoi there is no Buddhist pagoda, but in the nearby commune of Hai Van there are two, maintained and frequented regularly by the faithful (the majority of whom are old women) especially on the Buddhist feast days, and on the 1st and the 15th of the lunar month. Few inhabitants of Hai Van frequent these pagodas, and there exists, as a result of the religious difference, a certain social isolation between the two villages.

In the 'agreement' already cited there are some sections concerning Buddhism: it is especially stipulated that the bonzes (who, let it be noted, do not exist in the commune itself) must respect the directives of the Association of Unified Buddhists. With regards practice, the only authorized offerings are flowers, incense sticks, incense, fruits and glutinous rice cakes, all of which are in keeping with Buddhist traditions. Bells may be rung freely, but authorization of the popular committee is necessary to use the gong or the drum. The same 'agreement' decrees the elimination of animistic practices which frequently occur in Buddhist rites, and in particular, there is a prohibition of the cult of the 'Holy Mother', the equivalent of a female spirit, venerated either by domestic cultic practices, or in pagodas, which, sometimes, are the cause of extravagant expenditure.

There is, in Hai Van, a temple dedicated to the tutelary genie, Trieu Viet Huong, an 8th or 9th Century national hero, who died in the struggle against the Chinese. Legend has it that he died in the very place where the temple now stands. According to the writer Nguyen Tu Chi[3], the kings of the Le dynasty made use of the cult of the genies, which had been in existence since the beginning of the Chinese conquest, to integrate them into a monarchical hierarchy, by fabricating for each an adapted biography, which added a symbolic element to the tributary bond which bound the villages to the central authority. There also exist many other temples dedicated to the same hero and each of the villages concerned claims for itself the glory of having been the place where the hero died. The temple is not well maintained and a few old folk go there occasionally to burn sticks of incense.

Another cult is that of the founders of the great families. There were nine of them in the commune, but today they have dwindled to five, and are of little importance and the cult is tending to disappear. Their existence raises the question of how far these families pre-dated Catholicism, a question that historians have still to decide upon. Some animist practices have left behind them traces that still exist, e.g., the cult of the banyan (a sacred tree), or of the stone dog, but only a few old people still have recourse to these cultic practices and here too, there is evidence that this kind of practice is dying out. When the commune tried to link the principal canal of the district with the reservoir of the commune, some old peasants opposed it. According to them the dragon's head was to be found there. If the constructional operations were carried out, they believed, the head would spit out blood and there would result from it great misfortunes for the village. The question was discussed in the popular assembly and the majority decided to go ahead with the work of construction. The peasants who relate this story, not without a touch of malice, say that no ill-effects followed.

In former times there were a certain number of animist feasts or feasts dedicated to the tutelary spirit. With the advent of the revolution, these have disappeared together with the traditional feast of spring, of the wrestlers, of the old, etc. The only feasts that continue to be celebrated in Hai Van are the feasts of the great religions Tet, Christmas, Easter, the feast of the patron saint of the local church – and the new national and revolutionary feasts.

Among the religious practices of special significance was the ritual to bring down rain. Before the revolution they took the form of processions organized between March and April. Among non-Christians, it was the tutelary deity that was taken in procession through the village, and among Catholics, the local saint. Today, these practices too have disappeared. As for domestic cultic rites, universally observed among non-Christians, there was the cult of the ancestors, with a very special ceremony performed on the occasion of the anniversary of the deceased.

The nomenclature used in the 'agreement' of the commune regarding 'the practices which must be eliminated, or the bad manners and customs which do not correspond to our civilized way of life' is interesting, for if they are mentioned by name, it is because they have existed, at least, in the recent past or that they still exist. The 'agreement' states that to be excluded, are the practices of divination generally performed by the blind, who, on the basis of the date of birth, give some indication of the future by playing heads or tails. The same may be said of astrological practices, meant to determine favourable dates for the big events of life, and based on the position of the starts or by means of the random selection of sacred texts which are supposed to indicate one's fate. The 'agreement' also refers to the reincarnation of spirits or of the souls of one's ancestors who (it is claimed) can be made to reappear by means of magical practices. Forbidden also is the practice of placing esoteric writings in private houses to prevent the entry of demons or to chase them or other phantoms away. Forbidden also, on the occasion of funerals, are the practices of making paper reproductions of ingots of gold or money, spent on the occasion of the funeral procession in order to prevent demons from causing trouble during the ceremony and to help the deceased to find his way to his home.

The 'agreement' goes on to oppose the dedication of children to the 'Holy Mother' (the female spirit), the depositing of photographs of the dead in the pagodas, the imposition of burnt perfumes with incense on the head, and then of bringing them to the temple, a practice bound up with the cult of the 'Holy Mother'. The 'agreement' also condemns the practice of healers who use water mixed with the ashes of burnt incense for the cure of the sick, and the cult of the spirits of the forest as a remedy for sterility in women. But it is especially the cult of the 'Holy Mother' in the pagodas which has come in for the strongest condemnation: 'In Buddhism there is no 'holy mother',' said the text of the 'agreement', 'It is a superstition'. In 1975 the province of Nam Ha suppressed the feast of the 'Holy Mother' at Phu Giay. 'All altars in private houses must be eliminated, and they must be transformed into altars for the ancestors. Those who place burnt perfume at the altar in the pagodas are requested to remove them'. Finally, the 'agreement', which, let it be recalled, was decreed by the popular assembly of the commune, decided to eliminate all cultic practices dedicated to spirits in temples, for, it said, these are superstitions.

The study made of the religion of the population of Hai Van is insufficient ground for firm conclusions on the subject, but it is possible to formulate some hypotheses. It seems clear that the revolutionary process in Vietnam signifies the dissolution of those religious forms which we have described above. In fact, two of their fundamental bases have been progressively eliminated. The first is social, and concerns the former social relations generate by production. It is, in the first place, the tributary bond with the monarchy which was partly responsible for the cult of the genies and then the continuity by kinship of the families of the 'notables' who exercised, despite a real social mobility from one generation to the next, a solid predominance of the Confucian tradition, built up on the ownership of the means of production and on social and cultural prestige (royal titles and letters). The rapid establishment of the new social relations of production ensured the disappearance of those former cultic practices and symbolic expressions.

Further, the progress made in the level of the forces of production have also contributed to undermining the basis of certain protective rituals, especially those which were meant to activate the spirits (or the saints) and other natural forces, more or less personified, and make them influence the natural elements. This is the case with the problem of rain – mastered today by works of hydraulic engineering – and with the incidence of certain illnesses. One may well wonder whether, considering the gamble that the cultivation of rice fields becomes when there is no rain or when there are typhoons, some of these cultic practices would not have persisted but for the administrative measures taken against them. We have been observing here as elsewhere in non-socialist societies, a characteristic evolutionary process. The difference which exists between this religious group and the Catholic group poses an interesting problem from the point of view of the sociology of religion, to which we will come back in the conclusion of this chapter.

Elements of Religious Transition

We said at the beginning that Catholicism represented for the group a source of identity and of social cohesion. This is still a live force in the collective memory of the Catholic group, but there is no doubt that this is no longer today an exclusive source of its concern for group identity. Hence it is worthwhile making some observations on this question before passing on to the analysis of the more systematic inquiry concerning the contemporary religio-cultural models in the commune. We will divide these observations into three categories: the religious practices, the religious roles and the coexistence between Christianity and socialism.

Attendance at Sunday mass, or in group prayer in those rare cases where there is no place for mass, is very strong in the commune; even the young attend mass regularly. Among some adults there are those who abstain from the practice of Sunday mass, but continue to claim they are Catholics. The churches of the five hamlets, all of them well maintained, are full when a religious ceremony is organized. It is the Catholics who maintain the churches, but when large-scale repairs have to be effected the commune includes it in its budget, and the state grants the materials needed.

Religious funeral rites continue to occupy a prominent place in the life of Catholics. It is, in fact, the equivalent of the cult of the ancestors, prevalent among non-Christians. The cemetery is particularly well cared for, and it is a continuing practice to ask the priest to celebrate a certain number of masses for the deceased.

Children are christened within eight days of birth according to the parish priest who was consulted on this question. The Eucharist or communion is sometimes distributed by the laity to the sick, or again, on the occasion of the feast of Easter, when large numbers of the faithful approach the sacrament. As for confession or the sacrament of penance, it is given in a collective fashion on certain occasions. There are devotions to many Vietnamese martyrs, particularly to Thé, as well as to saints of European origin, e.g. St. Anthony, St. Theresa, St. Vincent and Spanish saints, who are often invoked for cures and for good harvests. The feast of the Immaculate Conception is celebrated with splendour in the diocese and is made an occasion for a pilgrimage to Fu Nhai, a place not very far from Bui Chu. Thousands of Catholics, not only from the region, but also from far beyond the diocese, from Hanoi and elsewhere, travel to the shrine. However, this practice is tending to diminish, especially on account of practical difficulties such as transport, food, lack of priests, etc. Pilgrims go there to pray for happiness and better living conditions.

Local religious feasts have acquired a very special importance, and are of different orders: first of all, there are the feasts of the universal Church, such as Christmas, or those of the patron saints of the different hamlets. Apart from the five new secular feasts, those are the only feasts that abide and in which the non-Christians are often associated. Thus the former village of beggars celebrates the feast of the patron of its Church, St. Joachim, on 16 July. The celebration begins with mass and is followed, until 6 p.m. by perpetual adoration in the Church, at which families assist in groups. The mass is celebrated at 8 p.m. in a packed church. One of the organizers of the ceremony who is present with his whole familiy, is the head of the work-group, and the secretary of the cell of the Party. The prayers receive their responses from all, and the singing which follows, is accompanied by an accordion. The *quans* in their traditional black robes are in attendance in orderly fashion. Hundreds of children in their Sunday best attend with the adults. The feast is prepared for several days ahead; the houses are cleaned; the neighbouring roads are spruced up; and during the day the organization of other activities ceases in order to enable all to participate in the adoration.

The houses of Catholics are decorated with religious signs; the new brick and tile houses each have a wall set apart for religious symbols, usually, Christ and the Virgin Mary, and sometimes saints who are the objects of family devotion. On the wall facing the entrance, the photographs of any dead parents are exhibited, with a bouquet of natural or artificial flowers placed in front. Those photographs invariably have a picture of Ho Chi Minh over them, while above the gate there is usually a portrait of Lenin, and sometimes Marx.

The religious education of children is started in the home by the family, where daily morning and evening prayers are still practised, even though there is a noticeable diminution of this practice among the youth. This practice is specially ensured in the young by the grandmothers. This teaching is prolonged by catechisms organized in the different churches of the commune. Contrary to what happens in other parishes, at Hai Van it is the priest himself who takes the catechism classes. This was caused by a conflict with the parishioners, the result of which was the refusal of the laity to co-operate in performing this task. In other parishes serviced by the same priest, lay catechizers ensure religious instruction in the churches. The content of the catechism bears on the gospel message, the duties towards God and neighbour, the Ten Commandments and the three fundamental articles of the faith: God; the future life; and reward and punishment for good and evil.

The priest who was questioned on the attitude of Catholics towards birth control said that it was not a problem for them to accept it in so far as it was a question of limiting the number and not suppressing life.

Before the revolution there existed several Catholic associations, but they are prohibited today because of their role in the anti-Communist struggle, or because of the rivalry with mass organizations which are equally open to Catholics. It should be noted however that the relative inactivity of some of the youths is due in some part to the desire for certain regroupings on a religious basis (choral etc.).

We have already noted that the parish priest of Hai Van serves five parishes. He himself believes that this load is too heavy, for there are more than 21,000 Catholics and he is not young any more. In this there is a problem for the Catholics of the whole region, but especially for those of Hai Van. It is interesting to note that the conception which the Catholics of the commune have of the priest and of his role seems to have been considerably transformed by its relationship with the past. One detail will show this: during the years 1974 and 1975, a conflict arose between the parish priest and the parishioners of Hai Van, and they were threatened with ecclesiastical sanctions if they criticized him. A meeting of more than a thousand persons was then organized to protest against this threat. The parish council met and expressed their disapproval of the parish priest, who retaliated by threatening the council and the Catholics critical of him by refusing religious funeral rites to their families. It was then the turn of the committee of the commune to bring pressure to bear on the parish priest, but nothing was done. Finally, the parishioners appealed to the bishop and demanded the replacement of the parish priest. The bishop replied that he was helpless since he had no one to put in his place. Finally, it was the secretary of the Party of the commune who intervened in order, he said when interviewed, to remind him of his sacerdotal duties and to tell him that it was intolerable that he should refuse religious rites at funerals to the faithful who asked for them, adding to his arguments threats of sanctions such as the denial of the supply of rice if he did not submit to the wishes of the parishioners. The conflict then subsided. Some Catholics, questioned about their attitude to the parish priest, said that this conflict did not prevent them from practising their religion any more than the former political attitudes of the parish priest. In fact, without the parish priest there would be no celebration of the Eucharist, which is essential for their religious life. They could not, therefore, pass over it, regardless of their personal opinion of him as a priest. As for his former political options, well, he has recognized his errors, so why rake up the past?

It is clear, then, that for the Catholic peasants of Hai Van, the role of the priest is no longer that of a social leader. He is a religious agent from whom one expects, above all else, the performance of religious rites which he alone can accomplish. This is confirmed by the fact that Sunday mass is hardly ever replaced by a ceremony directed by a layman when the priest is absent. But the social authority of the priest in the group has not completely disappeared. This was seen recently on the occasion of a meeting of the popular assembly of the commune, at which it was necessary to take a decision on whether or not to lend 35 tonnes of rice to the state. The parish priest spoke out for an affirmative decision and it was complied with.

The laity also fulfil some of the religious functions: there is first of all, the parish council, the president of which, in Hai Van, has been in charge for 23 years. He is elected by the Catholic population and approved by the civil authorities, for his role consists precisely in effecting a bond between the two. In former times the president was appointed by the priest. The role of the council and of its president consists of administering the parish together with the priest, organizing religious feasts, and managing its finances. In former times the parish had at its disposal lands, the revenue from which was used to defray the cost of cultic practices and to maintain the priest himself. This practice was confirmed by the law of agrarian reform. In 1977 the lands were integrated into the co-operative which furnished the priest his ration of paddy. It is also the council which attends to the repair of churches. Some proposals to this effect were presented by means of the Patriotic Front, which is the organ for co-ordination between the different groups and associations. The work was done during the off-season. The role of the president of the parish council is also to be in touch with the religious policies of the state; to see that they are effectively implemented at the local level; and that no abuses are permitted.

The *quans* are also elected by the Catholics, for six year periods. Their election is sanctioned by the priest, and the bishop supplies them with books for their training; there are as many women as men among them. They have the responsibility for maintaining order in the church, and they are also in charge of the singing. The acolytes – children between eight and ten – are trained in the performance of their tasks by one of the youths of the parish.

The question of the relations between Christianity and socialism was often touched upon by the peasants in the course of their conversations. In fact, the animated and sometimes, tragic, history of the Catholic group – animated and tragic because of the ambiguous policies into which it was dragged, and the philosophical position of the Party in power – posed problems both theoretical and practical. These problems sprang up spontaneously in our conversations with the peasants, especially when some of them recalled the past. Thus, for instance, the head of Work Group no. 1, ended his interview with these words:

> The teaching of Christ is inclined to equality and justice. Christians therefore must be enthusiastic in collaborating in the setting up of a socialist system, the precise aim of which is to attempt to realize in fact the Christian ideals. There is no contradiction between Christianity

> and socialism. The Bible says that one must work in order to live. This is a commandment of God which is also a socialist law. The Party educates the people to love their neighbour. There is, therefore, a real conformity between the Christian and Communist ideals.

Another peasant said:

> To be a good Catholic and a good Communist is not contradictory. Communism has always been opposed to poverty and oppression. This squares with the Christian ideal and this is what we are attempting to translate into reality in the commune.

A third peasant added: 'Jesus was crucified because he defended the poor.' The theology of the peasant is, therefore, essentially practical; he believes what he sees. When an attempt is made to lead him into the realms of theology, e.g. that of the relationships between Christianity and atheism, he is out of his depth and replies, as do the young Catholics of the Youth Movement: 'This question is too difficult for us. We must reflect more at length on it.'

The Cultural Models of the Catholic Population

In order to have a deeper understanding of the forthright observations cited above, we must attempt to discover in what measure the Catholic rural population has elaborated a synthesis of its religious values and the values which the population has experienced in the socialist experiment of Vietnam. Further, it is of interest to determine, from a sociological point of view, whether certain religious beliefs, peculiar to traditional Catholicism, continue or not to fulfil a regulative function in the relations of man with nature. It was, therefore, with this double function in mind that we elaborated a series of 16 propositions concerning which those questioned were asked to manifest either their total agreement with them or their simple agreement with them, or their disagreement with them. Their opinions were then submitted to factor analysis.

It was important here to devise a method which would have the advantage of disclosing the logic behind the opinions expressed by a group of persons, when those opinions constitute a coherent model of representations. From the technical point of view, it consists in the calculus of multiple correlations in all the opinions expressed by all the individuals, in such a way as to separate those opinions that form a group by association from those which are not commanded by a structural system of thought, even if they continue to be chanelled into the group. The sequel to all this is the search for the meaning of the opinions expressed.

Practical Compatibility of Christianity and Socialism

First, the factor analysis reveals the presence of a primary, fundamental logic

Table 8.1
Persons Sharing in the Three Cultural Models Concerning the Relations Between Christianity and Communism

			Age			
	Men	*Women*	*Less than 35*	*35-49*	*50 and over*	*Total*
Compatibility between Christianity and Communism discovered practically	13 (27.7%)	8 (29.6%)	12 (46.2%)	7 (23.3%)	2 (11.8%)	21 (28.4%)
Compatibility between Christianity and Communism legitimized religiously	22 (46.8%)	13 (48.1%)	12 (46.2%)	12 (40.0%)	11 (52.9%)	35 (47.3%)
Incompatibility between Communism and Christianity	3 (6.4%)	–	–	2 (6.7%)	1 (5.9%)	3 (4.0%)
Total	*38 (80.9%)*	*21 (77.8%)*	*24 (92.4%)*	*21 (70.0%)*	*14 (82.4%)*	*59 (79.7%)*

shared by 54 persons who were questioned, i.e. 73% of the whole. Its structure revolves round a single, central idea which expresses the proposition:

'A good Christian can be a good Communist'

which forms the base for the following additional propositions:

'To work at the co-operative is a good way of practising love of one's neighbour'

'Our faith sways us to participate in the building up of socialism'

'A classless society is the expression of the will of God'.

This model reveals a fundamentally pragmatic approach. It rests on an experience, on facts established, by persons who while being engaged in the process of the building up of socialism, have discovered that they can realize their Christian faith in it – a faith, however, more practical than intellectual, centred on the love of others.

It should be noted, however, that three people (men more than 40 years old) totally rejected this model, i.e. they believed that there existed, even at the practical level, an incompatibility between Christian faith and Socialism. Further, 31 persons out of the 74 (i.e. 41.9% of the whole), have a more complex model, in the sense that there is behind it another logic quite different from the first. It is founded on the proposition:

'The Parish is a large family'

on to which are grafted the following propositions:

'Jesus was the defender of the poor and of the oppressed of the Palestine

Table 8.2
Persons Without Systematized Cultural Model Concerning Relations Between Christianity and Communism

			Age		
	Men	*Women*	*Less than 35*	*35-49*	*50 and over*
Negative attitude with regard to the natural or psychological efficacy of religion	6 (12.8%)	1 (3.7%)	–	3 (10.0%)	4 (23.6%)
Religious and social conservatism	2 (4.3%)	2 (7.4%)	–	4 (13.3%)	–
Those without any cultural model	1 (2.1%)	3 (11.1%)	2 (7.7%)	2 (6.7%)	–

of His day'
'Social injustice is a grave sin'
'It is just that the young should work for the old'
'Religion helps us to accept the difficulties of life'
'Christian morality is opposed to the limitations of birth'
'A classless society is the expression of the will of God'
'It is good to pray in Latin'.

This second sequence of propositions introduces the legitimizing apparatus which justifies simultaneously the egalitarian relations within the religious group, within the parish and within society. It is of interest to establish that it is the same religious lesson of injustice, condemned, by virtue of the practices of the founder of Christianity, which legitimizes the exigencies which this group expresses with regard to those two systems (economic-social and religious) to which it pertains. Placed in this context, the proposition which affirms that 'religion helps us to accept the difficulties of life' does not signify a recourse to religion in a fatalistic sense, but rather a means to face the difficult events which characterize every human existence. As opposed to the cultural models which may be observed in other rural groups of Asiatic societies, one of the effects which induces a transformation of social relations in the very depths of the religious domain is the ability the peasant population acquires of discovering the profound values of Christianity and of demanding that they be put into practice, in the innermost recesses of the religious sphere.

Two propositions, one relevant to Christian morality in the matter of family planning, and the other concerning the use of Latin, are indicative of the persistence of the traditional religious content. Morality intervenes only with regard to the methods of family planning, and Latin is no longer the universal medium of expression in contemporary Catholicism.

Table 8.3
Attendance at Sunday Mass and Reception of Communion

	Attendance at mass				Reception of communion				
	Every Sunday	*Sometimes*	*Big feasts*	*Never*	*Sunday*	*Once a month*	*Feasts*	*Once a year*	*Never*
Sex:									
Men	40(85.1%)	6(12.8%)	1 (2.1%)	–	7(14.9%)	1 (2.1%)	11(23.4%)	26(55.3%)	2 (4.0%)
Women	25(96.2%)	1 (3.8%)	–	–	2 (7.7%)	–	5(19.2%)	16(61.5%)	3(11.0%)
Age:									
Less than 35	23(88.5%)	3(11.5%)	–	–	1 (3.8%)	–	6(23.1%)	15(57.7%)	4(15.0%)
35–49	29(96.7%)	1 (3.3%)	–	–	5(16.7%)	1 (3.3%)	5(16.7%)	18(60.0%)	1 (3.0%)
50 and over	13(76.5%)	3(17.6%)	7 (5.9%)	–	3(17.6%)	–	5(29.4%)	9(52.9%)	–
All	65(89.0%)	7 (8.6%)	1 (1.4%)	–	9(12.3%)	1 (1.4%)	16(21.9%)	42(57.5%)	5 (6.0%)

Table 8.4
Objects of Prayers of Petition (%)

	Men			Women	
Age:	*Less than 35*	*35-49*	*50 and over*	*Less than 35*	*35-49*
For preservation of health	91.7	86.3	94.1	92.9	100.0
For a good harvest	75.0	61.1	94.1	71.4	75.0
For the future of the children	58.3	50.0	70.6	42.9	41.7
Protection of the children or of members of the family in the army	16.7	33.3	64.7	28.6	33.3
For perseverance in the Christian life	58.3	33.3	64.7	57.1	41.7

Table 8.1 establishes, first of all, that 79.7% of those questioned had a well defined cultural model which expressed for them the conceptions which they had of socialism and of Christianity. While there is little difference between the sexes, the influence of age is much greater. In consequence, almost all the young belong to one or the other of the models expressing compatibility, while more than 25% of the older persons are not to be found in this latter type of category. Further, the 35s plus are less pragmatic than the younger group. It is true, that they have had experience, for the most part, of the pre-revolutionary situation and the social injustice, which would explain why they have not only sought to rationalize the condemnation, but continue to nourish their collective memory with remembrances of the past.

But what of the 15 persons whose logic does not correspond to those models? Factorial analysis reveals that six of them have no systematized cultural model concerning this question. The others share a double logic which is subtly differentiated by certain propositions.

Common propositions: 'The priest ought to occupy himself solely with religious matters'

'Today the young no longer respect their parents.'

Differing propositions:

primary logic	secondary logic
It is not necessary to pray to obtain rain	It is good to pray to obtain rain
Religion is not a help to accepting the difficulties of life.	Religion helps us to accept the difficulties of life.
	The good Christian recites his rosary every day.
	In the Commune the poorest are the laziest.
	It is unfair that the young should work for the old.

Seven persons have a model corresponding to the primary logic: six men and one woman, of whom three were of the age group 35-49 and four were 50+. It is a question here of an attitude of rejection which seeks to confine the religious agent within the religious field, and of affirming the uselessness of religion in spheres where traditionally faith had a say. Nevertheless, this denial does not seem to be supported either by a secular ideology or by a new conception of religion.

As for the remaining four persons (two men and two women), they express the secondary logic which reduces the traditional religious beliefs into a system of social conservatism. Put summarily, Table 8.2 indicates the distribution of these 15 persons.

When one considers the whole of the Catholic population studied in the commune, it becomes clear that the development of a socialist mode of organization of society at the village level, does pose, for the majority, the problem of confrontation of Christian values transmitted through numerous generations with a new system of values. Of the persons questioned, 75% accept the new organization of society. All in this group arrived at the conclu-

Table 8.5
Opinions on Certain Types of Prayer (%)

	Men			Women	
Age:	*Less than 35*	*35-49*	*50 and over*	*Less than 35*	*35-49*
It is good to pray to obtain rain	83.3	44.5	70.6	78.5	85.0
A good Christian recites his rosary every day	33.4	33.3	17.7	42.8	41.6
It was better to pray in Latin	8.3	–	17.7	7.1	100.0

sion that their faith was compatible with the new system. It stands out, however, that for two thirds of the persons concerned, particularly for those who have known the society of pre-revolutionary days, this transition demanded a profound reflection to make them discover the social dimension of that justice of which Christianity was the original vehicle. The younger generations, for whom the problem has never been posed in these very concrete terms, seem less explicit from this point of view.

It is important to underscore the fact of the very small number of those whose system of thought has very little structural organization in what is relevant to this question. This fact constitutes a major difference between the rural population of Hai Van, and those of other Asiatic societies, for whom the transition to capitalism produced a cultural void, in fact, an absence of knowledge (and therefore, of awareness) of social realities, the effects of which they are now being submitted to, without being able to discover their causes. At Hai Van, even if this knowledge is more practical than theoretical, it is, at least, sufficient, to allow the peasants themselves to construct their own proper synthesis, in the religious sphere.

Religious Practices and Their Content

Because of the exploratory character of this research we have been compelled to limit our attention to only four forms of religious practice: assistance at Sunday mass; the reception of communion; prayer; and marriages between Catholics.

For assistance at Sunday mass, the figure given for all persons questioned is 89%; the remaining 11% are irregular in this practice. These figures are slightly less for men (85%), particularly for those men who are 50+ (76.5%). Men of the 35-49 group, and women, are regular at Sunday mass (96.7% and 96.2% respectively).

If the figures for assistance at Sunday mass are considered high, those for reception of communion is very low. The majority (57.5%) are satisfied with fulfilling the annual obligation, and 22% receive communion only on big feast days. In the case of Hai Van, women receive communion less frequently than men, especially those of the less than 35 group, among whom 22% never

Table 8.6
Opinions on Mixed Marriages (One of the Spouses not Catholic) (%)

	Men	*Women*	*Age* Less than 35	*35-49*	*50 and over*
A mixed marriage can produce a happy household	72.3	65.4	76.9	60.0	64.7
A mixed marriage cannot produce a happy household	6.4	3.8	7.7	3.3	5.9
Happiness in the household depends on something else*	21.3	30.8	15.4	23.3	29.4

* The question posed did not include this opinion which was expressed spontaneously by the persons interrogated.

receive communion. These figures reveal a conception of the receiving of communion strongly tainted by 'Jansenism', i.e. corresponding to sacralization of the sacrament to such a degree that human beings are considered unworthy of receiving it. In this case, again, one sees how the group has been cut off from the renewal of Catholic thought during the last 50 years.

Family prayer is a religious practice prevalent among 85% of the cases studied; 31.5% of the families were faithful to it every day; 54% were rather irregular, according to their hours of work. Every house has an altar fixed in the wall where there are gathered together pictures or statues of Christ, the Virgin Mary, and some saints (usually Spanish in origin) towards whom the family's particular devotions are directed.

According to the persons interviewed, the end of this practice is both devotional (in 51% of the cases) and propitiatory or petitionary (in 100% of the families). Table 8.5 takes account of opinions concerning three propositions relative to prayer.

A scrutiny of the figures in Table 8.5 reveals, first of all, the spheres that seem vital for the rural population – health and economic production. In both cases, hazardous natural events, confronted by which one feels powerless, can perturb right order. This powerlessness is perhaps experienced all the more in the group considered in Table 8.5 where the level of education is low: 13.7% have had only primary education and 2.7% secondary education. But even in their cases, there is no perceptible difference between their opinions and those of others; at any rate, no more than is to be found among those who are not employed in agriculture. Thus of the 12 artisans and workers in the population studied, 11 pray for the preservation of health and for a good harvest. However, if one reckons with other indicators, one may surmise that one is not dealing here with a conception of religion that is purely magical or superstitious. It stands out that percentages are very low (except among older women) with regard to persons who regret the dropping of the use of Latin (a language which they did not understand) as a medium of expression of prayer. Further, Catholics who consider the recitation of the rosary as a sign of a good Christian are small in number. Thus they give little importance to practices firmly implanted in former times, such as the use of the sacred tongue or repetitive prayers, the meaning of which (though not understood) is often compensated for by the number of repetitions among a rural, illiterate population.

We are faced, therefore, with a population among whom the level of production forces is very low and who, because they are rural – and therefore very much exposed to natural hazards – feel very vulnerable. Their attitude contrasts very strongly with the synthesis which the study of cultural models with regard to representation of social reality revealed where may be obsered, among a very small number only, an attitude of a sacralized type. This appears quite logical in the light of the transition of which we spoke in the preceding chapters. In fact, the socialist regime has transformed the social relations of production, by stages, but in a systematic manner. These social relations present a new situation in contrast with the past. There has been an abolition of former relationships and a construction of new ones, even if they are not yet exclusively socialist relationships. There exists, therefore, at this level, a veritable social consciousness. However, those new relationships within the co-operative have been built up on a base productive force which is today striding towards a new start – preparation for production on a large scale.

Marriages between Catholics were considered in the traditional society of Vietnam as something to be taken for granted. The sharing of the same religion guaranteed the preservation of the faith of the spouses and therefore their mutual happiness. From a sociological point of view, even if the social agents were not aware of this, this practice was the surest means for guaranteeing the reproduction of the group and for safeguarding its identity. From this arises the question of knowing current opinion of Catholics on this subject.

It is striking that the problem is posed in terms quite different from what one would have expected. It seems that one may interpret this attitude as a socially significant indicator, i.e. that the group is tending towards extroversion. This could well be a form of rejection of the prior ghetto situation. This opinion is put forward, however, as a hypothesis. It is interesting also to note that the practice of giving dowries continues among Catholics though its forms have changed. The parents of the bride buy the wedding gown and a trousseau of eight garments, which involves expenditure of 1,000–3,000 dongs. The expenses of the wedding feast and the purchase of the furniture are met by the bridegroom.

Conclusions

We will end this chapter by making some tentative reflections on certain interpretations already expressed in the course of this study, and consequently, to orientate our thought towards what is to follow.

It is clear that the reactions of the Catholic group of Hai Van, like those of other groups in the region during the transition towards socialism have been, in the first place, motivated by the fact that they felt that their identity and social survival as a religious group were being threatened. This created the paradoxical situation of bringing together the oppressed and the oppressors, in the belief that collective power alone was the guarantee of survival for both. From this arises the sociological phenomenon of a strengthening of the power of the 'notables' and landlords, who found in this religious cohesion a foothold for their political positions, and hence, for their economic power. At the same time, this situation solidified the traditional structure of the internal leadership which was strengthened by the fact of collective defence. Well trained by the missionaries first of all, and by the Vietnamese priests thereafter, the Catholic groups, unlike the Buddhists, were directed by a clergy exercising the powers of exclusive and overall leadership. This explains also the strict discipline of these groups which was manifested, notably, after the exodus of half of them to the South, when they founded new and well organized communities.

But once the Catholics became aware of the possibility of survival for them under the new regime, and when they experienced this concretely in their day-to-day life, there were no more major problems for them of insertion into the new situation of material and moral growth. Without doubt, there still exists a collective memory of past incidents, but this is now seen in its true perspective. Problems still remain and, for the present, they are without any clear cut solution in the minds of the Catholics of Hai Van, e.g. that of the clergy, of its future replacement by younger priests, and that of the coexistence, in the long term, of atheists and believers. But these problems, on the whole, are in no way a hindrance to a positive attitude with regard to the organization of their lives today. One finds among Catholic youths, solid and even enthusiastic cadres with the same rigid discipline which characterized the group in the past; and these ranks are all for integration into an economic and social system which, for its part, demands it of them with equal insistence. The paradox, therefore, of the smooth functioning of an appreciable number of Catholic communes and co-operatives finds its sociological explanation here.

It seems that the ethical dimension of religion has acquired special significance through the rural Catholics themselves, e.g. to do one's duty to the collectivity, to be just and good, to be helpful to others. The expressive aspect of religion has also developed, as may be seen in cultic practices that are marked by stern discipline, efficient organization and effective realization. The internal organization of the group has given it a solid cohesion, all the more so because former social opposition has disappeared, thanks to the new regime. This organization – the parish, the hamlet, the family, with their corresponding roles – is today democratic, just like the commune

The experience of 30 years has left an indelible mark on the Catholics. Their beliefs have been thoroughly purged of much dross, and this is witnessed to both by the priests and the laity. The progress made by the forces of production has eliminated certain aspects of the animist type (superstitions), and the essentials of the Christian religion stand out more clearly even if, among many peasants, religious and ethical practices seem more important than the content of the faith. Further, the transformation effected in the leadership is remarkable; the laity is becoming important and is assuming responsibilities. This is part of the process of secularization that is met with everywhere, but it is being effected in an evolutionary manner, with a delicate balancing of forces, quite different from what has happened in certain capitalist societies in the Third World.

Another reflection is concerned with the non-Christian group which, let it be noted, is practically devoid of any Buddhists, and which is a minority in the commune. We noticed in this group a rapid and almost total dissolution of religious forms, save the cult of ancestors, while, among Catholics, the phenomenon of erosion touched only some individuals or practices of animist type, or the practices seeking protection against hostile forces. Only a few interpretative hypotheses can be advanced to this effect – hypotheses which might be helpful in making future research more specific.

Three factors play a key role: there is first of all an extra-religious element, on which we have already commented – the social cohesion of the Catholic group, so much the stronger as it was forged in the furnace of social and political changes, of which it was scarcely the agent, and which was set in motion by a party whose official ideology was atheistic; and in consequence, the group felt the necessity of safeguarding its identity and making sharper its precise nature. The progressive integration of the group into society as a whole, should have entailed, as its logical result, an erosion of the group's identity. Some signs of such an erosion may be perceived in some individuals especially among the youth but they do not constitute a major phenomenon, as has been the case with the non-Christian group. The sociologist must, therefore, look for other explanations.

Thus it comes about that a second factor must be taken into consideration, a factor bound up with the very content of belief. In Christianity as in Buddhism, though in a different manner, the elements of the religious system directly linked with the relations of man with nature or with the social relations generated by production, is clearly secondary, with regard to the total meaning of human existence, of the universe, of its origins and of its finalities. These last questions can be formulated according to different philosophical approaches, in different cultural contexts, and even in contexts that are foreign to each other. They are also largely influenced in their manifestations and in the modalities of their answers by the level of the forces of production in society at the time and by the social relations. But at the same time they transcend them fundamentally, thus realizing a particular dialectical relationship which allows this element in religion to survive all other functions. This does not signify that atheism cannot exist either in a practical form, as is the case with crude materialism which stifles, with its philosophy of 'eat, drink and be merry, for tomorrow we may die', every questioning by the human being of the meaning of existence, or, in a philosophical form, which makes its own proper response – also atheistic – to the same questions. But this implies the sociological possibility of the existence of religions with a meaning, transcending even the very conditions which an excessively simplistic and mechanistic form of Marxism has sometimes postulated as necessarily implying the automatic disappearance of religion.

The third sociological factor which we believe we can propose for heuristic reasons is linked with a certain type of institutionalization of religion. Institutionalization is indispensable for the reproduction of religio-cultural models, but the fashions in which the institutions can be clothed can be various. In Catholicism institutionalization has reached a very high degree both in the domain of beliefs and rites as well as ecclesiastical organization. Without doubt, the rigidity of the models has been made more flexible by the Second Vatican Council of the sixties. What can be a force for good, sociologically, can also become an obstacle to progress, especially in periods of change. This is what happened in North Vietnam during the 30 year period, 1945-75. But institutionalization, which, when made so formal, suffers from excessive rigidity in its reproductive functions, can also by paradox, become an instrument of adaptation and a means of avoiding dissolution. This is probably what began to happen, especially after 1975. This has been noticed in different spheres, especially with regard to cultic forms (the liturgy, for example), to social ethics (participation in a new mode of economic and social life, for example) and to the role of the laity within the religious institution. It is under a double impulse that this mechanism has been set in motion – that of the social practice of Catholics themselves, and of the transformation wrought at the level of the universal Church. There is therefore a complex dialectical process here at play. What we wish to emphasize is that the existence of an institutional framework, which can both assure reproduction and guarantee adaptation, is a factor of great social importance for the stability of a religious group. These, briefly, and by way of hypothesis, are the factors which we think we can offer as explanations of the phenomena established so far.

What can one say of the future? It is always a very delicate task for a sociologist to make pronouncements about the future. All that can be expressed as ideas have their foundation in present knowledge and in its analysis. The value of such reflections is coterminous with the extent of the study undertaken. It seems that the Catholic villagers of Hai Van will enter without difficulty into the phase of large-scale production, i.e. into the more advanced stage of socialist production. In any case, if there is an obstacle, it will not come from their adherence to religion. This is evident from the economic point of view; from the political point of view it will not be less so, for the local Catholic cadres have been well inserted into, and well accepted by, the social whole. The religious factor, as such, does not seem to play any particular role at this level. It would be an element of restraint only if a local cadre does not respect the general policy of the party concerning religions, i.e. respect for believers, and the chance for them to live their Christian faith freely; from the point of view of the sociology of religion, one may surmise that the internal transformation of Catholicism will go ahead, accompanied, more or less, by catechism and preaching, and that religious adherence will take on more and more the character of voluntary adhesion rather than social cohesion.

Notes

1. In 1980, the reorganization of the seminaries was the purpose of an agreement, in principle, between the government and the Church, in the wake of a plenary council of the episcopate. In the North, Hanoi and Vinh will probably be developed, starting with the existing nucleus.
2. According to surveys made in 1953, the Catholic Church in North Vietnam possessed, at this time, 23,928 hectares of land, i.e., 1.5% of the arable land.
3. Nguyen Tu Chi, Le láng Traditionnel au Bai Bo-sa Structure organisationnelleses problemes, *Le Village Traditionnel*, Etudes Vietnaminnes, No.61, Hanoi, 1980.

9. The Sociology of Social Transition

After an exploratory study such as we have just presented, it would be pretentious on our part to draw definitive conclusions from it. Further, it would also be tedious to repeat what we have already said in the course of the study where some interpretative hypotheses have been put forward, together with some suggestions for action. However, we will take up again, briefly, some of the ideas treated already, to indicate how sociological research can be simultaneously one of the components of the dynamics of action, and also be the basis for a discipline in its own right, at the theoretical level.

Relations Between the Infrastructure and the Superstructure

The question of the relationship between the infrastructure and the superstructure has been a controlling factor throughout this research, and it has been raised throughout most of the chapters. Still, it would be of interest to come back to it before concluding this study. This, in fact, is one of the key questions of a sociology of transition and of the contribution which sociology can make to social action.

We have been able to establish that change does not follow automatically in the superstructure when the infrastructure is transformed. This conclusion is quite obvious and, perhaps, much empirical research was not necessary to arrive at it. But what is important to determine is how this is so, and where one may situate the permanencies and the dissolutions of economic, social and cultural forms, in the process of willed change, i.e. change that has been planned.

As there is no infrastructure without a superstructure, and since the latter is not a simple reflection of the former but enjoys a relative autonomy, and consequently, is capable of reacting on the former, it could be a cause of retardation just as well as of acceleration where the transformation of the mode of production is concerned. It must be noted that in making this affirmation on grounds empirically established, we do not deny that, in the last analysis, the economic function is the determining influence (sociologically speaking, the social organization of the material base). We only emphasize the complexity of the problem by affirming that the intermediary links in the chain of explanations is often multiple and always of a dialectical type. This contradicts all simplistic conclusions of the mechanical or linear type.

As sociologists, we formulate the final determining influence of economics as a hypothetical point of departure, i.e. as an instrument for the investigation of social reality, which will help us always to push our questioning further and further, through all the intermediary stages, right up to the material base of the collective organization of the relations engendered by production. This base is not necessarily situated in the present. The way to explain the conditions from which certain phenomena have emerged may have origins many removes away. If thus one discovers a fundamental logic, one should not forget that the interaction between the diverse elements of the infrastructure and the superstructure is always dialectical, i.e. fully interactional.

The relative autonomy enjoyed by every sector of the political organization, or of a symbolic sphere, has this effect, namely, that the explanation of a certain number of forms of those diverse spheres and of their reproduction in time can also be situated, not directly in their relation with the material base, but in the process of institutionalization itself. Without doubt, this latter can be finally explained in its origin only in relation to the infrastructural functions which delimit the conditions of its emergence and the social functions which it fulfils. Finally, we must point out the importance of the non-economic factors in the orientation of the infrastructure itself, especially, in a planned economy. This is what we meant to say when we spoke of a retarding or an accelerating effect, without forgetting, however, that the deeper reason for this function being fulfilled by the superstructural elements finds its explanation, in the final reckoning, in the social conditions of its emergence. These social conditions cannot be separated from the particular systematization existing between the infrastructure and the superstructure, at least, at any particular moment of their history; a fact which is empirically verifiable.

This brings us back, in consequence, to the dialectic between the productive forces and the social relations of production, provided that one is aware that one, no less than the other, of these two elements, will cover up as many elements of the infrastructure as of the superstructure. The forces of production exist only as a human phenomenon and, therefore, also as a cultural phenomenon the state of the various branches of knowledge, the formulation of the representation concerning man's relations with nature; while the relations of production and all the other social relations find their denouement only in the very act of their representation, be it illusory, fetishistic or scientific. But if all this forms the backdrop of the theoretical foundation of our work, it must be well understood that a sociology of transition must enter into details about the mechanisms involved, in order to transcend the immediate explanation and thus to attempt to give a theoretical status to the processes observed. This is not an easy task, and only a comparison between various situations, not only in Vietnam, but also in other socialist societies, will enable one to make progress towards the goal. Some of the traces of this can already be sketched.

Thus, the introduction of the new relations of production seems to have an immediate effect on all the social elements implied as integrating parts of the former structure. For instance, the system of kinship and the totality of family relationships played a central role in the relations engendered by a tributary or tribal system of production. Certain vestiges of these relationships prevailed within the colonial system, or also in what is generally known in Vietnam as the semi-feudal system (history must help us to give precision to these terms). However, they lose their regulative function in the new social relations engendered by production. This has an immediate effect on the family system itself which loses its forms of the extended family and manifests itself in the form of the nuclear family. We have outlined in the chapter which concerns this process some hypotheses on its processes and mechanisms.

Another example can be given with regard to the introduction of the new social relationships of production, by the abolition of private ownership of the means of production. The transition between the real, if not the legal, appropriation of land by a minority, and its collective appropriation at the level of the co-operative, has, no doubt, in a commune such as Hai Van, caused a profound change in the participation of peasants in the taking of economic decisions and in the sense of their human dignity. One may say that the representation of man in his social dimension has been transformed, and that its repercussions have spread so far as to affect even his religious conceptions.

To continue this type of study, it would be necessary to reconsider all the elements that go to make up an agrarian society (and also an urban society), in order to find out what the process of their transformation is. This is the case, for instance, with regard to the role of the woman and the unforeseen effects which these changes can have on the forces of production. The introduction of three harvests instead of one acts directly on the work-load of the woman, and indirectly, on her low degree of participation in economic and social decisions.

To take another example, the change of production relations enables us to reallocate to the peasant the fruits of his or her toil, at least in an appreciable measure, and in a higher degree than before. This is realized by the system of the award of points, and through the benefits accruing from the domestic economy. The repercussions felt are made manifest in the values developed among the peasants, notably, in the field of education. To education, little value is given so long as the increase of the family revenue depends on the number of hands in the family available for work. The development of education has to await the precise moment when the peasants are able to surmount the limitations of material development in the matter of their houses, furniture etc.

To illustrate another sociological process, that of institutionalization, we could again refer to education. Though we have not been able to make a systematic study of its content, by studying its effects on the population it has been made possible for us to affirm, at least as a hypothesis, that its content has only a limited influence on some of the cultural behaviour. Could not this be due, once again. to a scholastic system of education, and to a pedagogy of inculcation inherited from the past, and not sufficiently rethought in the context of a process of transition to a socialist form of social formation?

The transmission of former models, in spite of some very important and even radical transformations of the infrastructure, could, in fact, have had its provenance in the institutionalization of those cultural models, which have been effectively resistant to change both in the teachers and in the taught – change, which would signify the necessity for rethinking not only the content of education but also the roles of the educators and the educated. The same remarks could be made with regard to preventive medicine.

All this only indicates the complexity of the changes that have taken place in society, and the need to be attentive to all its aspects. This enables us to establish the importance of research and of sociological reflection, in order to be able to measure the extent of the deviations of the reality from the plan – which is generally well done at the economic level – but also of the unintended from the intended – something that seems scarcely to have been realized, probably because of the lack of instruments for such measurements. This is equally a manner of explicating that which is a lived experience at the level of the masses, and of giving to them a supplementary means of expression – which is an indispensable condition for true development. It is in this sense that sociology is also one of the elements of social practice.

The New Dimension of Social Space

The development of the productive forces, in dialectical affinity with the renewal of the relations engendered by production, has enlarged 'social space', i.e. the number, the quality and the geographical dimensions of inter-human relationships. We have verified this phenomenon in studying the transition made from the co-operatives of the hamlets to the single co-operative of the commune of Hai Van. Certainly, the level of the threshold surmounted was not very high, and it was accomplished gradually, even though it reckoned with the diminishing number of workers who left the commune every day to practise their craft in other places of the district, not to speak of the youths who left for military service, or of those who, though smaller in numbers, went to school to follow the third or higher cycle of studies. There has been, therefore, a real enlargement of social space, due to changes in the infrastructure.

We have made in this study the observation that the co-operative appeared as an 'economic subject', while the work-group remained, even after having lost its character of 'economic subject', a 'social subject'. This is very important for a sociology of transition and if this is verified in the other communes of Vietnam, it would be a factor to be taken into consideration in the course of the transition to large-scale production. In fact, this would greatly enlarge economic space, and inevitably, social space. But it seems that if one was too quick to make inferences from the one to the other, one would run the risk of committing errors, the repercussions of which would be very grave.

It would probably be necessary, therefore, to dissociate the two spaces and to steer the transitions at the level of social space, in order not to create useless distortions. All the more so, because, according to our hypothesis, the peasants are in no way opposed to an enlargement of economic space; they even desire it, in so far as they have understood that it is necessary for the growth in the productivity of work; hence to an increase of their revenues. The only reservations one will have are those concerning social space, the place, namely, for group identification of the greater part of them. Such a cultural scheme can be transformed only according to the rhythm of the changes in generation, and one must avoid the situation that what has contributed to the cultural coherence of the changes effected up to today – for which one must be grateful to the social consciousness of the peasant – is not imperilled by too abrupt an enlargement of social space. In other words, one must be vigilant about the social roles of the units at the base, such as the head of the work-group and likewise, of the institutions functioning at this level – institutions concerned with education, health and culture, lest their values be denigrated or they themselves be destroyed in the process.

The Collective Aims

The study of the aspirations of the peasants, as well as of their modes of behaviour, enables us to make the following reflections by way of hypothesis. The desire for, and the hope of, change exist in the peasants and it would be erroneous to believe that they remain immovably attached to ancestral customs. The experience of 30 years of socialist transition has introduced them to an economic rationale which is getting closer to that of the workers involved in the process of industrialization, even if it is still in the embryonic stage.

It is very important, however, and probably very difficult too, to define the collective aims which are capable of making the peasants surmount the stages of transition that will occur in the future. National consciousness, traditionally a very live force in the people of Vietnam, was considerably revived during the war and also during the period of reconstruction. But this cannot serve as a motive force indefinitely, and one should expect the new generations, which have not experienced the sufferings (as well as the glories) of the armed struggle for the defence and integrity of the country, to live in the same mood. Further, the cultural aspirations of these same generations – the adults also have them – seem to be turned towards the future and towards the world outside, rather than towards the past and towards the values of traditional society. While not denying the importance of the cultural insertion of the people into the history of the country, so rich in literature, poetry and drama, which could today find new channels for transmission, they should not be immured in it. We only wish to underscore the inadequacy of those bases for the building of a collective transcendence of immediate interests, no matter how indispensable they may be for building society in the future.

The risk would, therefore, be of arriving gradually at a form of society purely materialistic – using the word in its pejorative sense – i.e. arriving at individual and collective aims determined solely by their increase of material welfare. This would be quite comprehensible as a social process for a peasant population which has come close, for the first time, to a minimum standard of living fit for a human being. The work accomplished by the mass organizations and by the Party is moving in this direction. But two questions may be posed on this subject: the first concerns the degree of real participation and the pedagogical content of the mass movements at the level of the small rural commune. It is averred, at least with regard to women's movements, that the physical impossibility of a more intense participation has rendered the work of organization more difficult. The second concerns the translation into terms concrete, accessible and realistic – for this is the way the peasant mentality apprehends reality – of the aims of the Party, i.e. of the aims of the collective masters, especially when, at the local level, the tasks both of exercising power and of inspiring and orienting the minds of the people devolve on one and the same person. These, simply, are questions which an enlightened sociology would help to clarify and, in a certain measure, to resolve.

Objective Conditions Versus Consensus

The new co-operative economic and political institutions, that is the commune or co-operative are viewed from a particular perspective: as pedagogical structures, i.e. as institutional *loci* of the social learning of new social practices and of new models of thinking, since changes at that level are not automatic and must be induced. Objective conditions must, therefore, be created. At the same time, to reproduce social practices and to institutionalize cultural models on a solid ground, the consensus of the social actors is required. We take such a viewpoint because not only is social transformation a matter of structural changes *in abstract*, but a process affecting and affected by social actors; and to speak of social actors presupposes social practices, cultural models, consensus.

The Effects of Induced Changes

The decisions taken by political actors at the macro-level towards the transformation of the social formation and, in particular, for changes of the rural society, correspond to a model which was not created by local peasants. It represents the part of constraints versus consensus, even if, in the actual process, both occur simultaneously.

The first aspect to be considered in this respect is the influence of the transformation of the various elements of the economic system on the cultural patterns of the social actors. It will be recalled that after a period of parcellization of the land, giving it to the tiller, the first new set of induced practices was the result of collective organization of the work, which, eventually, was followed by the collective ownership of the means of production. This new organization of labour introduced the social actors into a new dimension of economic rationality. Before the land reform and the socialization of the labour process, the peasant received the direct fruits of his productivity at the end of the process – when the crop was harvested – and thus was largely dependent on the natural elements and, therefore, could hardly represent himself as the main actor in the process. With the new organization he began to receive a reward, according to the time spent and the efficiency with which he performed the work; this latter being measured according to norms and points for the various steps of productive labour, which are immediately estimated and immediately rewarded. It introduces a new rationality, together with the need for economic and social accountability, and the peasants are acquiring a greater awareness of their role as social actors.

Such an impact on cultural models is, however, different according to some objective factors, in particular the former class character. For example, the middle peasants will have a different experience in the field of economic behaviour from that of the poor peasants or the agricultural workers. This influences the way that new practices are accepted and new cultural models internalized, the first group having a greater facility to enter into the new economic rationality. It also has its repercussion on the exercise of new roles, in particular in the co-operative. All this shows how a new reality is always built with the elements of the old one.

This series of facts raises the question of the 'ideal part of reality' according to the expression of Maurice Godelier, which is too often only implicitly recognized. The function of ideas is to represent, to classify, to interpret, to explain, to legitimate the reality, in one word the ideas are forming the organizational schemes of the action of social actors. Meanings are produced by social actors starting from a series of representations of reality, which are simultaneously a reflection of this reality and an active production of thought. Such representations are organized in cultural models, socially transmitted through language and education. Of course these various processes, whether for the genesis of social practices or for their reproduction, are always concrete, related with the actual level of productive forces as much as with the place of the actors in the social relations of production.

Once produced, cultural models of social practices acquire a certain autonomy through their institutionalization. This means that when performing a function of social reproduction, they obtain a possibility of continuity, even when the social conditions in which they have been produced are disappearing or have been transformed. This explains some of the contradictions revealed by this research, namely between new objective conditions produced by the transformation of some aspects of the social relations of production and the permanence of some cultural schemes of the past. True enough, such contradictions are at the origin of new actions, but this is not automatic. It requires a social awareness linked with a political will to solve the contradictions; that some are tackled, when others are ignored, seems to be a good instrument of the measure of social and political consciousness.

All this indicates the dynamic role of such models and representations, as a part of the transformation process or as obstacles against it. It is central in a process of transition, which is always the fruit of the action of social actors facing new objective conditions. *A fortiori* is it the case in a planned transition, intending to create new social relations of production and a new level of productive forces. In both of them, indeed, the part of thought is central for the creation of models of practices able to create and to reproduce the new social relations and to increase the level of productive forces.

To produce a formal subsumption of capital to labour (the contrary of the logic of the capitalist mode of production), means to induce an infinite number of social practices among an infinite number of actors. It means also, the progressive creation of cultural models able to orientate the reproduction of the practices. The process of real subsumption, i.e. the constitution of the material basis for the reproduction of the social relations of production, supposes also a smiliar process. In the first case the social actors are producing social structures, in the second, they produce material conditions able to reproduce them without counting exclusively on such non-material conditions, as political, juridical or ideological ones. All this constitutes the objective conditions of the process of transition.

The Formation of the Consensus

The second condition for ensuring the stability of any social process and particularly of a planned process of social transformation, is the consensus of the social actors, or a subjective condition – obviously the distinction between objective and subjective conditions is an abstraction. In reality both aspects are intrinsically related in a dialectical process which on the one hand unites objective factors inducing social practices, and the consciousness of the social actors. For a better understanding of this we can make a parallel with Marx's well known distinction between a class in itself (objective aspect) and a class for itself (subjective aspect); in this case Marx was describing a situation. In a perspective of action, we can affirm with the same logic that the struggle of a dominated class to change the social structures, at the same time supposes an objective situation of a class division and a subjective situation of a class consciousness.

In the study of the Vietnamese commune we have noted that this subjective aspect, or the consensus of the peasants as to the social transformation, was present in the various steps of the process, with, evidently various degrees of intensity or of contradiction according to the former class structure or to conjunctural factors of economic successes or failures. As a whole we have been able to assert that the peasants were aware of the fact that they have been the 'masters' of the process, even if they knew that they were not the exclusive ones. A real consensus about the social and economic transformations had been created.

The research in Hai Van helped us to reflect on the conditions which have made such an awareness possible and to propose some answers. First, among peasants, a consensus as to a socio-economic transformation can emerge only when they are convinced of the material advantages of the innovation. This can be verified as much in the field of new forms of appropriation of the means of production, as in the field of labour organization, or even in the concrete aspects of the transformation of the productive forces; it corresponds to a strict, logical reasoning. For a peasant, to accept a risk for his production, has for centuries been a question of life and death and only when he is totally convinced of the positive material result of the innovation will he adopt it. It is the type of cultural model that the accumulated experience has produced in the group. This is why the transformation of productive forces in their aspect of technical organization of production (irrigation, fertilizers, etc.) is such an important factor in creating the bases of new advantages in the productive process, at the moment of transformations of the social relations of production. The latter will be accepted easily when the correspondence with the material basis results in a higher productivity, or improved distribution of the social product. New experiences will result in new representations, new cultural models and new social practices. This is a first and *sine qua non* condition for the consensus, but is not, however, the sole one.

Others are situated directly in the field of representations. In particular, one quite central condition is related to the conception of man in the universe, and more precisely the extent to which human beings are represented as actors or as having to submit themselves to a fixed social order linked with the functioning of the natural forces. The emergence of a consensus as to a planned transformation is conditioned by the cultural, and particularly the religious models prevailing among the rural population. These may constitute a serious obstacle to the acceptance of new social practices, but they may also become incentives for a consensus. In other words, their function is ambivalent and this can be verified even in the field of religion. When religious representations are no longer a substitute for an analysis of the social relations of production or for an objective explanation of the relations to nature, and when they become a moral incentive for the construction of new social relations of production (a classless society) or for the development of the productive forces, they acquire new social functions.

In the same area of representation we have already mentioned the perception of social space. Inevitably, in a society where precapitalist forms of production, collective organization and representations are still numerous, a transition to socialism supposes dimensional changes in the organization of the space. This representation is, however, linked with the previous social experience of the social actors, and is why the identification with the former *lång* (village), which became the basis for the organization of the work brigade, remained so profound. Often, the great difficulty in a rural population is to create a representation of new intermediary spaces between the local unit – very concrete and linked with daily life – and the national one, which, however real – especially after national wars or struggles for national liberation – remains rather abstract. To create a consensus and thus to promote the social actors as builders of new economic dimensions and of corresponding social interactions, requires the existence of a perception of social space going beyond the traditional dimensions. Such a perception is changing through concrete experience, in a dialectical process with the newly created conditions of production, with political participation, with educational techniques, etc. However, the rhythm of change is often slow, because of the profound institutionalization of the representations of space and because of their affective dimensions.

This brings us to a third aspect: the ethical and affective adhesion to the process of a planned transition. Consensus being a subjective reality supposes that the social actor should be motivated for acting and thinking in a new way. Positive material results offer a basis for action, but any human enterprise requires also an ethical legitimation. Only this can create a real consensus. Not without reason, in class societies an important ideological product is elaborated to build up systems of legitimation, religious or not, according to the types of social formations. In societies in transition, where the first phase is characterized by a formal subsumption of capital by labour, a moral justification of the process is also necessary, i.e. the legitimation of the revolutionary moment it presupposes, and of the various steps of the subsequent transformations of the constitutive elements of the social relations of production (appropriation of the means of production, labour process and distribution of the social product). The affective adhesion to the process is conditioned by the ethical justification and both of them form a fundamental prerequisite for a consensus and for action.

The last aspect we want to stress – not in chronological order, but following a social logic – is the degree of real participation of the social actors in the process. It is of course intimately related to the former ones, because there is no participation without positive effects in the production, without new representations, without ethical justification and affective commitment. At the same time, participation is also a condition for the creation of the other elements. This is the lesson which appears clearly from our study and it corresponds to other similar social experiences. Participation is opposed to technocracy and bureaucracy as social processes. It, however, supposes, in a planned transition, the existence of skill and the intervention of the State, otherwise it would end in a purely illusory populist project. Again a dialectical process is created, however, unifying the contradictory elements in one social process which exists in a permanent stage of provisional equilibrium. Any break in this equilibrium has its repercussions on the participation and hence on the consensus.

A Pedagogy of the Planned Transition

Many elements enter into a pedagogical process and we do not intend to consider them all. We want to call the attention only to the pedagogical function of the correspondence between social practices necessary for the transformation of the social relations of production, and a change in the material basis, i.e. in the level of productive forces. From the intellectual viewpoint it is important to keep the theoretical character of the two concepts of social relations of production and of productive forces, in order not to reduce them merely to descriptive categories. The concrete process of action means the initiation of new social practices of production, that are producing new forms of social organization of production and finally, new social relations of production. Such an initiative appears evident to social actors when corresponding material bases have been created. In this case a consensus is more easily given for the reproduction of such new social structures, hence the importance of a balanced transformation of the social forms of production and their material bases. It becomes a real pedagogical tool, when the aim is not only economic growth, but the integration of human beings (here the peasants) as active social actors in a social process, which presupposes a consensus.

Certainly, many other elements are also playing a role and we have alluded to some of them: the social representation of space, religious representations, other cultural models related to the family, the habitat, etc. Pedagogical initiatives, such as formal education, mass organizations, party, are also parts of such a process, but we formulate the hypothesis that the basis of them all is the dialectical equilibrium between the two elements indicated above.

With those considerations we end this study of a Vietnamese commune, conscious of the incompleteness of such an enterprise, but with the hope of having made a contribution – however limited – to a sociological approach to a transition to socialism, within the framework of a Marxist approach. We wish also to thank especially the inhabitants of Hai Van, who were so sympathetic towards us and accepted to behave as 'masters' for the team of sociologists who had come to question them and who have thus also contributed to the progress of a knowledge necessary to proceed with the transformation of society.

Index

agent: religious, 164; social, 59, 63, 76, 84, 90, 93, 124, 164, 187, 198-202
army (people's), 11, 15
avant-garde, 17

Bao (Revd.), 165
Bao Dai, 11, 166
Bettelheim, C., 6, 20, 25, 27, 50
Bible, 180
blood-relationship (system of), 21
Bourdieu, P., 69
bourgeoisie: national, 10; rural, 13
British troops, 10
Buddhism/Buddhist, 116, 162, 164, 171, 173, 174, 175, 188, 189

cadres: administrative, 14, 45, 62, 74, 76-9, 89; economic, 76, 78, 79; militant, 15; political, 15, 77-9; religious, 77-9
capital, the, 2, 20
capitalism: *see* mode of production
caste: Brahmin, 95, system, 5, 46
Catholicism: Catholics, 21-5, 41-3, 54-68, 71, 73, 75, 78-84, 90, 118, 132-52, 162-80, 185, 187, 188, 190; Catholic church, 21, 28, 132, 163, 166, 169-72, 174, 176-9, 190, 191; Catholic militia, 166, 168; parish council, 73, 77, 165, 178, 179; Second Vatican Council, 190
Charism, 53
Chiang Kai Shek, 10
Christianity/Christian, 116, 122, 151, 163, 164, 179-83, 185, 186, 189; minorities, 162, 173, 176, 177, 189
clan, 22, 28, 46
class: alliance, 9, 10, 16, 17; consciousness, 10, 15, 199; dominant, 83, 84, 116, 169; dominate, 199; hegemonic, 116; landowners, 13, 17, 19; middle-, 55; struggle, 9, 16, 17, 168; subalternate, 9, 116
colonialism, 9, 21, 95, 194; French, 7, 9, 11, 19, 95, 164, 167
committees: central, 18; district, 44; popular, 10, 11, 174; provincial administrative, 16; reform, 14
communities, religious, 14
Confucius/Confucianism, 9, 83, 94, 95 116, 162, 176
consciousness: class, 10, 15, 199; collective, 16; national, 10, 196; political and social, 7, 27, 30, 196, 198, 199
council: of management, 52, 58, 62-4; of peasants, 16

Dien Bien Phu, 11, 19
distribution: 25, 26, 37, 39, 40, 45, 48, 49, 58, 64, 98, 100, 109, 200; of land 141, 165
domestic economy, 26, 27, 33, 39, 40, 42, 43, 46, 49, 68, 95, 106-8, 111, 112, 117, 118, 132, 135, 138, 140-43, 146, 148, 156-8, 161, 194
Duan (Revd.), 167

economy: collective, 33, 68, 108, 122, 132, 135, 161; domestic, *see* domestic economy; welfare, 121; *see also* new economic zones
elite (Westernized), 9

Fall, B., 18, 20
family planning, 92, 96, 99, 103, 182
feudalism: anti-feudal struggle, 12, 16, 17; *see also* production, mode of
force, productive, 2, 4-7, 12, 19, 25, 27, 28, 34, 43, 44, 48, 49, 69, 73, 80, 81, 90, 99, 105, 121, 155, 158, 164, 173, 176, 186, 187, 189, 193-5, 198, 202
French: troops, 10, 166, 167; *see also* colonialism
functionalism, 2
Fu Nhai, 177

Geneva Accords, 29, 162, 168

Godelier, M., 4, 198
Gramsci, A., 47

Hai Hau, 21, 163
Hai Phong, 22
Hai Xuan, 165
Ha Nam Binh, 10
Hanoi, 21, 163, 165, 168, 173, 177, 191
Ho Chi Minh, 12, 18, 165, 167, 169, 177
Hong Gai, 25
Hong Hai, 22
Hung Yen, 18

imperialism: 9, 12; cultural, 116; French, 9; Japanese, 9; anti-imperialist struggle, 12, 16, 17
India, 5, 95, 156
infrastructure, 2, 4-8, 24, 44, 45, 47, 96, 131, 168, 192, 193, 195
irrigation, 22, 24, 26, 35, 45, 132, 200

Jansenism, 185
Jesus, 180, 181

Kerala, 95
Khan (Revd.), 165
labour, division of, 24, 114
labour-force, 32-7, 44, 46, 48, 69, 95, 98, 107, 108, 115, 151
labourers, 16, 74, 96; landless, 12, 14, 18
land reform, 5, 9-24, 40, 95, 165, 168, 169, 179
landlords, 22, 23, 46, 165, 167, 168, 188
landowners, 9-20, 56, 165, 166, 168, 169
Latin-America, 5, 84
laws, objective, 3, 6
Le Duan, 43, 44, 51
Le Huu Tu, 165, 166
Lenin, V.I., 177
liberation, national, 112, 200

mandarin, 46, 81, 132
material base, 8, 46, 131, 192, 193, 199, 200, 202
materialism, historical, 2
Marx, K., 2, 3, 5-7, 20, 95, 177, 199; Marxism, 190; Marxism-Leninism, principle of, 16
means of production, *see* production, means of
medicine, 90-93, 135, 144, 195
migration, 24, 30, 31, 95
Ministry of Health, 91
missionaries, Spanish, 73, 162, 167
mode of production, *see* production, mode of

model: cultural, 4, 7, 8, 65, 69, 75, 84, 85, 90-96, 111, 114, 116, 119, 121, 132, 135, 146, 168, 173, 175, 180-83, 186, 190, 192, 195, 197-202; political, 8

Nam Dinh, 90
Nam Ha, 175
National Assembly, 12
National Front, 9-12
new economic zones, 25, 27, 30
Nghe An, 18
Nguyen, 21, 164
Nguyen Cong Tu, 21
Nguyen Tu Chi, 50, 174, 191
Nhan Dan, 18
notables, 13, 16, 22, 23, 94, 165, 167-9, 176, 188; village, 10, 12, 21

parties, 52, 53, 55-60, 62-75, 79, 133, 135, 137, 142-52, 157, 158, 160, 167, 169-71, 177-80, 197; Vietnamese Communist Party, 9-11, 13, 15-18, 25, 162; Party of the Workers, 47
patriarchy, pattern of, 7, 116
Patriotic Front, 71, 73, 77, 166, 179; of Hai Van, 165
peasants, 9-12, 15-30, 37, 40, 45-50, 55, 66, 69, 70, 74, 75, 82, 84, 91, 95, 103, 104, 111, 121, 132, 135, 148, 152, 162-5, 167-70, 174, 179, 180, 185, 189, 194, 196-202; class, 7, 9, 79; landless, 13, 16, 17, 55, 95; middle, 9-19, 40-43, 54-69, 78, 169, 198; poor, 11-19, 25, 28, 41-3, 54-69, 78, 167, 198; rich, 11-19, 169
Pham Van Dong, 51
Phat Diem, 163, 165, 166
Phu Giay, 175
planning, 3, 7, 47, 71, 79; family *see* family planning
poor, 9, 17, 22, 56, 152, 180, 181, 183
population, active, 31-3
practice, social, 81, 96, 99, 168, 196-202
production: means of, 5-7, 23, 35, 44, 45, 94, 95, 172, 176, 194, 197, 200, 201; mode of, 5, 20, 45, 161, 192; feudal, 3-5, 12, 13, 46, 194; tributary (Asiatic), 7, 21, 47, 49, 94, 95, 194; capitalist, 2-5, 7, 9, 44, 46, 185, 189, 199; socialist, 3-5, 7, 17, 183, 187; social forms, 4, 5, 8, 49, 202; social relations, 2, 4-8, 21, 44, 46, 48, 49, 73, 76, 100, 122, 130, 131, 173, 176, 187, 193, 194, 198

Red River (Delta), 1, 5, 7, 46, 99, 165, 166

religion: popular syncretistic, 116; traditional, 122, 182
representations, 7, 8, 135, 173, 180, 186, 193, 194, 198-202
revolution, 13, 17, 18, 21, 22, 28, 79-84, 94, 95, 116, 163, 165, 170, 174, 178; national, 11, 18; popular, 18; social, 11; Vietnam, 9
rupture, 5

Scott, J., 70
Secularization, 189
socialisation, 81, 85, 197
socialist mode of production, *see* production, mode of
sociology, 1, 7, 8, 73, 80, 164, 168, 173, 188, 189, 192, 193, 195, 197; Marxist, 2, 202; of religion, 7, 162, 176, 191; in socialist society, 1-3; theory, 2
South-East Asia, 69
Spanish missionaries, *see* missionaries, Spanish
Sri Lanka, 46, 70, 156
stock, 69
structure: economic, 169; juridicial, 5; political, 4, 5; social, 4, 28, 70, 195, 199, 202; socialist, 162, 195
subject: economic, 25, 27, 28, 195; social, 27, 28, 195
subsumption: formal, 4, 199, 201; real, 4, 199
superstructure, 2, 4-8, 44, 96, 131, 168, 192, 193
symbolic (universe, sphere), 44, 121, 122, 131, 193
symbolism, 5, 90, 173
system, patriarchal, of families, 21

Taoism, 162
temples, 21, 22, 132, 174, 175
Thai Binh, 42, 43
Thailand, 156
The, 177
Thuong Oank, 165
Tongkin Peninsula, 164
transition, 2-8, 17, 22, 27, 44-6, 49, 50, 73-5, 80, 81, 92, 96, 112, 115, 124, 131, 135, 163, 168, 170, 173, 176, 185, 187, 188, 192-202
tribunal: people's popular, 16; special, 14
Tributary mode of production (Asiatic), *see* production, mode of
tribute, 21, 95
Trieu Viet Huong, 21, 95
Truong Chinh, 11, 18, 20

unemployment, 14, 95
U.S.A., 11
Utrecht, E., 18, 20

Viet Minh, 9, 166-9
Vinh, 191
Vo Nguyen Giap, 16

war (second world), 9, 162
workers, 10, 12, 14, 19, 25, 26, 37, 45, 48, 52, 59, 63, 65, 66, 74, 78, 95, 98, 99, 103, 109-112, 121, 123, 152, 165, 179, 186; agricultural, 19, 32, 95, 98, 99, 198; rural, 14, 52
work-group, 25-9, 50, 196
working class, 9, 108, 111